JEWS, MONEY AND
SOCIAL RESPONSIBILITY

About our cover: The Hebrew words, *Keren Shefa,* translate into English as both "The Shefa Fund" and "horn of plenty" or "cornucopia." The Shefa Fund's goal is to promote ethical approaches to the creation of shared abundance for all the world.

JEWS, MONEY AND SOCIAL RESPONSIBILITY

Developing a "Torah of Money" for Contemporary Life

Lawrence Bush
Jeffrey Dekro

A Resource Book, with Supplementary Essays by
Letty Cottin Pogrebin and Arthur Waskow
Foreword by Jonathan Schorsch

The Shefa Fund שפע קרן שיפעו

To Sidney Shapiro

"The Torah teaches you a good rule of *mentshlikh* living,
namely, that when you do a *mitzvah*, do it with a joyous heart."
— *Leviticus Rabbah 34:8*

Published by The Shefa Fund, 7318 Germantown Avenue, Philadelphia, PA 19119, 215-247-9704.

Library of Congress Catalog Card Number: 92-085145
ISBN 0-9635684-1-8

Printed on 100% Recycled Paper

Table of Contents

Acknowledgments and Credits

FUNDS FOR RESEARCHING, writing and distributing this book came from The Albert A. List Foundation, the Gimprich Family Foundation, Boston P'nai Or, the Trio Foundation, Viki Laura List, R. Max Samson, Deborah Winant, and the Progressive Philanthropy Project. We are deeply grateful for their involvement and their generosity.

For important information and perspectives on socially responsible financial activities, we thank Robert Schiller, Jonathan Schorsch, Arline Segal and Ellen Stromberg. We are especially grateful to the Council on Economic Priorities, whose groundbreaking resources serve as a major springboard for our discussion.

For guidance in our various discussions of class, the "psychology of money," the politics of philanthropy, and the teachings of Judaism about the "Torah of Money," we thank Martha Ackelsberg, Joanie Bronfman, and Sidney Shapiro.

Praise is due to all the participants in The Shefa Fund's annual retreats. Their courageous explorations of their own feelings and histories regarding money and Jewish identity have inspired and guided us. Our thanks, also, to Congregation Beth Am Israel in Philadelphia, to Rabbi Marc Margolius, and to Rabbis Jeff Roth and Joanna Katz, in whose spaces The Shefa Fund held workshops from which materials for this book were drawn.

Several people gave sharp critical feedback as our manuscript evolved, including Chela Blitt, Joanie Bronfman, Harry Chotiner, Ellen Cassedy, Debra Cohn, Gary Ferdman, Nan Fink, Rabbi Marc Margolius, Andy Rose, Sidney Shapiro, Arline Segal, Rabbi David Teutsch and Deborah Zucker. All were immensely helpful. For contributing to our "questions to consider and discuss" at the close of each chapter, we especially thank Deborah Zucker.

For sharp-eyed proofing and editing, thanks to The Shefa Fund program officer, Betsy Tessler. For compiling our index, obtaining permissions to use copyrighted material, performing a hundred different editorial tasks and providing steady encouragement, we are grateful to The Shefa Fund administrator, Henry Goldschmidt.

Our thanks to The Shefa Fund Board of Directors for serving as midwife to this project.

119, and the Rockefeller collage on p. 130; Dick Codor, for his cartoons on pp. 4, 34, 39, 69, 70, 72, 152, and 164 (all but the first of which appear in *Babushkin's Catalogue of Jewish Inventions* by Lawrence Bush, Dick Codor and Bruce Sager, 1988); Netta R. Gavin, for the photo on p. 146, and Yugoslav Vlahovic for the drawing on p. 84.

Our book was designed and put together by Lawrence Bush. The cover is by Mixed Media of Madison, WI —design by Nancy Zucker, art by David McLimans. Our special thanks to both.

About the Authors

Lawrence Bush is a writer and consultant for the Union of American Hebrew Congregations (the Reform synagogue movement). He is the author of *Bessie,* a novel (1983) and of two works of fiction for adolescents, *Rooftop Secrets* (1986) and *Emma Ansky-Levine and Her Mitzvah Machine* (1989). His fiction, essays and poems have also appeared in *Moment, Reconstructionist,* the *Village Voice, MAD* magazine, *Reform Judaism* and other periodicals, primarily of the American Jewish press. Bush was editor of *Genesis 2* during its final three years of publication (1987-1989), and served as assistant editor of *Jewish Currents* magazine from 1979-1984.

Jeffrey Dekro has been an organizer of people and money in progressive and Jewish renewal movements since coming to Brandeis University in 1969, during which time he has organized millions of dollars in support of small non-profit organizations dedicated to political and spiritual transformation. Dekro is president and founder of The Shefa Fund, a public foundation in Philadelphia that promotes Jewish renewal in America. He was also one of the creators, in 1989, of the Jewish Funders Network, and in 1985 he was a founding board member of the Delaware Valley Community Reinvestment Fund. Dekro has had articles published on politics and public affairs, Jewish ethics and spirituality, and has taught at Hebrew Union College in New York and at the University of Pennsylvania.

Foreword

by Jonathan Schorsch

KABBALAH, the secret and mystical self-proclaimed inner core of Judaism, saw in the *mitzvot*, the commandments, an opportunity for righteous Jews to help God repair the world. These days, we are still being asked to save the planet. The metaphysical has been made physical: Personal and spiritual crises intermingle with global, ecological ones. Future generations are being punished for the sins of their parents and grandparents: profligate consumption, industrially-promoted narcissism, an addiction to endless growth, and others. The environmental crisis, according to many, is only the clouds presaging the flood to come. Like Noah, we have had fair warning. How will we respond?

Jewish tradition provides a story whose acute hindsight should stir us. The *Zohar*, in Daniel Matt's sparkling translation, says that when Noah came out of the ark

> *he opened his eyes and saw the whole world completely destroyed*

> *He began crying for the world and said*
> *"Master of the world!*
> *If you destroyed Your world because of*
> *   human sin or human fools,*
> *then why did You create them?*
> *One or the other You should do:*
> *either do not create the human being*
> *or do not destroy the world!"*

How did the Blessed Holy One respond? "Foolish shepherd!". . .

> *[Before the flood] I lingered with you and*
> *   spoke to you at length*
> *so that you would ask for mercy for the*
> *   world!*
> *But as soon as you heard that you would*
> *   be safe in the ark,*
> *the evil of the world did not touch your*
> *   heart.*
> *You built the ark and saved yourself.*
> *Now that the world has been destroyed*
> *you open your mouth to utter questions*
> *   and pleas?*

We are faced with similar conundrums: the fate of the planet hangs in the balance and we hide in our ark with the indifference spawned by

JONATHAN SCHORSCH is a writer and environmental researcher who has worked with Shomrei Adamah, The Data Center, Lenore Goldman Associates, The Green Seal, and the Council on Economic Priorities (CEP). At CEP he established the corporate environmental data clearinghouse, the first centralized database network to collect comprehensive data on corporate environmental performance. He is a co-author of CEP's *The Better World Investment Guide* (Prentice Hall, 1990), a sourcebook on ethical investing, and *Shopping for a Better World* (Ballantine, annual since 1989), a bestselling guide to socially responsible shopping. He and his wife Gail live in Berkeley, California.

good fortune, with excuses of personal power-lessness, with rationalizations about nature's resilience or the inevitability of human history.

Is there any way we can avert this *ro'ah gezayrah,* this severe judgment?

Rambam, Rabbi Moshe ben Maimon, the great 12th-century philosopher and Talmud-ist, provides one avenue in his *Mishneh Torah,* his guide to Jewish Law. In the 10th chapter, on the laws of gifts to the poor, Maimonides clas-sifies eight levels *(ma'alot)* of *tzedakah.* The highest level, "above which there is no other,"

> *is that of the person who assists a poor Jew by providing him with a gift or a loan or by accepting him into a business partnership or by helping him find employment — in order to strengthen his hand until he no longer needs to ask aid of others."*

Rambam echoes here the Talmudic sage Rabbi Shimon ben Lakish, who said that "one who lends money is greater than one who just gives it. And one who forms a partnership is the greatest of all."

What is the operating principle elucidated here? It is that true *tzedakah* attempts to rem-edy a situation by eliminating its root causes, not just by ameliorating its current painful-ness. To paraphrase the Reverend Martin Lu-ther King, Jr., while we laud philanthropy, we should not forget to address that which makes philanthropy necessary. The apocryphal *Ec-clesiasticus* (14: 20-22) expresses a potent ver-sion of this idea, with prophetic rage: "Whoever brings an offering of the goods of the poor does

as one who kills the son before his father's eyes. The bread of the needy is their life: he that defrauds him thereof is a man of blood. He that takes away his neighbor's living slays him; and he that defrauds the laborer of his hire is a bloodshedder."

This passage, incidentally, was used by Bar-tolomé de Las Casas, the human rights-minded Dominican cleric who accompanied Columbus to the New World, in describing the treatment of the native *Indios,* the Taino. (Las Casas is thought by many scholars to have been a "New Christian," a Spanish Jew whose family was forced to convert to Christianity during the persecutions that racked Spain through the 14th and 15th centuries.) Watching the Span-ish exploitation and extermination of native peoples in the Americas, Las Casas grew so indignant and appalled that he became his generation's most ardent defender of the Indi-ans and most vocal advocate for New World social reform. Las Casas even won permission from the Spanish crown to start an "alternative" plantation in what is now Venezuela, where "equal pay" was offered to Africans, Indians and Europeans for equal and shared labor. The fledgling utopia proved too fragile for the tu-mults of its time, however, and lasted but a few short years.

A later New World exemplar of what we might now call social responsibility is John Woolman (1720-1772), an early Quaker leader who was prominent in the religious reform movement that swept the United States in the mid-18th century. David Shi, in his book, *The Simple Life:*

Plain Living and High Thinking in American Culture, tells the following about Woolman:

> *In 1746, at the age of 26, he visited Quaker meetings in Virginia, Maryland, and North Carolina. There for the first time he saw "the dark gloominess" of slavery practiced on a large scale, and he determined to do all he could to end such a barbaric practice. During his trips to the southern colonies, he paid for his lodging in the houses of Quaker slave-holders rather than accept their hospitality, since it was unpaid slave labor that made such hospitality possible. He also gave up using both sugar in his food and dyes in his clothing because they were products of slavery. . . In 1758, he. . . convinced the Philadelphia meeting to disown Quakers who continued to buy slaves.*

Today's (mostly secular) *tikkun olam*, repair of the world, offers its own updated techniques for change. The organizations and strategies for change so excellently covered in this book and in other resources — companies such as The Body Shop, Co-Op America, Working Assets, banks such as the South Shore Bank of Chicago or the Grameen Bank of Bangladesh, books such as *Shopping for a Better World*, organizations such as Mazon, the New Israel Fund, Amcha for Tzedakah, strategies such as social investing — all attempt to live up to the Maimonidean challenge of infusing true *tzedakah* into our activities. All seek to remedy a situation by eliminating its root causes; all seek to address that which makes philanthropy necessary. They act out of the belief that our local economies and global interactions are as ripe for ethical consideration and judgment as is our personal behavior. They are unwilling to separate ethics from everyday life. They see everyday business as precisely the locus where true *tzedakah* needs most to be made manifest.

True social responsibility, true *tzedakah*, does not segregate spheres of decision-making. Understanding the connections between things helps prevent the crises that come from creating separations: from pretending, for instance, that there is no connection between toxic emissions into the environment and toxic contamination of food supplies. For the most part, however, we are ignorant of the extent to which things are connected.

In northern Quebec, for example, a dam built in the first phase of the massive James Bay hydroelectric project meant the flooding of thousands of acres of land. Scientists are only now discovering that the flooded rock is releasing mercury as it decomposes undewater; incidents of toxic poisoning from eating contaminated fish are surfacing among the local Cree inhabitants. In the Amazon River basin, on the other hand, natural seasonal flooding keeps people alive, as they depend on the abundant fish from the overflowing rivers. In these areas, the trees and the water life have forged delicate, often symbiotic relations. Deforestation, however, is killing off the trees at whose submerged base roots many of the fish feed. With declining fish populations, local people face even greater difficulty meeting basic survival needs.

In central Asia, the Aral Sea is literally disappearing because its two feeder tributaries were diverted for cotton production under a Stalinist agricultural plan. The drying up of the sea (formerly the world's fourth largest) means the surrounding population's drinking water has become salinated. The once-thriving fishing industry is dead. Many say the sea's shrinking has led to dangerous climatic changes, especially considering the agricultural importance of the area: severe dust storms, longer winters, drier rainy seasons. How many more connections don't we recognize?

True social responsibility, true *tzedakah*, requires true seeing. Ecologist David Orr calls us the generation of "landscape illiteracy." Gary Paul Nabhan, a pioneer and saint of seed diversity protection, writes that "fewer and fewer people can read the landscape about them for indications of its health and hidden wealth. . . More tractors, but fewer eyes and feet upon the land, mean that we fail to notice the impoverishment of the biological community and the loss of soil: an erosion of both genetic and environmental resources that have evolved over millennia. The ecological crisis, in a very real sense, is a failure of vision."

Sadly, much of this strikes most people as mere rhetoric or, worse, heresy. In Hebrew there is a curious idiom for heresy: *l'katsets benetiyot,* to apostatize. The apostasy of one Talmudic figure, Elisha ben Abuye, earned him the notorious title of *Aher,* the Other. He is described in the Talmud as *kitsets be-netiyot,* that is literally: He cut down the shoots (young trees). He cut the endless circle of God's creation; he denied the connectedness of the Whole and all its parts. In the concise and fertile words of Wendell Berry, "If we represent knowledge as a tree, we know that things that are divided are yet connected. We know that to observe the divisions and ignore the connections is to destroy the tree." These days, we realize, with growing bewilderment to our comfortable, rationalist worldview, that the heretics are we: we who believe in endless economic growth (driven by endless population growth, among other things), limitless resources, the separation of nature and culture; we who believe that the earth and God's splendors are ours for the taking, that downtrodden people don't demand justice; we who are cutting down the tree of life.

And here we have come full circle. The new integrative biology, the Gaia hypothesis, the Newtonian laws of thermodynamics, even the Einsteinian universe of energy and matter, affirm what nearly every traditional culture knew from time immemorial, whether it be the Kabbalistic verity that deeds in the lower worlds affect the upper worlds, or the Native American sacred hoop of the Creator's intertwined universe and all its beings: actions have reactions; pollution (in every meaning) has severe repercussions; connections unmade can only be mended at great cost, if at all. Charles Darwin, an abolitionist in his day, wrote: "If the misery of our poor be caused not by laws of nature, but by our institutions, great is our sin." Amen to that.

Berkeley, California
March, 1992

JEWS, MONEY AND
SOCIAL RESPONSIBILITY

Rabbi Yishmael said:
> One who wishes to acquire wisdom should study the way
> that money works, for there is no greater area of Torah-study
> than this. It is like an everflowing stream. . . .
>
> *Bava Batra 175b*
>
> *Bava Batra* is a tractate of Talmud within the Mishnaic order of *Nezikim,* which deals with
> criminal, commercial and civil codes of law.

Derived from Danny Siegel's wonderful anthology of midrash and halakhah, *Where Heaven and Earth Touch* (1989, Jason Aronson, Inc., New Jersey and London), pp. 161-162. Used by permission.

Introduction: Money — Eek! — and Social Responsibility

IN THE 1977 PUBLICATION of The Vanguard Foundation, *Robin Hood Was Right: A Guide to Giving Your Money for Social Change,* Laura Bouyea wrote about how difficult it is for people of wealth to discuss money. The subject, she said, "is more taboo than sex. . . . laden with embarrassment, guilt, secret pleasure, and the fear of other people's envy." Add to her list sorrow, anger, anxiety, shame, pride, lust and disgust, and you only begin to catalogue the emotions that the topic of money stirs up for people of *every* income bracket — emotions that produce silence, secretiveness, exaggeration, absent-mindedness and other awkward behaviors when we are faced with the need to discuss money matters. Intimate relationships are stressed, parent-child relationships are sorely tested, partner-

1

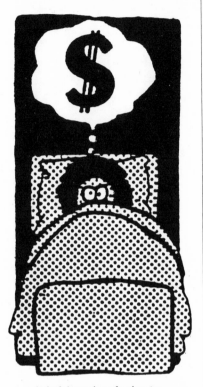

Ackelsberg is referring to Richard Sennett and Jonathan Cobb, *The Hidden Injuries of Class,* 1982, Alfred A. Knopf, New York.

ships founder, over issues of money. Why this tremendous ambivalence about something that is, after all, only a tool of exchange, a tool required for everyday living?

At the founding retreat of The Shefa Fund in 1989, Prof. Martha Ackelsberg of Smith College answered this question succinctly: Money, she said, is not only a tool of exchange, but a measurement of power and status used to create rankings among people. This system of ranking ("class status"), supposedly based on personal merit, is reinforced through unequal opportunities and privileges, class-bound cultural identities and states of mind, and cross-class prejudices, all of which ultimately serves, in Ackelsberg's words, to "legitimize vast inequalities of income, wealth and respect" and "generate feelings of isolation, powerlessness and inadequacy *for virtually everyone.* . . . No matter what class we were raised in," she emphasized, "it always feels 'wrong.'" Ackelsberg explained:

As Sennett and Cobb emphasize in their analysis, U.S. society places a high value on freedom, autonomy and independence. But we think of achieving freedom, autonomy and independence by differentiating ourselves from others (i.e., being the best student in the class, the most obedient, the most outrageous, etc.). This creates a basic paradox. . . . On the one hand, we feel good (or, at least, are supposed to feel good) about ourselves when we demonstrate that we are different from, better than, or at least independent of, others. This perspective is reinforced clearly in many of our school systems; it is also present in the ideal — pervasive in U.S. society — of the independent entrepreneur. In this context, as Sennett and Cobb make clear, class becomes a contest for dignity.

But a situation where dignity and (self)-respect are achieved through differentiation effectively denies us ties of community and connectedness. . . . Our society accords respect and dignity at the cost of isolation from peers.

> **The class system hurts everyone — including rich people.**

Steven M. Cohen quoted in *The Jewish Week,* October 5, 1990.

Part of this "cost of isolation" is our inability to speak of money matters without high anxiety. Anxiety: that we will be stereotyped and judged for our wealth or lack of same; that we will be asked to give it away; that we will be blamed for inequities that are societal in scale and not within our power, even on a case-by-case basis, to alter very significantly; that we will be held morally accountable for a system that is amoral in its functioning and often immoral in its results.

FOR JEWS, anxieties about money are vastly heightened by our historic experience of persecution and displacement, particularly in Europe, against which Jewish wealth (bribery) and professionalism (indispensability) were often our only available, though far from infallible, defenses. Jews cannot afford to be glib about money issues; money has been, for us, a tool not merely of status and power but of survival. Jews are also constantly contending with classic, enduring stereotypes linking us to affluence and greed; we have reason to worry about visibly thriving within a system that is marred by inequity, for we have often been scapegoated for problems not of our making.

Thus when we read the estimate of Steven M. Cohen, one of the leading demographers of American Jewish life, that "One third of multi-millionaires [in the U.S.] are Jews, and Jews are 40-50% of elites in professions such as medicine, law, and the

JEWISH CAPITALISTS, JEWISH COMMUNISTS

Judaism and Jewish culture have been idealized and appropriated as a paradigm by proponents of both free-enterprise and socialist ideology, writes Meir Tamari, Former Chief Economist in the Office of the Governor of the Bank of Israel in Jerusalem, in his study, *"With All Your Possessions" — Jewish Ethics and Economic Life* (1987, The Free Press, New York). "(C)hampions of capitalism," he notes, presented the Jew "as a model for private enterprise" due to the Jewish "need for political freedom ... ability to transcend national boundaries, and Judaism's legitimization of the profit motive in the accumulation of capital. . . . The problem with these arguments is that they divorce Jewish economic practices from Jewish sources. These sources impose important restraints on the free market model, restraints that derive from peculiarly Jewish concepts of mutual responsibility, the sanctification of everyday living and God-given absolute morality." From the other camp, Tamari quotes A. S. Lieberman, "one of the fathers of Jewish socialism": "'For us, socialism is not strange. The community is our existence, the revolution our tradition, the commune the basis of the Torah, which has been made concrete in the laws that land is not to be sold in perpetuity, in the law of the Jubilee and Sabbatical years, a system of equality and tranquility.' But," Tamari argues, "despite Judaism's insistence" on economic justice, charity, and mutual assistance, "it also recognizes the legitimacy of private property, the profit motive, and market mechanism" (pp. 1-2; used by permission).

Why Marxism Failed!

Religion is the opiate of the people.

Where can I get some?

The *Harvard Business Review* study by Frederick Sturdivant and Roy Adler is reported in *Jews in the Protestant Establishment,* by Richard L. Zweigenhaft and G. William Domhoff (1982, Praeger Publishers, New York).

The American Jewish "Success Story" — Some Statistics

• The Council of Jewish Federations' 1990 National Jewish Population Survey reports that while the median annual income for housholds with at least one Jewish member is $39,000, between 10% and 14% are low-income (under $20,000 for a multi-person household). 70% of American Jewish households earn under $50,000. Some 10% — 600,000 Jews—are estimated to live at or below poverty levels (compared to 13% of the general population)
• Of the 400 richest Americans listed by *Forbes* magazine each year, 25% consistently are Jewish.
• Fewer than 3% of Jews in the work force any longer work in family businesses; 15% are government workers, 16% are self-employed, 9% work in the non-profit sector.

media," a lot of us become nervous: the "rich Jew" stereotype hovers dangerously close to our heads.

When we read, on the other hand, of a 1976 *Harvard Business Review* study of 444 top executives of major U.S. corporations that found only 5% were Jewish (although Jews make up a significantly higher percentage of college graduates, who comprise the pool for potential corporate executives), we may feel some of our anxiety relieved ("Whew, Jews don't have disproportionate economic influence after all!) — even while we feel vaguely suspicious about anti-Semitism in corporate life.

THE TALMUDIC PASSAGE quoted at the opening of this essay may be alarming as well. Rabbi Yishmael's assertion that "there is no greater area of Torah-study" than "the way money works" may feed our worries about anti-Semitic perceptions of Jews and Judaism. It should also intrigue us, however, as a startling spiritual assertion about money — one that is potentially far more empowering than the usual religious preachments against worldliness and materialism.

In fact, Judaism does very much concern itself with "the way that money works" — as it concerns itself with every aspect of daily living. *Judaism is a discussion about life, both its mundane and cosmic aspects — a discussion in which the sanctification of creation and the amelioration of the human condition are central, intertwined concerns.* Within Jewish thought, the wresting of our livelihood through labor sanctifies the connection between the human being *(adam)* and the earth *(adamah),* while reflecting the daunting-yet-elevating fact that human beings are formed in the image of God, whose creative labor shaped the universe. Work is one of the means by which the Jew participates in the re-creation of the world, as a partner with God. "As the Torah was given as a covenant," the

5

Judaism for Agnostics

A 1991 national survey of Jews by the American Jewish Committee shows that while two-thirds of American Jews say "definitely yes" when asked if they believe that "there is a God," only 18% believe that "God intervenes in the course of human events." It is altogether probable, therefore, that many readers of this essay do not base their Jewish identities upon a faith in deity and may even be uncomfortable with "God-talk" that does not make explicit a sense of metaphor (that is, non-literal reality). Of course, there is no space here for full-blown theological discourse on God as a Being (or Spirit or Intelligence) vs. God as a convenient appellation for what we perceive as the "unity of the universe" or what we feel as the human will to redemption — except to say that Judaism, with its lack of dogma and its varied sources of interpretive authority, can function as a pragmatically oriented ethical tradition with *either* definition. This essay is non-literalist and non-fundamentalist in spirit; it views a Jewishly religious life as entailing (in Rabbi Arthur Green's words) a "leap of consciousness" rather than a "leap of faith." It is written in the belief that, whether the word "God" needs simultaneous translation for you or not, progressive Judaism, which essentially seeks to heal the world through "sanctification" (ritualized appreciation) and *mitzvah* (constructive deed or constructive restraint), offers great redemptive potential for human beings.

"Work as covenant" from
Avot de-Rabbi Nathan,
derived from Avraham
Shapira's essay on "Work" in
*Contemporary Jewish Re-
ligious Thought,* edited by
Arthur A. Cohen and Paul
Mendes-Flohr, 1987, The
Free Press, New York, p.
1056.

sages said, "so was work given as a covenant. " The "ways of money," then, are considered to be imbued with potential holiness that human beings need to recognize and actualize; the ways of money can be rendered into a "Torah of Money," rooted in the ethical imperatives of Judaism via injunctions, restrictions and other tools of influence.

CENTRAL TO THIS "Torah of Money" are Jewish teachings that reinforce our awareness of interdependence and mutual responsibility — an awareness so obvious during our dependent childhoods, yet all but obliterated from our consciousness by the requirements of "growing up" and "making a living" in the modern world. "The individual," writes Jewish feminist theologian Judith Plaskow in her 1990 work, *Standing Again at Sinai,* "is not an isolated unit who attains humanity through independence from others. . . Rather, to be a person is to find oneself from the beginning in community. . . . *The conviction that personhood is shaped, nourished and sustained in community is a central assumption that Judaism and feminism share.* . . . The covenantal history that begins with Abraham, Isaac and Jacob finds its fulfillment only at Sinai, when the whole congregation answers together, 'All that the Lord has spoken we will do' (*Exodus* 19:8)" (italics added).

Judith Plaskow, *Standing Again
at Sinai,* 1990, HarperCollins,
San Francisco, pp. 76-77. Used
by permission.

This affirmation of interdependence and mutual responsibility is one that the American capitalist system little acknowledges. Rather than affirming the communal obligations of the human being — and the communal sources of society's wealth — the capitalist system simply affirms the rights of the individual (including the rights of corporations, which are "individuals" in the eyes of the law). Capitalist theorists argue that the needs of the community are best met by a well-functioning marketplace in which individual self-interest (i.e.,

Wealth and Community:

Writing in the Spring, 1992 issue of *Israel Horizons,* economist Gar Alperovitz takes note of the "community investment" involved in the production of wealth: "the build-up of highways and waterways, the evolution of overall skill levels, repeated generations of schooling. . ." and, "still more fundamental. . . the much longer and larger community investment which provides centuries of science — from before Newton to after Einstein — and in the development of technologies and inventions among hundreds of thousands of scientists and engineers and millions of skilled working people. This very broad community investment is the most important factor. When a bright young computer inventor produces an innovation that makes him a millionaire, he commonly thinks he 'deserves' all that he receives. His 'invention,' however, is literally unthinkable without the previous generations — indeed, centuries — of knowledge, skills, wealth. He picks the best fruit of a tree which stands on a huge mountain of human contribution."

Buber quote derived from *The Way of Response: Martin Buber, Selections from His Writings,* edited by Nahum N. Glatzer (1966, Schocken Books, New York), p. 55. Used by permission.

financial profit) is pursued, and that other economic systems that attempt to build structures based upon perceived communal needs ("the greatest good for the greatest number") at best surrender efficiency and innovation, at worst decline into coercion and totalitarianism.

Given the horrors, dire failures and ultimate bankruptcy of the communist systems of Eastern Europe, our capitalist system seems the safer road, the "lesser of two evils" by far. Yet our rejection of a system that crushes the individual in the name of "community" does not mandate our uncritical acceptance of a system that ignores the demands of community in the name of individualism. The fall of communism does not mean the success of capitalism — a system which has produced, in the America of the 1990s, gross economic inequities, real poverty for over 32 million people, and a dimming economic future for the majority. As in the Jewish tale of the rabbi who is negotiating a dispute and judges both disputants to be correct — and, when asked by a witness, "How can they both be right?," responds, "You're right, too" — so are we entitled to judge both systems as unbalanced and incomplete.

Martin Buber did so in 1943, when he posited a "genuine third alternative," arising from the human apprehension of God ("on the narrow ridge. . . where I and Thou meet"), and "leading beyond individualism and collectivism, for the life decision of future generations." His words are potent for our time, given the collapse of communism ("collectivism" that was totalitarian and murderous) and the increasing human and environmental toll of capitalism ("individualism" that is rootless, one-dimensional and unjust).

YET BUBER'S WORDS are vague, if wonderfully suggestive. What, in fact, would comprise a "genuine third alter-

Martin Buber, 1878—1965, considered himself a "religious socialist." "(R)eligion and socialism," he wrote, "are essentially directed to each other. . . each of them needs the covenant with the other for the fulfilment of its own mission. *Religio,* that is the human person's binding of himself [sic] to God, can only attain its full reality in the will for a community of the human race, out of which alone God can prepare His [sic] kingdom. *Socialitas,* that is humankind's becoming a fellowship. . . cannot develop otherwise than out of a common relation to the divine center, even if this be again and still nameless. Unity with God and community among the creatures belong together. Religion without socialism is disembodied spirit, therefore not genuine spirit; socialism without religion is body emptied of spirit, hence also not genuine body." Quoted from *The Way of Response,* as cited on the previous page, p. 158. Used by permission.

Martin Buber

native. . . leading beyond individualism and collectivism. . ."? The Jewish religious tradition (which has, curiously enough, been considered a paradigm of both capitalism and socialism by proponents of either system — see p. 4) offers teachings

In affirming human interdependence and mutual responsibility, Judaism gives significant clues about how to reform the "ways of money."

Progressive Asset Management,1814 Franklin St., 7th floor, Oak-land, CA 94612, 510-834-3722 or 800-786-2998. PAM advises and manages some 3,500 accounts containing over $300 million. PAM clears its financial transactions through Paine Webber, thereby giving clients access to a full range of investment products and services, including stocks, bonds and mutual funds.

about *shabbat* (sabbath), *tzedakah* (charity, redistribution), stewardship instead of ownership, and the unity of creation, that were the building-blocks of Buber's vision. These and other core concepts of Judaism are to be explored in this essay, as we attempt to envision what we might call a "covenanted economy" or a "Torah of Money."

Judaism, however, by no means has a monopoly on such concepts. Among many other religious and secular voices for economic justice, there has been in the U.S. for well over 20 years a "socially responsible money movement" that has sought to join a sense of communal responsibility to corporate individualism through shareholder initiatives, socially screened investments, consumer activism and other tools that can influence corporate behavior. Ellen Stromberg, an investment broker who helped found Progressive Asset Management of Oakland, California, one of a handful of socially responsible investment firms and banks in the U.S., describes "the movement" as follows:

> Socially responsible investing involves the consideration of social and personal values in deciding where to invest our dollars. We do so in recognition that *everything we do involving money makes a moral statement;* every time we spend or invest money, we are making ethical, political and economic choices. Ten years ago, when I trained to be a stockbroker, this awareness was not an element in my training; I learned to make investment suggestions to people without thought as to where the money involved was going, or whom it was affecting or not affecting.

In fact, Stromberg was significantly influenced by Jewish teachings:

> Yet I also had the Jewish tradition to reckon with — the critical attention paid within Judaism to the responsible use

of wealth. Much of Jewish thought stresses the cultivation of holiness within everyday life, including the application of the teachings of Torah to the marketplace.

When I became a bat-mitzvah, my *parshah* was *Leviticus* 19: "When you reap the harvest of your land, you shall not reap all the way to the edges of your field, or gather the gleanings of your harvest. You shall not pick your vineyard bare, or gather the fallen fruit of your vineyard; you shall leave them for the poor and the stranger. . ." *Leviticus* 19 also gives instructions guiding the payment of fair wages and other business practices. It made explicit to me a connection between Jewish tradition and the socially responsible use of money.

For most activists within the social responsibility movement, however, judgments about "social responsibility" are rooted more consciously in the American peace and social justice movements of the past three decades (civil rights, feminist, gay and lesbian, environmental, etc.) than in any Jewish religious or historical concepts. Fair labor practices, reduced environmental impact, opportunities for minorities and women, divestment in South Africa, limited military involvement, no nuclear involvement, ethical management, truthful public relations, respect for law and regulations — these are some of the specific criteria for corporate conduct that concern socially responsible money managers, analysts, consumers and investors.

A disproportionate number of American Jews participated in those movements of the 1960s, '70s and '80s, and share some of the vocabulary and priorities of the social responsibility movement. Many of us, however, feel both connected to and frustrated by liberal political values and alliances. We have been alienated by the anti-Semitism and anti-Israel preachments of sectors of the left and Black communities; we have felt unsupported by progressive forces in our struggles

> **The social responsibility movement has been pursuing justice within a marketplace economy for over two decades. It deserves Jewish involvement and support.**

on behalf of Soviet Jewry or religious freedom; we have been actively courted by neoconservative and fundamentalist Christian would-be allies; we are wondering where we stand.

Likewise do many Jews feel both connected to and variously alienated by Jewish life and Judaic tradition. We may be angry about its sexism and its resistance to reinterpretation; we may be turned off by the bureaucracies and hierarchies of organized Jewish life; we may be agnostic in our faith and ignorant of our traditions; we may feel trapped in all sorts of contradictions by our concern for Israel.

Neither "tradition," in other words, is clearly authoritative in guiding our ethical lives. Yet both are influential — and many of us are actively involved in reinterpretive and reconstructive efforts on both fronts.

THIS ESSAY will therefore attempt to wrestle with both traditions in order to advance towards the paramount goal that they clearly share: to influence what Rabbi Yishmael called "the way that money works" in a direction that might free us from the suffering, the anxieties, the silences, the less-than-whole sense of self that the existing money system foists on us; to begin to develop, in other words, a modern "Torah of Money" in which the dictates of the "bottom line" and the teachings of the "Most High" are harmonized.

Through our wrestling, we hope also to help awaken readers to the existence of the social responsibility movement *and* to the richness of pertinent Jewish teachings. We hope to empower readers of whatever economic status to begin to deal consciously with their money as a tool for *tikkun olam,* the righteous reordering and healing of the world. In short, we aim to help make a *shiddukh* (marriage) between the Jewish community and the social responsibility movement, to the benefit of both:

• To the benefit of the social responsibility movement, because American Jewish wealth is significant enough to have enormous political clout if Jews would "put their money where their mouths are" and use it to leverage social change. Gerald Bubis, founding director of the School of Jewish Communal Services and Alfred Gottschalk Professor Emeritus at Hebrew University College-Jewish Institute for Research in Los Angeles, has developed figures that show that Jews, less than 3% of the population, now control some 15% of the Gross National Product. In addition, Jews offer the social responsibility movement outstanding examples of effective political organizing, and a vocabulary of religious humanism that has great power and currency in modern America.

• To the benefit of the Jewish community, because the issues confronted by the social responsibility movement are real-life issues that confront Jews, as they confront all Americans, at home, at work, and in the marketplace. Involvement with these issues can help revitalize and democratize Jewish communal life, heighten the importance of Jewish organizations for their constituents, and help attract the large plurality of American Jews who, sadly enough, have deemed Judaism as essentially irrelevant to their lives.

WE HOPE our readers will gain from this essay both facts and new perspectives about the business world and the world of Judaism. We warn in advance that it is, of necessity, superficial in its treatment of both worlds. For this reason we have supplemented the essay with as many tidbits as we could — sidebar information, bibliographies, addresses and phone numbers, etc. — to enable readers to pursue whatever interest we manage to provoke about the socially responsible money movement and about Judaism. In general we have used popularly written books as sources for quotations and insights from the texts of the Jewish tradition, so that even readers who are unequipped to read original Judaic texts can easily follow the advice of the great humanistic Talmudic sage, Hillel, to "Go and study."

Read in good health.

Questions to Consider and Discuss

What kinds of feelings arise in you concerning the role of money in your life? Pride? Embarrassment? Worry? Excitement? Pleasure? Have you compared notes on these feelings with others, or do you keep them to yourself?

How would you describe your "class status?" To what extent does money indeed translate into "status" (or lack of it) in your life? In what ways do your finances intersect with your self-esteem?

What do you think of as the "essential values" of Judaism? What do you consider to be your essential political or social values? Which wellspring of values seems more relevant or active for you?

What factors, if any, tend to alienate you from your Jewish identity or your political identity? In what ways do your Jewish consciousness and social consciousness support each other or seem in conflict?

Instant **Renewal**® 3-Lb. Box **99**¢	Assorted **Explanations** Mix 'n'Match! **2**³⁹ lb.	**Belly Laughs** guaranteed fresh **69**¢
Pure Pleasure Limit One per Customer **49**¢	**Thighs & Loins** Family Pac **79**¢	Multi-Purpose **Dough 89**¢
Imagination As seen on television Bunch **2** **49**	Premium **Guts 49**¢	**Space 79**¢
Facades Choose from a wide variety of designer styles **1**²⁹ 6-pack	**Guile 1**²⁹	Unconditional **Love 69**¢

Buy One, Get One Free!
Imported **Romance**
with this coupon **2**⁹⁹ Frozen

Buy One, Get One Free!
Satisfaction
with this coupon **1**⁷⁹ while it lasts

Manager's Special
Attention
with this coupon **1**⁸⁸ undivided

On Sale This Week!

IN THIS CHAPTER: Consumption, the "Wasting Disease". . . The Environmental Impact of American Consumption. . . Judaism's Sense of Limits and Borders: Shabbat and the *Sh'ma* . . . Judaism on Individual Responsibility: The Story of an Illiterate Tailor. . . The Council on Economic Priorities: Empowering the American Consumer. . . Other Strategies of "Shopping for a Better World.". . . The Socially Responsible Synagogue.

No one should taste anything without first reciting a blessing over it, as it is said, "The Earth is the Lord's and the fullness thereof" (Psalm 24). Whoever enjoys the goods of this world without reciting a blessing is like a thief.

Berakhot 35a

Berakhot is a tractate of the Talmud within the order of *Zeraim*, which deals with laws of agriculture.

Derived from Meir Tamari's *"With All Your Possessions," Jewish Ethics and Economic Life,* 1987, The Free Press, New York and London.

Consumption: Curing a Modern Disease

"**W**HEN THE GOING GETS TOUGH, the tough go shopping." "Whoever dies with the most toys wins."

Amid the bumpersticker humor and the relentless barrage of multi-million-dollar advertising aimed at whetting America's acquisitive appetites, a pattern of helplessness and addiction emerges. The warning uttered in the book of *Ecclesiastes* that "All is vanity!" is acknowledged by the commercial culture and perversely stood on its head: All is, indeed, vanity, so why not "shop until you drop?"

"Consumption," the "wasting disease" — these were the common names given to pulmonary tuberculosis, the health scourge of the immigrant generation of working-class Jews in America. Their profound exploitation in sweatshops bred both the disease (which literally consumed victims' lungs) and, for those who managed to maintain their health, a terrible sense of alienation from their own lives. The popular Yiddish sweatshop poet, Morris Rosenfeld (1862-1923), expressed that alienation with painful eloquence:

17

I work, and I work, and I work without pause,
produce and produce and produce without end.
For what? And for whom? I don't know, I don't ask.
Since when can a factory machine comprehend?

Today, the prevailing meaning of "consumption" has changed — as has the class composition of American Jewry. While poverty remains a Jewish problem, particularly among the Jewish elderly, and while the broadly middle-class American Jewish community is struggling to maintain itself against the pressures of "downward mobility" in the 1990's, our general affluence has enabled us to leave the sweatshop far behind. Few American Jews any longer feel the unrelenting, dehumanizing pressure to "produce and produce and produce without end" simply in order to survive. Still, the alienated, pressurized imagery of Morris Rosenfeld's poem does seem descriptive of our own lives: of the pressure we feel to consume, to be "plugged in," "hip" and fashionable; to turn our homes into fully-equipped, self-sufficient modules and our lives into over-scheduled athletic events; to "save time," to value "convenience," to distance ourselves in every possible way from the inhuman rigors of the sweatshop poet's era — and the inhumane poverty and suffering of our own.

The Environmental Impact of American Consumption

THIS LATTER-DAY version of "consumption" does not result solely from personal susceptibility to bumpersticker messages, or from personal unhappiness, greed or addictive tendencies — any more than tuberculosis was the "fault" of its victims' temperaments. Rather, it is the very structure of our

Tuberculosis, before it was curable, was mystified as the disease of the "hypersensitive, the talented, the passionate," writes Susan Sontag (*AIDS and Its Metaphors,* 1988, Farrar, Straus and Giroux, New York). Similarly, the as-yet incurable diseases, cancer and AIDS, are today mystified: cancer as striking the "psychically defeated" and "repressed," while AIDS affects the "indulgent" and "immoral."

It is the very structure of our urban and suburban lives in the U.S. — lacking even the familial and communal networks that buoyed our ancestors — that reinforces manic activity and wasteful consumption.

Jeffrey A. Hollender is a founder and chairperson of Seventh Generation, a catalogue shopping company that features "products for a healthy (*Continued next page*)

post-World War II, urban and suburban lives in the United States — lacking even the familial and communal networks that buoyed our ancestors — that reinforces manic activity and wasteful consumption. Certainly, the garage full of machinery that the average American Jewish family possesses could adequately serve a much larger community — as Israeli *kibbutzim* have amply demonstrated. But there are no such mainstream communal institutions on the American landscape. Instead, each separate nuclear family *requires* for its smooth functioning its own cars, food processor, VCR, lawnmower, etc. The maximization of consumption and the maximization of individualism and isolation thus become mutually reinforcing, systemic patterns.

Of course, that such abundance is available to many families, that life *has* materially improved for most Americans since Morris Rosenfeld's day, must be counted as a blessing (a blessing that American Jewish immigrant entrepreneurs in no small way made possible by helping to develop the U.S. retail industry). Nevertheless, modern consumption poses a broader threat than anything faced by our immigrant forebears, for while the consumption of Morris Rosenfeld's day shortened many a life, our latter-day version of the wasting disease is eating away at the vital organs of our very planet:

• "Americans throw out 10 times their weight in trash every year, or about one-half ton for every person," according to Jeffrey A. Hollender, author of *How to Make the World a Better Place* (1990, Quill/William Morrow, New York). "We throw away enough aluminum to rebuild the entire American airfleet" four times over, enough steel "to reconstruct Manhattan, and enough wood and paper to heat five million homes for 200 years" (or every American home for well over a decade). Of this trash, containers and packaging accounts for nearly 50%, writes Hollender, with 50% of our paper, 30% of our plastic,

19

(Continued from previous page) planet" (800-456-1177). The catalogue began as a project of Renew America, a non-profit environmental group that maintains *America's Environmental Success Index,* a clearinghouse of more than 1,000 products that are enhancing and restoring the environment. Contact: Renew America, 1400 16th St. NW, Suite 710, Washington, DC 20036, 202-232-2252.

In fact, one in every six American trucks is a garbage truck, according to *The Recycler's Handbook,* published in 1990 by The Earth•Works Group, 1400 Shattuck Ave., #25, Berkeley, CA 94709. Such trucks average only six miles per gallon in fuel consumption. Eighty percent of their load is buried in landfills — which are closing across the U.S. at the rate of two per day (14,000 of 20,000 landfills closed between 1978 and 1988). "Most landfills were built before safety standards became a high priority," writes The Earth•Works Group. "They're not equipped to stop toxic leachate from seeping into groundwater. How many landfills might eventually leak? According to the Environmental Protection Agency, *all* of them."

40% of our aluminum, 75% of our glass, and 8% of our steel used "solely to package and decorate consumer products." Overall, Americans spend more for food packaging than the nation's farmers receive in net income.

• We also throw away 18 billion disposable diapers (made from 21 million trees), 25 billion Styrofoam cups (the manufacture of which threaten the ozone layer of the planet), and two hundred million automobile tires per year. "Americans generate four to six pounds of garbage per day," according to Hollander, "about double that produced by the typical Japanese, Swiss. . . German or Swedish citizen. . . . enough to fill about 40,000 garbage trucks or to load up an armada of 125 ocean-going garbage barges."

• We dump the equivalent of one ton per person of hazardous waste into the ground every year. Groundwater in more than 30 of the 50 states has been contaminated with agricultural pesticides. Of the nearly 50,000 permitted chemicals listed in the inventory of the Environmental Protection Agency, fewer than a tenth have been tested for cancer-causing or reproductive effects. Meanwhile, the few chemical bans that are enacted in the U.S. rarely extend to overseas sales by American chemical companies. "DDT and benzene hexachloride (BHC), both banned in the U.S. and much of Europe," writes Hollender, "account for about three quarters of the total pesticide use in India. Residues of these compounds," both presumed carcinogens, "were found in all 75 samples of breast milk collected from women in India's Punjab region. . . Similarly, samples of breast milk from Nicaraguan women have shown DDT levels that are an astounding 45 times greater than tolerance limits set by the World Health Organization." Our poisonous exports, of course, return to us as imports — off-season strawberries, for example — and as toxic detritus from the tides of the global environment.

Graphic from *The Big Stick,* Yiddish humor newspaper, June 27, 1919. The Yiddish on the bandage says, "Di Velt" — the world.

ETCETERA, ETCETERA: After a while, statistics about pollution, vanishing species, global warming, and so on — similarly to statistics about worldwide starvation and poverty — tend to bore as much as they horrify. The problems we face seem so large and multi-layered as to be beyond solution or even discussion ("It's too depressing"). Our alienation thus redoubles on itself, and we are left to experience the pain of human disaster individually: in individual tumors and birth

21

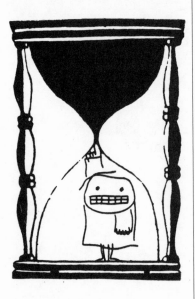

defects and infertility, in individual choices not to linger here, not to travel there, not to read this, not to think about that, but simply to hug our loved ones, apply more suntan lotion and hope — or pray — for the best.

Judaism's Sense of Limits and Borders

THE WORLD indeed seems damned, if not doomed. Some non-Jewish religious teachings even view life from that perspective (e.g., "original sin") and urge us to respond to society's failings by "dropping out." Asceticism, chastity, renunciation — each is a mark of religious devotion, and may have its place in the struggle against modern "consumption." Judaism, however, has hardly any renunciate tradition; rather, Judaism associates abundance with holiness, as exemplified by the sabbath feast that we spread on our tables. "The holy law imposes no asceticism," wrote Judah Halevi, the Hebrew poet of medieval Spain, in his book of religious dialogue, the *Kuzari* (c. 1135). "It demands that we. . . grant each mental and physical faculty its due." The Talmud agrees: Each of us will be called to account in the hereafter, says *Kiddushin* 4:12, for each pleasure we abjure without sufficient cause.

Eighteenth century Hasidic folk-mysticism went further, noting that although the tradition calls us to sanctify certain specific activities with blessings and prayers, other endeavors, notably sexual and business activities, have no intrinsic holiness and are "neutral." Hasidic teachings maintained that a goal of human life is nevertheless to sanctify these mundane areas, to "redeem the holy sparks" by engaging in sexuality and business and financial affairs with full, focused consciousness.

The problems we face seem so large and multi-layered as to be beyond solution or even discussion. Our alienation thus redoubles on itself, and we are left to experience the pain of human disaster individually: in individual tumors and birth defects and infertility, in individual choices not to linger here, not to travel there, not to read is, not to think about that, but simply to hug our loved ones, apply more suntan lotion and hope — or pray — for the best.

Judith Chalmer, Karen Brooks and Rebecca Sherlock, "Celebrating the Cycles of the Sun and Moon Together," *Genesis 2,* Autumn, 1988, Vol. 19, No. 3.

Our multifaceted tradition, in short, bids us not to abstain from this "corrupt" world, but to make it holy through our participation. Judaism asks that we discipline ourselves to *measure the impact* of each of our actions, upon the world and upon ourselves. "Judaism is a religion of distinctions," write Judith Chalmer, Karen Brooks and Rebecca Sherlock, co-leaders of Rosh Chodesh (new moon) celebrations in Montpelier, Vermont. "We are constantly delineating. . . *living within the boundaries that we need to be survivors in this world and creative participants in its making.* . . . The very word for 'holy,' *kadosh,* means 'set apart' — yet our concern as Jews is with this world, not a separate kingdom. . ." (italics added).

Even God is required to set boundaries and limits in order to preserve the universe, according to Jewish mystical accounts of Creation: The limitless Force of Creation must *limit* its holy radiance so as not to shatter the new vessel of reality. Rabbi Levi Yitzhak, an 18th century Hasidic teacher, describes the late stages of this process of cosmic creation while implying a powerful lesson about redeeming our world:

The Levi Yitzhak passage is derived from David R. Blumenthal's *God at the Center, Meditations on Jewish Spirituality* (1988, Harper & Row, San Francisco), p. 66. Used by permission. We have altered this passage so that references to God are not gender-specific. Levi Yitzhak ben Sarah (1740-1810) was an intense, mystical Hasidic leader in the early days of Hasidism in the city of Berditchev.

What was the grievous sin, the "lawlessness" (*Genesis* 6:11), that provoked the Flood? The Reform movement's *The Torah, A Modern Commentary* (1981, Union of American Hebrew Congregations), notes (p. 61) that "The Midrash speculates that it was unbounded affluence that caused men to become depraved. . ." And the sin that led to the "confusion of tongues" in the Babel story (*Genesis* 11: 1-9)? Again, the Midrash (p. 85): "The problem of the people of Babel was their mindless affluence" and the fact that "bricks became more precious than human life."

At creation, everything derived from the power of the Infinite and so it was capable of expanding indefinitely, without border or limit. Therefore God. . . was forced to say "Enough!" and to give order and boundary to all the worlds. For this reason, [God] is called "Shaddai" (usually translated, "Almighty"), that is "[The One] Who said to (the) universe: "Dai," "Enough.""

Biblical human beings before Abraham, however, do not show the capacity of God to say "Dai," "Enough!" Instead, they proceed to the Flood (*Genesis* 6:5-9:29) and the Tower of Babel (*Genesis* 11:1-9) — to fill the vessels of reality to bursting. The latter-day equivalents of such folly, from our vast stockpiles of nuclear bombs to our vast pools of toxic waste, from our vast, gratuitous suffering to our vast alienation from meaning, are so obvious as to make the Biblical myths seem all the more potent.

BUT LET'S GET REAL, now — after all, the messages of television are more present than the metaphors of Torah as a daily influence in most American Jewish households. (In fact, American households *throw away* several million television sets a year!) Torah teachings about creation and boundaries may or may not interest you; certainly they are not binding upon you as they might be in a theocracy or in a small, ideologically coherent community. In fact, that very question of how *voluntarily* to define limits and draw borders, how to implement a religious (or social) sensibility without indulging in coercive measures, is one that actively challenges the non-Orthodox Jewish world — as it challenges any who would have us move beyond the "shop-until-you-drop" ethic of capitalism into a "Torah of money" that would include some obedience to the commandment, "Dai!"

"Dai!" — yet we want a free market, with the opportunities and innovations it can bring.

"Dai!" — yet we are loathe to accept regulations that impose conformity or bureaucracy or undue expense upon us.

"Dai!" — yet the television keeps urging us to buy!

The challenge is to blend our freedom with a sense of obligation in order to achieve a better harmony. The challenge is to protect the ideal of "Life, Liberty and the Pursuit of Happiness" — that seminal phrase from the Declaration of Independence that envisioned the liberation of the individual from all coercive communal identities — without surrendering our sense of communal responsibility. The challenge is to find a compromise between "Buy!" and "Dai!," freedom and obligation, the enlargement of our lonely selves and the preservation of our communal self.

JUDAISM OFFERS such a compromise in its concept of human custodianship, rather than ownership, of wealth. *"The Divine origin of wealth,"* writes Meir Tamari, *"is the central principle of Jewish economic philosophy.* Since Judaism is a community-oriented rather than an individual-oriented religion, this means that the group at all levels. . . is thereby made a partner in each individual's wealth" — wealth that derives from, and belongs to, God. Rabbi Ezekiel Landau of Prague (1713-1793), an outstanding *halakhic* authority of his day, reiterated this principle when ruling in a dispute between two

---

The challenge is to find a compromise between "Buy!" and "Dai!" (Enough!) — between freedom and obligation, the enlargement of our lonely selves and the preservation of our communal self. . . . Judaism, in fact, offers such a compromise in its sense of custodianship, rather than ownership, of wealth.

Meir Tamari, *"With All Your Possessions" — Jewish Ethics and Economic Life* (already cited), pp. 36-37. Used by permission.

The story about Rabbi Landau is told by Rabbi William B. Silverman in *The Sages Speak, Rabbinic Wisdom and Jewish Values,* published by Jason Aronson, New Jersey and London, 1989, p. 107.

The rights of private property are not sacred in Judaism, Meir Tamari notes. Individual rights are limited by religious observances, concern for the welfare of others, and concern for the "public welfare." Indeed, the rabbis of the Talmud held that the central sin of the wicked city of Sodom was its citizens' refusal to share their wealth with the poor and with strangers, and their insistence on the absolute rights of private property. "When a poor person would come to Sodom," says *Sanhedrin* 109b, "everyone would give him a coin upon which was written the giver's name. But they wouldn't sell the poor person any bread. When the poor person died, each came and reclaimed his coin."

Jews who claimed ownership of a tract of land. Landau is reputed to have put his ear to the ground and then announced: "The earth has rendered its decision: 'I belong to neither of you, but both of you belong to me.'"

Reinforcing this sense of stewardship rather than ownership are the Jewish cycles of work/acquisition and rest/restoration: the weekly sabbath, and the sabbatical year and Jubilee Release that are detailed in *Leviticus* 25: 1-13:

The sabbatical year *(shmitah)* : "Six years you may sow your field and six years you may prune your vineyard and gather in the yield. But in the seventh year the land shall have a sabbath of complete rest for the land." (*Deuteronomy* 15:1 also calls for the cancellation of debts every seven years; this was abrogated shortly before the beginning of the Common Era by Hillel, leader of the Jewish governing body, the Sanhedrin.)

The Jubilee Release *(yovel):* ". . . (Y)ou shall hallow the fiftieth year. You shall proclaim release throughout the land for all its inhabitants. It shall be a jubilee for you; each of you shall return to his holding and each of you shall return to his family" — that is, twice each century, land taken as debt shall be restored to its original owners.

The intent of these laws is made clear in the text: ". . . the land must not be sold beyond reclaim; you are but strangers resident with Me" (*Leviticus* 25: 23). Both the Land and People of Israel ultimately belong to God, according to the Torah; thus no individual is permitted to acquire relentlessly or use unremittingly either property or person. These work/acquisition and rest/restoration cycles serve as a hedge against exploitation, and therefore mediate the power relations between the empowered and the disenfranchised of society.

Neither the sabbatical nor Jubilee year, however, is observed in modern Jewish life. Even in Israel, the seven-year sabbatical cycle has always been averted by rabbinic decree

"Divine Authority" and the Environmental Imperative

The Biblical process of mediation or justice-making is not based on abstract principles of human equality or democracy, but on divine, sometimes coercive, authority. This often offends contemporary sensibilities. However, environmental awareness can perhaps grant new tolerance for the prescriptive voice of the Torah and new willingness to listen to it interpretively. Environmental imperatives do, after all, have a certain "do this or else" urgency to them; the recognition of deep ecological interdependence carries implications of "covenant" that often seem as binding as any divine commandments. Creation, in other words, speaks its mind and makes its demands in no uncertain terms.

Arthur Waskow, "Rest," in *Contemporary Jewish Religious Thought,* eds. Cohen and Mendes-Flohr (already cited), p. 795. Used by permission.

(on the grounds that it would cause undue hardship for the Jewish state). The Jubilee, meanwhile, has for two thousand years been explained away as inoperative for as long as Jews were in exile; it has evolved into a messianic vision rather than a mandated event.

The weekly sabbath, on the other hand, is a living, definitive observance for many Jews. Few non-Orthodox observe it in accordance with the tradition's "forty minus one" restrictions regarding work and consumption, yet many are discovering within *shabbat* a sense of personal respite and healing that has social reverberations. *Shabbat,* writes creative theologian and activist Arthur Waskow, is a "reflection and expression of cosmic rhythms of time embedded in creation," as well as "an affirmation of human freedom, justice and equality. The biblical tradition views these strands not as contradictory but as intertwined. . . . What moderns call social justice is, in this biblical outlook, treated as one form of rest — as social repose or social renewal."

Indeed, Waskow envisions a society-wide *shabbat* as the likeliest cure for modern "consumption." "*Shabbat,*" he writes, "is precisely the cure for modernity turned cancerous. . ."

For modernity — like a cancer cell — doesn't know when to stop growing. Maybe every seven years, we should give

"The earth has rendered its decision: 'I belong to neither of you, but both of you belong to me.'"

—*Rabbi Ezekiel Landau of Prague (1713-1793)*

27

one year off to all of the people who specialize in research and development — for it is "R and D" that speeds up our speeding — not only the Bomb-builders, the Holocaust-makers, but even those who are speeding up our most benign technologies. "Take this year off to sing, dance, sit down and read together. . . Let's talk about what it's all for, let's rest a year together. "

Now, when the earth itself is endangered. . . when better to reconnect the liberation of humankind with the resting-time of earth?

ANOTHER JEWISH SOURCE for guidance in responsible living is the *Sh'ma,* the best-known prayer of the Jewish liturgy: "Hear, O Israel, the Lord our God, the Lord is One." "This powerful, simple *sui generis* of yiddishkeit," writes Andrea Cohen-Kiener, an environmental activist and Hebrew school educator,

teaches us that all of our actions, interactions and reactions are part of a single reality field. An environmental way of stating this idea might be, "We are all downstream. . ." We are challenged by this unifying world view to drive less if we fear air pollution and to turn off our lights if we want to reduce radioactive debris.

The second ecological lesson of the *Sh'ma* is this: the place where we demonstrate our love for God and the place where God expresses approval or disapproval for our efforts is the natural world. If we turn away from God, the heavens will close up and we will perish quickly from the land. (God "will shut up the skies so that there will be no rain and the ground will not yield its produce; and you will soon perish from the good land that the Lord is giving you." —*Deuteronomy* 11:17.) One can easily draw sharp parallels to acid rain, drought, ozone depletion and other forms of environmental degradation that result from our having been "lured away to serve other gods and bow to them" (11: 16).

Arthur Waskow, "Mystery, Wholeness and the Breath of Life," a secular-religious dialogue with Lawrence Bush, *Genesis 2,* April/May, 1986, Vol. 17, No. 2.

Consciously secular Jews have also taken to sabbath observance in recent years; see, for example, *We Rejoice in Our Heritage,* a book of secular Jewish rituals by Judith Seid (Kopinvant Secular Press, 910 Arbordale, Ann Arbor, MI 48103). Seid is a "Certified Secular Humanistic Jewish Leader" who directs the Ann Arbor Jewish Cultural Society.

Andrea Cohen-Kiener, "The *Sh'ma* and Ecology," *Genesis 2,* Spring, 1989.

Jews are used to believing and behaving as if small actions reflect great issues. How we pick our crops, for example, hints at our commitment to hunger and social action. . . How else could we integrate lofty ideals into our daily regimen if not by small, concrete acts? This is the brilliance and challenge of Judaism: *Kideshanu b'mitzvotav* — we are holy because of our actions.

Demands, demands! The *Sh'ma* makes so many demands! "Take to heart these instructions with which I charge you this day. Impress them upon your children. Recite them when you stay at home and when you are away, when you lie down and when you get up. Bind them as a sign on your hand and let them serve as a symbol on your forehead; inscribe them on the doorposts of your house. . ." (*Deuteronomy* 6: 4-9). Many Jews reject Judaic observance, including *shabbat,* on this very basis — that it seems so extensively demanding, rather than simply inspiring.

Likewise do many American householders complain about recycling and other socially responsible consumption practices: too inconvenient, too expensive, I'd like to but. . .

As the *Wall Street Journal* sarcastically puts it:

It's a shame Todd Putnam can't walk on water.

He sorely needs a new pair of shoes, but he can't wear leather — that would be cruel to animals. He won't touch Nike sneakers — the company has been accused of exploiting the black community. Rubber and plastic are also out, because they don't recycle well. And he has even had to stop buying his Chinese all-cotton shoes because of the Tiananmen Square massacres.

But Mr. Putnam, 28 years old, one of a new breed of ultra-conscious consumers and the founder of the Seattle-based National Boycott News (circulation 7,000), would rather do almost anything than compromise his principles. . . . He may even miss this article because he only reads second-hand newspapers, to save trees.

"Being a Consumer Isn't Easy if You Boycott Everything," by Dana Milbank, *Wall Street Journal,* April 24, 1991.

The National Boycott Newsletter, irregularly published, obtainable from Todd Putnam at 6506 28th Ave., N.E., Seattle, WA 98115, 206-523-0421. Co-op America also publishes boycott news as a regular feature in *Co-op America Quarterly,* obtainable along with many other benefits for a $20 annual membership from Co-op America, 2100 M St., N.W., #310, Washington, DC 20063, 800-424-COOP.

The Michael Peters Group survey is reported in the Council on Economic Priorities' *Research Report,* April, 1990.

Recycling facts are from *The Recycler's Handbook,* already cited.

Overall, however, we are still recycling only 10% of our ever-mounting refuse.

Yet Americans are not scoffing at the notion of socially responsible consumption, at least not in regards to environmental responsibility. A July, 1989 survey taken for the Michael Peters Group design firm found that 89% of Americans are concerned about the environmental impact of the products they buy, 53% had declined to buy something during the survey year out of concern for the effects the product or its packaging might have on the environment, and 78% said they were willing to pay extra for a product with recyclable or biodegradable materials. Recycling programs are being undertaken in thousands of communities. Each year we now recycle about 60% of 80 billion aluminum cans (which cuts related air pollution and curbs related energy use by 95%, according to the Earth•Works Group), about 27% of our newspapers, about 20% of our plastic soda bottles, about a million tons of stainless steel and a 20-square-mile parking lot's worth of cars. Much of this effort is mandated by law, but rarely do municipalities have the budgetary means of enforcing environmental laws; recycling is, in truth, largely a voluntary activity in which people are participating on a household-by-household basis, prompted by genuine concern.

Consumer boycotts are also becoming a major weapon of environmental responsibility, according to the Council on Economic Priorities (CEP), which identifies "a new breed of environmentally aware citizen. Not necessarily considering themselves activists, these people care enough about the environment to reconsider the way they shop, invest and live." When organizations such as Greenpeace or INFACT bring critical information about environmental abuse or other acts of corporate irresponsibility to the public, they meet increasingly with a positive response — as evidenced by the successful Greenpeace-led consumer boycott of tuna companies that were using fishing methods that involved the slaughter of hundreds of thousands of dolphins. In response, "dolphin-free" tuna has become the boast of leading tuna companies.

JEWS ARE PARTICIPATING in such efforts as socially conscious consumers, but also in specifically Jewish contexts. *Hadassah* magazine, for example, gave up 20% of its advertising revenues in 1987 by no longer carrying cigarette ads — a move that aligned it with only 36 consumer magazines in the U.S. The Greater Miami Jewish Federation in 1992 began to use only recycled paper for all its communications. Shomrei Adamah ("Keepers of the Earth"), a unique Jewish environmental resource center in Philadelphia, has developed a set of "green synagogue" suggestions regarding congregational use of styrofoam and non-recyclables — and the New York Board of Rabbis has sent these materials to its 1,100 members. Jews who are vegetarians, motivated by *tza'ar ba'alei chayim,* the mitzvah of respect for animals, and by concern for the disproportionate resources used to raise animals for slaughter in the face of worldwide human starvation, have organized themselves to produce and disseminate holiday materials and other vegetarian resoures.

Most recently (March 10, 1992), 16 religious and secular Jewish leaders (including three Jewish U.S. senators and the heads of the Reform, Conservative, Orthodox and Reconstructionist movements), issued a call for synagogues and organizations to initiate educational, legislative and leadership programs to promote environmental protection and curb global warming, deforestation, animal extinction, toxic waste and population growth.

Despite these breakthroughs, however, the organized Jewish community has hardly begun to engage itself with issues of socially responsible consumption. For example, the "Joint

Jews and the Grape Boycott: One of the most widely observed boycotts in the U.S., mounted by the United Farm Workers in the 1970s and again in the late '80s, targeted California-grown table grapes. At its 1987 convention, the Rabbinic Assembly of Conservative Judaism endorsed the boycott "until all people involved in the growing and harvesting of such grapes are treated with the justice which our tradition demands." The boycott was also embraced by the Reform movement.

Dena S. Davis, an attorney and teacher of social and biomedical ethics, writes: "The observance of the dietary laws serves to remind Jews of the moral dimensions of everyday life. . . . In my own family, aggressively secular, the dietary laws were viewed as quaint or pernicious. . ." Nevertheless, "my shopping basket is also defined by my Jewishness. . . by my refusal to support a migrant worker system so antithetical to what I understand as the kingdom of righteousness. It's a little thing, not eating grapes,

(Continued on page after next)

INFACT's Boycott Campaigns

Among the most widely supported consumer boycotts have been those mounted by INFACT (Infant Formula Action) against the Nestlé Company from 1976 until 1983, and presently against General Electric.

The Nestlé boycott was provoked by the company's mass-marketing of infant formula to impoverished nations, where inadequate water sanitation, illiteracy and other factors turned bottle-feeding into a major cause of infant mortality. The efforts of hundreds of local INFACT chapters forced Nestlé to adopt a code endorsed by the World Health Organization regarding the marketing of infant formula — a code which several other companies, including Bristol-Myers, American Home Products, and Abbott/Ross Laboratories, continue to ignore.

The consumer-product boycott of the General Electric Company is in protest of G.E.'s nuclear weapons-related work, which comprises a decreasing percentage of G.E. sales — according to INFACT, nearly 12% in 1988, approximately 6% today, due in part to the impact of the boycott. G.E. was the third top defense contractor in 1990, with over $5.5 billion in contracts. It is one of the country's worst polluters, with responsibility for the largest number of Superfund (PCB and radioactive) toxic sites of any corporation in the U.S.

As of 1991, INFACT claimed more than four million consumer supporters of its boycott, as well as 450 endorsing groups and institutions (including hospitals, which can wield major influence through their purchase of costly medical equipment). INFACT's documentary film about G.E., *Deadly Deception,* directed by Debra Chasnoff, won an Academy Award in 1992. INFACT can be reached at 256 Hanover St., Boston, MA 02113, 617-266-7173 or on the West Coast at 818-799-9133.

Susan Meeker Lowry notes (in *Economics As If the World Really Mattered,* 1988, New Society Publishers, POB 582, Santa Cruz, CA 95061): "If you decide to join the G.E. boycott, or any other boycott, it is important to write the company to tell them why you have stopped buying their products . . . it's very hard to find light bulbs produced by companies not involved in nuclear weapons. . . GTE (GTE, Sylvania, Grolux, Lumalux), Westinghouse, Emerson Electric (Day-Brite, Emerson) and North American Philips all are. 'Nuclear-free' light bulbs can be obtained from Duro-test (Duro-lite), Dio-Light Technologies (47 W. Huron St., Pontiac, MI 48508) and NOUAH (4445 S. Telegraph, Dearborn, MI 48124)."

(Continued from page 31)
but it reminds me and my son, in the middle of the press of our daily lives, that our lives must include a moral dimension or they lack in meaning." (From "On Not Eating Table Grapes, *Genesis 2,* Vol. 19, No. 2, Summer, 1988.)

Shomrei Adamah, Ellen Bernstein, director, publishes a newsletter, *Voice of the Trees,* and can be contacted at Church Road and Greenwood Ave. (the Reconstructionist Rabbinical College), Wyncote, PA 19095, 215-887-1988.

On Jewish vegetarianism see, for example, *Haggadah for the Liberated Lamb* by Roberta Kalechofsky and *Judaism and Vegetarianism* by Richard Schwartz (Micah Publications, 255 Humphrey St., Marblehead, MA 01945 — also the address for "Jews for Animal Rights"). Jewish Vegetarians of North America can be reached at POB 1463, Baltimore, MD 21203, 301-752-VEGV. Meateating is viewed by them as wasteful and unethical in light of the following statistics: Over 1/5 of the human population of the planet could be fed annually by the grain and soybeans now consumed by U.S. livestock; global starvation could be entirely remedied by the grain saved if Americans reduced their meat intake by only 10%. Sixteen pounds of grain and soybeans are needed to
(Continued on page after next)

Program Plan" for 1990-91 of the National Jewish Community Relations Advisory Council (NJCRAC), umbrella group for 11 major national and 111 local Jewish organizations, offers no comment on environmental concerns but to repeat an annual call for "the promotion of energy conservation." Worse, the legitimate fears of the Jewish community regarding the influence of oil-producing (i.e., mostly Arab) nations have prompted NJCRAC to endorse the development of nuclear energy throughout the past decade (with the National Council of Jewish Women consistently dissenting and calling for a moratorium on nuclear development).

Neither major organizations nor individual synagogues have, with rare exception, vigorously pursued recycling, energy conservation, or purchasing programs designed with socially responsible values in mind. In short, the Jewish community is in sore need of the energy of activists who will lead us into what Shomrei Adamah calls the "renewal of Jewish ecological wisdom."

Judaism and Individual Responsibility

YET PERHAPS ALL these exhortations to recycle, to boycott, etc., seem petty. Though the Talmudic injunction quoted at the start of this chapter may be startling —

> Whoever enjoys the goods of this world without reciting a blessing is a like a thief.

— the thievery it describes is petty larceny at worst! After all, on a household-by-household (or even synagogue-by-syna-

ETERNAL LITES

Cancer-Shmancer, as long as you're healthy!

The Tobacco Industry: Public Relations and Public Health

Philip Morris Companies, owner of General Foods (since 1985), Kraft Foods (since 1988), and four beer brands, is the world's largest consumer products company and the second largest food company. It is also the largest corporate sponsor of dance in America and has become a major donor to the arts in general (although its charitable giving is pegged by the Council on Economic Priorities at less than one percent, below the corporate standard). Such visible philanthropy has greatly enhanced the company's public image, which was damaged over the past two decades by Philip Morris's active lobbying against restrictions on tobacco use and advertising, its vigorous distribution of political action committee (PAC) monies to create a favorable legislative climate for the tobacco industry, and its strong support for Senator Jesse Helms (R-NC) — who, ironically enough, has become the liberal arts community's leading political foe. Public relations aside, however, Philip Morris' chief product remains an international killer. Writing in *The Progressive,* May, 1991, Morton Mintz reports that as American tobacco use declines, the three largest U.S. tobacco companies — Philip Morris, R. J. Reynolds, and Brown & Williamson — are aggressively expanding foreign markets with sophisticated advertising and considerable legislative support in the form of tariff and trade agreements. According to the World Health Organization, roughly a million people per year will die from smoking-related causes in underdeveloped countries during the 1990s (two million in industrialized countries). Nevertheless, in 1990, Philip Morris shareholders firmly rejected resolutions aimed at getting the company out of the tobacco business.

(Continued from page 33)
produce one pound of feedlot beef; 20,000 pounds of potatoes can be grown on the acre of land needed to produce 165 pounds of beef. In addition, cattle produce prodigious amounts of manure, which chokes rivers and lakes with excess nitrogen; huge tracts of forest are being cleared to sustain cattle grazing; 55% of the antibiotics produced in this country are mixed with livestock feeds; 55% of pesticide residues in the U.S. diet are consumed in meat. Statistical source: *How to Make the World a Better Place,* by Jeffrey Hollender, already cited.

gogue) basis, how much despoilation of the earth do we indulge in? Wouldn't we be better served by reciting a word of prayer — or protest! — each time the Exxon Corporation ships oil in single-hulled tankers, rather than reciting a blessing each time we purchase a tankful of gas for our car? Don't we need to tackle these issues at the level of *production and corporate responsibility,* rather than at the level of consumption and individual responsibility? Isn't all this "million-and-one things you can do to save the earth" politically light-weight at best, irrelevant at worst?

YES, THERE ARE systemic causes to the problems that plague us, though our mainstream news media tend to portray world-historic events as matters of individual behavior and will. The 1989 Exxon *Valdez* oil spill disaster, for example, was attributed in most news reports only to the ship captain's negligence, without much mention of the contributing systemic factors of oil dependency, cost-cutting expedi-

Consumer Empowerment According to Ralph Nader

The founding father of modern consumer activism, Ralph Nader, on February 1, 1992 presented to all Presidential candidates a list of ten principles to "strengthen citizens in their distinct roles as voters, taxpayers, consumers, workers, shareholders, and students." These "Concord (N.H.) Principles" are aimed at reversing the "pervading sense of powerlessness, denial and revulsion" that is "sweeping the nation's citizens as they endure or suffer from growing inequities, injustice, and loss of control over their future and the future of their children."

"(D)emocracy," Nader declares, "must be more than a bundle of rights on paper; democracy must also embrace usable facilities that empower all citizens" to obtain information from their government, communicate opinions, and "band together in civic associations." "We lack the mechanisms of civic power. We need a modern tool box for redeeming our democracy." Nader's specific recommendations include several for consumer empowerment that are provocatively simple:

• "Periodic inserts" in electric, gas and telephone bills and in bank statements that "invite customers to join their own statewide consumer action group to act as a watchdog, to negotiate and to advocate for their interests. A model of this. . . is the Illinois Citizen Utility Board which has saved ratepayers over $3 billion since 1983. . . . Had there been such bank consumer associations with full-time staff in the 1970s, there would not have been a trillion-dollar bailout. . . for the S & L and commercial bank crimes, speculations, and mismanagement debacles. These would have been nipped in the bud at the community level by informed, organized consumer judgment."

• Empowerment of the "citizen consumers" who are the viewers and listeners of television and radio through the establishment of an "Audience Network." "Federal law says that the public owns the public airwaves which are now leased for free by the Federal Communications Commission to television and radio companies. . . . Modern electronic communications can play a critical role in anticipating and resolving costly national problems when their owners gain regular usage, as a community intelligence, to inform, alert and mobilize democratic citizen initiatives."

• Worker control over the investment of the $3 trillion in pension monies that they own. "During the 1980s the use of pension monies for corporate mergers, acquisitions, (and) leveraged buyouts showed what does happen when ownership is so separated from control. . . . Pension monies are gigantic capital pools that can be used productively to meet community needs."

• Shareholder democracy, such that the "small or institutional. . . owners of corporations should be able to prevent their hired executives from. . . abusing shareholder assets and worker morale with huge salaries, bonuses, greenmail, and golden parachutes, self-perpetuating boards of directors, the stifling of the proxy voting system and blocking other shareholder voter reforms."

For a copy of the Concord Principles contact the Center for the Study of Responsive Law, Box 19367, Washington, D.C. 20036, 202-387-8030.

Even with stiffer penalties for corporate polluters being legislated across the U.S., enforcement remains the "weak link in protecting the environment," writes Josh Barbanel in the *New York Times,* May 13, 1992. He reports on a Suffolk County, N.Y. "sting operation" in which undercover detectives, posing as illegal dumpers, "went into the business of disposing of toxic waste from small businesses for $40 a barrel, no questions asked, and . . . found the competition so fierce that they had to lower their price. . ." The investigation was "perhaps the first of its kind in the nation," and resulted in indictments against four companies and six individuals.

Pirkei Avot (Ethics of the Fathers) is a treatise on the principles of Jewish conscience, containing many ethical statements by famous rabbis. It is a part of the Mishnah, the code of laws compiled by Judah the Prince in 188 C.E.

ency, insufficient safety regulations and the very lenient punishments meted out to polluting corporations.

It is extremely difficult, moreover, for individuals to dissent and survive within the powerful and overarching systems of our society; harder still for dissenting individuals to effect actual change. Corporations and governments have whole internal cultures, codes of behavior, gender biases, rewards and punishments, uniforms, etc. that stifle or marginalize dissent.

Nevertheless, to view those power structures as beyond the reach of individuals — and to view the problems that those power structures generate and perpetuate as beyond the realm of personal responsibility — is to embrace and breed alienation. It means separating yourself from citizenship — very possibly from the ethical dilemmas posed by your own job or home or community life! It means despairing of the significance of personal actions and the value of democracy; it means belittling the very concrete achievements of social activists, past and present. It means abandoning a basic principle of Jewish faith: that the covenant between God and Jew is a yoke placed upon each of us:

> Rabbi Tarfon said, "It is not incumbent upon you to complete the work; but neither are you free to desist from it."
> *Pirkei Avot* II: 21

> "Surely this Instruction (Torah) which I enjoin upon you this day is not too baffling for you, nor is it beyond reach. It is not in the heavens, that you should say, 'Who among us can go up to the heavens and get it for us and impart it to us, that we may observe it?' Neither is it beyond the sea. . . No, the thing is very close to you, in your mouth and in your heart, to observe it."
> *Deuteronomy* 30: 11-14

The entirety of Jewish "history," in fact, begins with an

individual couple — Abraham and Sarah — who are full of weaknesses and limitations, like all human beings, yet are called upon to abandon idolatry and "go forth" to a new, holy consciousness. Their endeavors climax centuries later with the giving of the Torah at Mt. Sinai — an event at which all 600,000 of the former Egyptian slaves are gathered, *each to receive the revelation.* "There are no representatives here," wrote Rabbi Leo Baeck about the assembly at Mt. Sinai, "no one who could assume the task for others."

Perhaps Judaism's thesis about individual responsibility is best expresssed, however, in the tale (paraphrased here from a version by Nathan Ausubel in *A Treasury of Jewish Folklore,* 1948, Crown Publishers) about Rabbi Levi Yitzhak's questioning of an illiterate tailor on the evening following Yom Kippur, the Day of Atonement. Levi Yitzhak wants to know what the tailor, unable to read the prayers, had said to God on this holiest of days.

The tailor replies, "I said to God, 'Dear God, my sins are so minor! A few times I failed to return to customers some leftover cloth; a few times I ate food that was not kosher, when I could not help it. Is this so terrible? But you, God — examine *your* sins! You have robbed mothers of their babes and have made helpless babes into orphans. Your sins are much more serious than mine, so what do you say we call us even?'"

"Foolish man!" cries Levi Yitzhak. "You let God off so easily! Just think — you could have forced the messiah to come!"

The Leo Baeck quote is taken from the UAHC's *The Torah, A Modern Commentary,* already cited.

The Council on Economic Priorities: Empowering the American Consumer

THIS NOTION that the prayers of an illiterate tailor might

The organized Jewish community has hardly begun to engage with issues of socially responsible consumption. NJCRAC, umbrella group for 11 major national and 111 local Jewish organizations, has even repeatedly endorsed the development of nuclear energy.

force the redemption of the world is analogous to the faith in individual initiative that the Council on Economic Priorities expresses in its best-selling consumer guidebooks, *Shopping for a Better World,* of which over 700,000 copies have been printed since 1990, and *Rating America's Corporate Conscience* (1987). These books rate 2,400 brand-name supermarket and food products (in *Shopping. . .*) and numerous household appliances and non-food items (in *Rating. . .*) on the basis of their manufacturers' conduct in ten areas of concern (including but not limited to the field of environmental impact). The ratings are aimed at empowering consumers to shop "responsibly," to spend money "politically," using information that is hard to track down on one's own. "You can have substantial impact on a company," say the authors of *Shopping for a Better World,* "by switching brands and telling the chief executive officer why. . . Ultimately, companies want your business and the sensible ones will change their ways if enough people let them know they care." Addresses and phone numbers of corporate officers are included in CEP's books.

CHARITABLE GIVING is one of the ten areas of evaluation. Corporations that give 2% or more of net pre-tax earnings

A specialty chemicals firm with an excellent environmental record, H. B. Fuller was recently tainted by disclosure of the fact that thousands of Central American youngsters were addicted to one of the company's glue products, a situation that the company could have altered (with some loss of profit) by adding an ingredient that induces nausea if the glue is sniffed. Following an exposé of its record of neglect in this matter, H. B. Fuller withdrew the product from its Central American markets.

Sara Lee, which in addition to its foods produces Hanes clothing, Fuller brushes, Electrolux vacuum cleaners and Kiwi waxes and polishes, was cited in 1987 by the U.S. Office of Antiboycott Compliance for *(Continued next page)*

(including in-kind donations and matching gifts) are considered leading performers in this realm (the average is 1.5%). Some companies have joined the flagship 2% and 5% clubs, including, in the latter group, Black & Decker, Parks Sausage, Dayton Hudson Corp., H.B. Fuller, and several banks. The cause attracting most attention, notes CEP, is education — particularly as corporations reckon with an increasingly ill-educated American work force.

Several Jewish-owned and/or founded companies are particularly generous in their charitable giving. Ben and Jerry's Homemade (ice cream), for instance, gives over 9% of its earnings, and has additionally helped establish "1% for Peace, Inc.," a non-profit national organization with the purpose of promoting peace activities. (By contrast, most corporate giving is to "safe," non-controversial groups such as those funded through United Way groups.) The Fel-Pro Corporation, manufacturer of automotive gaskets and sealants in Skokie, IL, gives about 5% of its earnings, principally to vocational training. The Merit Gas Company provides consumers in the Northeast the opportunity to save a few pennies per gallon at the gas pump and to support environmental and Jewish renewal causes through the Max and Anna Levinson Foundation, named for the founder of Merit Gas, Max Levinson, and his wife (the foundation holds a stake in the company).

Noteworthy, too, is the charitable giving of the Sara Lee Company, half of it for job and literacy training, homelessness relief, and other anti-poverty efforts, mostly in the Chicago area where the company is headquartered. (The Nathan Cummings Foundation, a family foundation named for Sara Lee's founder but run separately from the company's philanthropic arm, has been a major supporter of environmental groups and such Jewish organizations as the National Foundation for Jewish Culture and *Shomrei Adamah*.)

(Continued from previous page) violating the Anti-Boycott Provision of the Export Administration Act, which forbids U.S. companies to cooperate with the Arab boycott of Israel. CEP notes that the citation may have been "an overreaction to business activities by Sara Lee" and that the company is itself blacklisted by the Arab states for "a joint venture with an Israeli chemical concern in 1976."

Some of the corporate information in this section comes from CEP's *The Better World Investment Guide* (by Myra Alperson, Alice Tepper Marlin, Jonathan Schorsch and Rosalyn Will, 1991, Prentice-Hall, New York). Other information comes from the files of The Shefa Fund.

CEP's ratings are aimed at empowering consumers to spend shop "responsibly," to spend money "politically," using information that is hard to track down on one's own. "You can have substantial impact on a company," say the authors of *Shopping for a Better World,* "by switching brands and telling the chief executive officer why. . . Ultimately, companies want your business and the sensible ones will change their ways if enough people let them know they care."

Stride Rite Corp., the maker of Keds, Sperry and Stride Rite brand shoes, is another member of the 5% club whose recently retired chair, Arnold Hiatt, is an outspoken Jewish voice for corporate responsibility. "We look at public service as an investment," he told *Newsweek* magazine (May 4, 1992) upon announcing his assumption of full-time responsibility for the Stride Rite Foundation, following 24 years at the company helm. "We believe that the well-being of a company cannot be separated from the well-being of the community. If we're not providing the community with access to day care and elder care, if we're not providing proper funding for education, then we're not investing properly in our business. . . . Have our stockholders suffered? Well, those that invested $10,000 in 1984 would now have $155,000. Not bad." Among its many socially responsible deeds, Stride Rite pays its employees to do mentoring in inner-city schools for two hours a week.

"One gives generously and ends with more," says the Torah (*Proverbs* 11:24). "Another stints on doing the right and incurs a loss." *Shopping for a Better World* and *Rating America's Corporate Conscience* can empower us to help make this proverb

41

THE RUNAWAY BESTSELLER—
OVER 700,000 COPIES IN PRINT

SHOPPING FOR A BETTER WORLD

THE UPDATED & EXPANDED
1991 EDITION
THE QUICK AND EASY GUIDE
TO SOCIALLY RESPONSIBLE SUPERMARKET SHOPPING

". . . This could be seen as the mother of all guides . . .
A comprehensive and effective guide to corporate
winners and sinners." — *Washington Post*
The Council on Economic Priorities

The Council on Economic Priorities

CEP was founded in 1969 when Alice Tepper Marlin, a financial analyst and manager in Boston, was asked to design for a local synagogue a "peace portfolio" consisting of companies uninvolved in the manufacture of weapons used in Vietnam and Laos. The portfolio was offered through a *New York Times* ad that received 600 responses. CEP was then founded as an independent, non-profit public interest research group supported by national membership and individual and foundation grants. Members receive an annual update of *Shopping for a Better World* and a monthly *CEP Research Report.*

CEP annually produces the "America's Corporate Conscience Awards" ceremony, chaired by chief executive officers of companies that are past winners. The event honors corporations for outstanding citizenship in a particular field of concern and also gives "dishonorable mention" to corporations that have disregarded the public interest.

"Companies," writes CEP in *Shopping for a Better World,* "are responding. For example: Borden executives requested a meeting with CEP staff to see what policy changes could improve their ratings. After the meeting, they planned to recommend specific improvements and new programs to their chief executive officer. And Eden Foods put a woman on their board and reorganized their charitable giving program, in part as a response to the guide. In 1989, nearly 150 Fortune 1000 companies appointed women to their Boards of Directors for the first time."

We are using CEP's work as a springboard for our discussion of socially responsible consumption and investment for Jews, for CEP's work is probably the most widely known and available in the field of corporate responsibility.

The Council on Economic Priorities can be reached at 30 Irving Place, New York, NY 10003-9990, 212-420-1133.

a prophecy, at least in the aisles of the supermarket or department store.

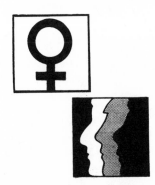

Corporate Anti-Semitism?
Anti-Semitism is not mentioned by CEP in its discussion of corporate hiring and promotion practices. Twenty or 30 years ago, such an omission would have been a significant oversight. However, studies today show that job discrimination against Jews is greatly overshadowed by anti-Black, anti-Hispanic and sexist discrimination. "An important difference," writes Richard Zweigenhaft in *Who Gets to the Top? Executive Discrimination in the Eighties,* published in 1984 by the American Jewish Committee, ". . . is the almost total absence of women and Blacks in senior corporate positions. . . . Jews were not likely to be inside directors of companies neither founded nor owned by Jews, but were still more likely to occupy such positions than
(Continued next page)

WOMEN'S ADVANCEMENT and MINORITY EMPLOYMENT are two more of the ten areas of concern in CEP's corporate evaluations. American women working full-time earn only 71¢ for every $1 a man earns, notes *Shopping for a Better World,* while Black Americans earn $331 per week, $98 less than white Americans' average. At the upper echelons of employment, women and African-Americans do no better: As of 1989, "289 Fortune 1000 companies had no women on their boards. Minorities had even less representation."

Campbell's Soup Company, with over 1,000 products, is one example of a corporation praised by CEP for its "commitment to promoting women to upper levels of management." General Mills is another, cited for having "systems in place to eliminate barriers to the advancement of qualified women and minorities," including "Upward Mobility Committees, mentoring programs" and "advertising in women's and minorities' publications." Such efforts to increase women's opportunities in business especially benefit Jewish women, by the way, given the high level of educational attainment among them (45% are college graduates, compared to 17% of women generally).

CEP also encourages companies to participate in minority purchasing programs and to keep funds in banks owned by minorities or women, or in banks committed to community reinvestment. (We'll have more on banking in our chapter on investment and financial planning.) A leader in this field is the Kellogg Company, which has up to $3 million deposited in below-market rate certificate-of-deposit accounts in minority-owned banks, according to CEP.

43

(Continued from previous page)
either women or Blacks. There were invariably Jewish inside directors of companies founded or purchased by Jews, but there is no corresponding pathway open for women or Blacks." Nevertheless, corporate recruitment practices show vestiges of anti-Semitism — see, for example, our note about Sears Roebuck on page 88.

A toll-free line to answer questions about green consumerism has been established by the Pennsylvania Resources Council: 800-468-6772.

The Social Investment Forum, 430 First Avenue, Suite 290, Minneapolis, MN 55401, 612-333-8338, is a trade organization founded in 1981, open to individuals, businesses and organizations interested in the social investment field. SIF produces an annual directory, *Social Investment Services,* and engages in many other educational and research activities.

American Jews and Divestment from South Africa
   While the majority of the financial portfolios of major American Jewish organizations were divested of South Africa
(Continued next page)

OTHER REALMS of scrutiny by the Council on Economic Priorities are the TREATMENT OF ANIMALS, especially in the cosmetics and pharmaceutical industries (to a lesser extent in the food industry); COMMUNITY OUTREACH ("programs promoting education, housing and/or volunteerism"); ENVIRONMENTAL IMPACT, and DIVESTMENT FROM SOUTH AFRICA. This latter issue is, of course, in great flux: The apartheid system is being dismantled and, at this writing, South Africa stands at the brink of inaugurating a multi-racial, democratic system, though struggles for peace and justice in that tormented land clearly lie ahead. Suffice it to say that the divestment movement and the international sanctions it won against South Africa have significantly contributed to the downfall of apartheid. In fact, the great bulk of the $600 billion that the Social Investment Forum currently counts as socially "screened" monies earned that title simply by being withheld from investment in the apartheid system.

WORKPLACE ISSUES, including FAMILY BENEFITS, are also scrutinized by CEP, which considers the marks of socially responsible companies to include: "competitive salary, comprehensive health insurance. . . opportunities to improve skills. . . job security or adequate notice. . . a grievance apparatus for complaints, protection" for whistle blowers, "a bonus program for ideas that make a difference, and rewards for work well done" *(Shopping for a Better World)*. Of these, health insurance is a particularly acute concern for Americans, given our lack of a national insurance plan. Nearly a third of the population now reports that they or someone in their household have remained in jobs they wanted to quit for the sole purpose of holding onto health benefits, according to the *New York Times* (September 26, 1991). This phenomenon,

(Continued from previous page)
holdings over the past few years, several groups have declined to support sanctions. The American Jewish Committee, for example, in the National Jewish Community Relations Council's *Joint Program Plan* for 1989-90, expressed the belief that "divestment. . . would hurt the people of South Africa" and regretted "the decision to leave of U.S. companies which aided blacks by adhering to fair employment practices." The Anti-Defamation League, Hadassah, Women's American ORT and the Orthodox Union of Jewish Congregations took similar positions. NCJRAC has, however, consistently supported sanctions despite these dissents — and despite opposition to divestment from the South African Jewish community itself.

The Rabbi Salanter story is adapted from a version in Nathan Ausubel's *A Treasury of Jewish Folklore,* already cited.

known as "job lock," is hardly a reliable coping strategy, as many companies have been dealing with recessionary pressures and spiralling medical costs by shifting a greater proportion of medical premiums to employees or eliminating coverage altogether. In such a climate, the 1991 announcement by the Lotus computer software company (with some 3,000 employees) that it would extend medical benefits to unmarried and unrelated household partners — for example, to the domestic partners of gay and lesbian employees — was a shining example of responsible corporate behavior.

Family benefits such as parental leave, flextime, job sharing, child care and flexible benefits humanize the workplace. Sadly, the United States is far behind other countries in this realm. "At least 127 countries. . . require parental or maternal leave," reports CEP. Yet the Family and Medical Leave Acts of 1990 and '92, mandating 12 weeks of unpaid leave for childbirth, adoption or family illness without loss of job, rank, or benefits were vetoed by President George Bush. These bills had wide support from Jewish organizations, led by the National Council of Jewish Women.

Workplace issues should interest consumers if for no other reason than that worker dissatisfaction is likely to be reflected in product flaws. Rabbi Israel Salanter of early 19th century Lithuania made this point one year when he was too sick to supervise the Passover matzo-baking, about which he was ritually scrupulous. His disciples volunteered to take over for him, if he would simply instruct them as to what precautions they should take to assure the purity of the product.

"See that the women who bake the matzos are well paid," Rabbi Salanter instructed them, and said nothing more.

DISCLOSURE OF INFORMATION is another realm of corpo-

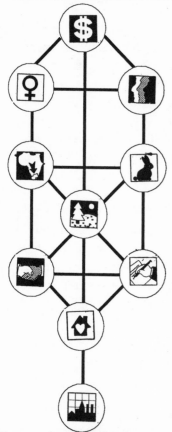

Diagrammatic of the *sefirot*, the divine manifestations according to the *Kabbalah,* combined herewith the Council on Economic Priorities' illustrations for the 10 categories of corporate responsibility used in *Shopping for a Better World.*

Workplace issues should interest consumers if for no other reason than that worker dissatisfaction is likely to be reflected in product flaws. Rabbi Israel Salanter of early 19th century Lithuania made this point one year when he was too sick to supervise the Passover matzo-baking, about which he was ritually scrupulous. His disciples volunteered to take over for him, if he would simply instruct them as to what precautions they should take to assure the purity of the product.

"See that the women who bake the matzos are well paid," Rabbi Salanter instructed them, and said nothing more.

rate behavior scrutinized by CEP, in belief that a company's "willingness to share information on its basic operations and its social endeavors. . . is an indication of corporate good citizenship." Jews, however, have an interest in one aspect of corporate disclosure of information that is *not* discussed by CEP — namely, corporate participation in the Arab boycott against Israel. Most Arab states require companies to disclose information about dealings with Israel, and will boycott those companies that have such dealings or that refuse to provide the information. Disclosing such information in order to comply with the boycott is illegal, however, under U.S. law. Thus the Pepsico Corporation, which receives nearly identically positive ratings for social responsibility from CEP as its main competitor, Coca Cola, might win the "taste test" for Jewish consumers thanks to Pepsico's defiance of the Arab boycott. The Ralston Purina company, on the other hand, compounded

Boycott Report, issued nine times annually by the American Jewish Congress, 15 E. 84 St., NYC 10028, 212-879-4500.

According to the weekly Jewish *Forward,* Eugene Schueller, president of L'Oreal, was a French fascist sympathizer , and the company's sole U.S distributor, Cosmair, is headed by Jacques Correze, a pro-Hitler French terrorist who was imprisoned for eight years for collaborationist crimes.

American Jewish Committee press release, "Japanese ignorance about Jews Leads to Disturbing Stereotypes," August 12, 1992. The American Jewish Committee is headquartered at 165 E. 56 St., New York, NY 10022, 212-751-4000.

its lousy record on women and minority advancement with a $22,000 fine in 1990 "for answering a nine-point [boycott] questionnaire as part of its effort to register a trademark in Iraq," according to the American Jewish Congress' *Boycott Report.* Two other consumer-product companies accused of participating in the boycott are L'Oreal and Lancôme cosmetics, both owned by Nestlé, the Swiss-based company targeted for consumer boycott for over six years by INFACT (see p. 32).

Japanese corporations have been notoriously compliant with the Arab boycott of Israel. "Until the mid-1980s," notes the Pacific Rim Institute of the American Jewish Committee, ". . . no Japanese companies had ever invested in Israel; Japanese banks refused to finance trade with Israel; Japan refused to allow El Al to land in Tokyo and Japan Air Lines chose not to land in Tel Aviv; Japanese ships did not dock in Israeli harbors; and the Japanese government supported companies' adherence to the Arab-led boycott of Israel." Nissan, Toyota and Mazda did not break the boycott until 1991; Honda not before 1989. These policies were rooted, the AJCommittee explains, in Japan's dependence upon Persian Gulf oil; the situation has significantly improved since the mid-1980's. Nevertheless, Jewish consumers might factor in this history of anti-Israel discrimination when considering whether to buy Japanese products, which are already being boycotted by some on the basis of Japan's persistent refusal to halt its whaling and other environmentally irresponsible activities.

Other Strategies of "Shopping for a Better World"

IN ADDITION to the CEP system of "shopping for a better

There are numerous other pathways for consumers to express their social concerns. These include the use of socially responsible credit cards, phone services and financial services; socially responsible travel; holding companies accountable for their advertising images and for violence-laden products for children; and no-nukes purchasing.

world," there are numerous other pathways to socially responsible consumption. Among these are:

• Socially conscious consumption of **financial services** from banks, insurance companies, credit unions, etc. We will deal with this at some length in our chapter on investment and financial planning.

• The use of **socially responsible credit cards** such as the Working Assets Visa. Each time you use the card, Working Assets contributes a nickel to non-profit organizations selected through voting by cardholders. Working Assets also offers IRA accounts, a money market mutual fund, a travel service, and a long-distance phone service that pays one percent of your bill to non-profit groups.

The Jewish Federation Council of Greater Los Angeles also offers a credit card, the "Mitzvah Card," through the State Street Bank and Trust Company of Boston, MA. By using this Visa, you help the L.A. Federation supports its many humanitarian services in the U.S., Israel and elsewhere. There is no consumer involvement, however, in the selection of recipients for credit card-generated funds.

Of course, the offering of credit to encourage consumption, even with a "kickback" on behalf of social justice, poses its own moral problems. In light of the discussion of the "wasting disease" and our environmental crisis that inaugurated this chapter, credit card applications should probably be required to include a warning label: "The Rabbi General has determined that this product may induce acute creditcardiovascular disease, a condition marked by excessive consumption that can be dangerous to your health and the health of our planet!"

• Involvement with **Alternative Trade Organizations** (ATOs),

From an 1876 cartoon strip about "greenback dollars" — the perils of credit

which assist Native American and other indigenous or poor peoples to market their crafts and commodities without middleman exploitation. ATOs pay producers in accordance with the fair market value of their products *in the countries where they are sold,* which helps break the cycle of poverty and exploitation that Third World craftspeople usually face. ATOs also tend to do business with worker cooperatives and other alternative economic models by which indigenous peoples are raising their standard of living. In Europe, ATOs have thrived for decades. They are also active as importers in Japan, Aus-

49

Co-op America is a non-profit membership organization (55,000 members, including 500 organizations) of socially responsible businesses and individuals that publishes a catalog of its members' products, as well as the very informative quarterly publication, *Building Economic Alternatives.* Members also receive *Boycott Action News,* the *Socially Responsible Financial Planning Handbook,* and access to innovative health and life insurance plans. Co-op America also offers a VISA card through the Socially Responsible Banking Fund of Vermont National Bank, and "eco-tours" to environmentally sensitive lands through Co-op America's Travel Links. Individual membership in Co-op America costs $20; $50 for institutions.

Other Alternative Trading Organizations include Trade Wind — Fair Trade with Native America (156 Drake Lane, Summertown, TN 38483, 800-445-1991)) and SERRV Handcrafts (international crafts), 500 Main St., Box 365, New Windsor, MD

(Continued next page)

tralia, Canada and the U.S., and as exporters in Africa, Asia and the Americas. The ATOs of North America have been meeting annually for nine consecutive years. For a list of these groups, contact Pueblo to People, an ATO that works with Latin American craftspeople (2105 Silber Road, Suite 101, Houston, TX 77055, 800-843-5257). Pueblo to People, like most ATOs, sells mainly through mail-order catalogs; many of these can be obtained through Co-op America, 2100 M Street, N.W., #310, Washington, DC 20063, 800-424-COOP.

• **Socially responsible travel:** Every hour more than 5,000 tourists from industrialized countries become tourists in less developed countries, according to Jeffrey Hollender's *How To Make the World a Better Place* (already cited). Yet "most tourist dollars. . . end up right back in the coffers of the countries from which the tourist came, since the industrialized nations control the hotels, airlines," etc. "Native communities are pushed aside to make way for high-rise hotels and private beaches. Fishermen and farmers and craftswomen are turned into barmen and hotel maids. . . . Natural environments are

(Continued from previous page) 21776-0465, 301-635-8775). The Company of Women merchandising catalog, though not an ATO, deserves mention here as well; its profits go to support the Rockland Family Shelter, an agency for women suffering domestic violence, rape or homelessness (6 South Broadway, POB 742, Nyack, NY 10960-0742, 800-937-1193).

For more information about socially conscious travel opportunities, see *Bridging the Global Gap,* $10.95 from Global Exchange, 2940 16th St., Suite 307, San Francisco, CA 94103.

often laid to ruin." Today, dozens of U.S. groups are organizing alternative travel packages that seek to maximize respect for, rather than exploitation of, the places we visit. At a time when many poor countries are examining whether environmental protection and the tourism it fosters can be as profitable as resource exploitation, the growth of socially and ecologically responsible travel has major implications for environmental policy around the globe.

• **No-nukes purchasing:** CEP gives negative citations in *Shopping for a Better World* to companies with "conventional weapons-related and/or fuel contracts" totalling $500,000 or more per year (among which are Bayer, Eastman Kodak, and Ralston Purina, among others whose products are found on supermarket shelves). Many Jews and Jewish organizations, however, remained mute about the sharp conventional military buildup of the Carter-Reagan-Bush years, largely out of concern for a steady flow of military aid to Israel, which has security needs that are strikingly more obvious than those of the U.S.

Opposition to the nuclear arms race, on the other hand, has been the consistent position of the Union of American Hebrew Congregations, the American Jewish Congress and other liberal Jewish organizations. This Jewish opposition to nuclear weaponry has been mobilized with particular effectiveness by The Shalom Center (7318 Germantown Avenue, Philadelphia, PA 19119, 215-247-9700, Arthur Waskow, Director). The National Jewish Community Relations Advisory Council, representing the broadest Jewish consensus, in its 1990-'91 Joint Program Plan expressed opposition to "Star Wars" (the Strategic Defense Initiative) and acute concern about nuclear and chemical arms proliferation — in a statement published *before* the Persian Gulf War brought proliferation fears to a new height.

51

Could G.I. Joe Fight Fires Instead?

Hasbro is not alone in the $3 billion toy industry in being a Jewish-owned company. Toys are "the one industry in the United States that Jews do have a lock on," writes Gerald Krefetz in *Jews and Money* (1982, Ticknor and Fields, New York). "Jewish families are heavily represented" in "Mattel, founded by Elliot and Ruth Handler," and there is "a strong Jewish presence in Hasbro by the Hassenfeld family of Rhode Island, in Ideal by the Weintraub family of New York, in Marx by Louis Marx, and in Gabriel by Jerome M. Fryer." This presence of Jews, in combination with the Jewish influence in the television and film industries, lends a particular responsibility and opportunity to Jewish activists and organizations concerned with violence-linked entertainment.

Myriam Miedzian's *Boys Will Be Boys: Breaking the Link Between Masculinity and Violence* (1991, Doubleday) offers good reason for that concern. Miedzian outlines the overwhelming dimensions of male violence in American culture and its link to the "masculine mystique" promoted by television, film, music, toys, sports (especially football) and other sources of cultural influence. She evaluates biological, psychological and other roots of male violence and details concrete suggestions, both educational and regulatory, for altering the picture.

Miedzian suggests, for example, that films and television programs featuring "stories of rescuing victims of tornados, floods, accidents and so on" are as exciting and marketable as "adventure films based on armed conflict between enemies." "The regulation of violence toys," she writes, "should be accompanied by research and development of toys that fulfill. . . desires for adventure, excitement and danger. . . while encouraging pro-social values." Toy manufacturers, she urges, should get tax credits for such product development.

The ending of the Cold War has not eliminated the need to pursue nuclear weapons-free economics. The threat of nuclear holocaust has diminished somewhat, but the vastly radioactive pollution of nuclear weapons production and testing, past and present, remains with us. The consumer boycott group INFACT estimates that the Hanford, Washington nuclear weapons facility alone will require $60 billion to be cleaned up. Factor in the medical and insurance costs of radioactivity-linked disease and mortality in the U.S. since the days of atmospheric testing in the 1950s, and the scope of the damage that we suffer thanks to nuclear weapons production becomes clear.

Consumer Brand Names. . . is available for $3 from Nuclear Free America, 325 E. 25th St., New York, NY 10011.

Perhaps the cessation of the Cold War and the genuine need for a domestic "peace dividend," if coupled with effective international control of the sale of arms to the Middle East, will free more American Jewish organizational voices to oppose the bloated and corruption-ridden Pentagon spending that we suffer. A household strategy of no-nukes product purchasing can be launched by obtaining *Consumer Brand Names of the Top 50 Nuclear Weapons Contractors,* published by Nuclear Free America.

• **Non-violent toy/music/video/film consumerism:** The Jewish-owned Hasbro toy company, which has given generously to Jewish Federation drives and to the American Jewish Committee, unfortunately derives a significant part of its profits from the sale of "G.I. Joe" dolls and accessories. Of course, Hasbro is not alone in the children's entertainment industry in profiting from violence-linked products: According to Myriam Miedzian's important study, *Boys Will Be Boys: Breaking the Link Between Masculinity and Violence,* 71% of Nintendo's video games (which are in 20% of American homes) are high in violence, and violence "has been injected into every type of toy sold to boys. . . . today's violence toys, in conjunction with TV and film violence, encourage violence at all levels — domestic, criminal and international. . . . We need to encourage boys to play with toys that reinforce nurturing, caring, fathering — not killing."

Miedzian points out that there is virtually no government regulation of media depictions of violence for children (as there are, for example, for depictions of sexuality). Parents are the sole regulators of slasher films, satanic rock videos, violence-as-fun wrestling matches, and other relentlessly violent entertainments to which young people have access. Indeed, the adversarial challenges that the commercial marketplace pre-

53

Family Pastimes, RR4, Perth, Ontario, Canada K7H3C6.

sents to socially conscious parents are, for many, a painful introduction to the idea of practicing socially responsible consumption; that to which we adults are inured becomes freshly offensive in light of our children's innocence and impressionability.

Letters of complaint to manufacturers and distributors of violent products, discussions with store owners, educators and, of course, children, and the purchasing of products from the few manufacturers of "alternative" entertainments for children (such as Family Pastimes, a Canadian manufacturer of very entertaining cooperative board games) are all part of the pursuit of socially responsible consumption in this crucial realm.

• **Accountability for advertising images:** Manufacturers of perfumes and cosmetics, cars, cigarettes, clothing and alcohol have long relied upon "image" advertising that stresses not the

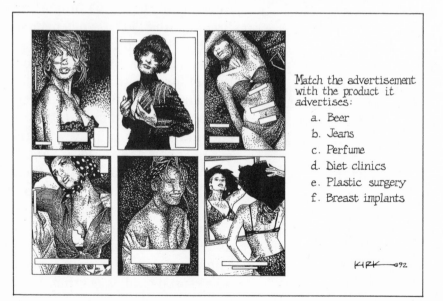

Match the advertisement with the product it advertises:

a. Beer
b. Jeans
c. Perfume
d. Diet clinics
e. Plastic surgery
f. Breast implants

KIRK ○92

virtues of the product but a lifestyle image which consumers are led to associate with the product. Such image advertising is now standard for nearly every class of consumer product —and much of it promotes artificial, exploitative images of women's sexuality, "tough" masculinity, the joys of being drunk, competitiveness and materialistic social values, etc. Holding companies accountable for their "advertising personalities" — personalities that profoundly influence American culture — is a key part of being a socially responsible consumer. Engaging in a private, disdainful boycott of an offending company is not enough, however; the *mitzvah* requires letter-writing, telephoning and other forms of organized protest that corporate board members can hear.

Positive feedback is important too: The efforts of such companies as Esprit, a California clothing manufacturer that touts itself as "a company that is trying" and runs public service messages in lieu of ads ("A Plea for Responsible Consumption" in *The Utne Reader;* "End racism and the killing of my people in the street" in *Vogue*), deserve active consumer support.

• **Affirmative shopping:** When you purchase an item from the Co-op America catalog, 30% of your money goes to print and mail the catalog and service orders; 70% goes to the cooperatives, worker-owned businesses, women-owned businesses, family farms, non-profit organizations, and other worthy groups that produce the things sold through the catalog. Thus you are "employing visually handicapped people in North Carolina, building roads, schools and banks in rural Mexico, planting trees in rainforest areas, improving health conditions in Senegal, West Africa, assisting victims of domestic violence and homelessness in New York, supporting art classes and other creative outlets in Harlem. . . helping organic

---

Jews can also be active within synagogues, Jewish Community Centers and Jewish organizations to encourage socially responsible consumption on a scale beyond that of individual households. Is trash being recycled and are non-recyclables avoided? Are maintenance staff and other employees receiving fair wages and benefits? Is the building special-needs accessible? Are leaders accountable? Are gifts accepted and honors bestowed with an eye to Jewish ethics, rather than opportunistically?

The Seventh Generation Catalog, founded by Jeffrey Hollender (see p. 20), derives its name from the following line from the Great Law of the Six Nations Iroquois Confederacy: "In our every deliberation, we must consider the impact of our decisions on the next seven generations."

New York Council on the Environment, 212-566-0990. One good source of information on alternative economic networks, in addition to Co-op America's *Building Economic Alternatives,* is Susan Meeker-Lowry's *Catalyst*, a quarterly newsletter now in its eighth year of publication. *Catalyst* focuses on small businesses, worker-owned firms, co-ops, non-profit groups, alternative banks, and responsible, publicly traded companies. Subscriptions are $25 (POB 1308, Montpelier, VT 05601, 802-223-7943).

and sustainable farms," and more, according to Co-op America — simply by assuring that the profit from your purchases becomes *social capital*.

Likewise, when you buy from The Seventh Generation Catalog, you not only assure yourself of receiving environmentally safe household products (thereby helping to sustain their manufacturers, usually small-scale businesses), but you build the organization's "Green Fund," which has in three years contributed about $150,000 to environmental causes.

Affirmative shopping can mean seeking out the newly burgeoning farmers' markets in many cities, which help to sustain small-scale farms. (New York's program, run by the New York Council on the Environment, is a model with over 25 greenmarkets operating on different days throughout the city, including several in low-income areas.) Affirmative shopping can mean joining a bartering network, a gardening cooperative, a food co-op — any of the many existing networks that emphasize community interdependence, a sense of place and a conscientious environmental attitude.

The Socially Responsible Synagogue

JEWS CAN ALSO BE ACTIVE within synagogues, Jewish Community Centers (JCCs) and Jewish organizations to encourage socially responsible consumption on a scale beyond that of individual households. Taking a cue from the Council on Economic Priorities, which encourages readers to apply the CEP rating system to their own workplaces, Jews might ask of their Jewish institutions:

Is trash being recycled and are non-recyclables avoided?

The Talmud (*Shabbat* 67b) warns against allowing lamps to burn too quickly, as this is wasteful of fuel.

Rabbi Arthur Gross Schaefer, "Ten Commandments for the Synagogue," *Reform Judaism* magazine, Fall, 1991. Schaefer, a lawyer and business ethicist, also discusses religious school violations of copyright laws, ethical decision-making, avoidance of gossip and other issues. See also: "Synagogue Ethics Manual: A Resource for Consideration of Ethical Issues in Synagogue Life," published by the UAHC Ethics Committee (838 Fifth Ave., New York, NY 10021, 212-249-0100).

Are light bulbs energy efficient and manufactured by a nuclear-free company? Are maintenance staff and other employees receiving fair wages and benefits? Is their working environment safe?

Are temple operating funds deposited in a financial institution that is helping to stabilize and improve neighborhoods?

Is the building wheelchair accessible? Are the books purchased for bar- and bat-mitzvah training non-sexist in theme and characterization? Are there women on the synagogue/JCC board? Are gay men and lesbians, families with non-Caucasian members, converts to Judaism, poor and working-class Jews, and other "minority" members within Jewish life given access to participation and advancement?

Are decision-making processes reasonably democratic? Are rabbinic and professional leaders accountable? Do leaders view themselves, in the words of Rabbi Arthur Gross Schaefer, "not as business managers but as trustees of Jewish tradition?" Are gifts accepted and honors bestowed with an eye to Jewish ethics, rather than opportunistically?

People might blanch at the notion of "shopping" for a Jewish life (though synagogue and communal organizations are indeed marketing themselves), yet the voluntary nature and high cost of Jewish affiliation in America, and the fortunate abundance of Jewish resources, have very much combined to create a "buyer's market" in which the "chosen people" are choosing their affiliations carefully! By including ethical considerations in our decision-making, we are speaking truth to the Jewish tradition —

> The Holy One, blessed be, wants the heart.
> *Sanhedrin* 106b

— while sparking the kind of discussion, debate, and values clarification that can render a synagogue or JCC "commodity" into a community.

Questions to Consider and Discuss

To what extent is consumerism prompted in your life by a feeling of necessity? Of fun? Of psychological comfort? Of compulsion?

What examples of "shopping for a better world" are already active in your life? How could you most easily intensify your participation in socially responsible consumer activity?

Do you feel yourself to be the "owner" or the "custodian" of your resources?" If you could transform your relationship to your resources, what changes would you make? How would you like to manage those resources differently from how you do now?

Which of Judaism's disciplines or boundaries feel congruent with your world view? Which feel foreign to you? Are there any disciplines to which you aspire to achieve a better "balance," whether personally, socially or environmentally?

Hot Tips

IN THIS CHAPTER: American Jews, from Rags to Riches, from Junk to Junk Bonds. . . Ethical — and Profitable — Alternatives to "Business as Usual". . . The Dollars and Sense of Socially Responsible Investment. . . Social Responsibility According to Judaism. . . The Covenant Idea: Power Made Accountable. . . A Fence for the Torah, a Fence for the Earth: No Nuclear Poisons . . . Idolatry-for-Profit? The Complicated Choices of Socially Responsible Investing. . . A Radical Critique of Socially Responsible Investing. . . Investing in Community Development Corporations. . . "Genuine We-ness" — The Centrality of Community in Jewish Thought. . . Why Have Jewish Institutions Not Participated in the Social Responsibility Movement?

I don't know how it happened; I don't know what possessed me to take my hard-earned money and put it in a bank. But that's what I did. . . .

"I call on all these customers standing here in line to be witnesses. Fellow Jews," I cried, "you are witnessing that I just deposited in this bank twenty good, crackling American dollars."

And I went home with my little green book. It goes without saying that I did not sleep a wink that night. All through the long hours I dreamed that the bank had been robbed — all the money was gone, down to the last penny. . . .

At the crack of dawn I rushed to the bank. It hadn't been touched! . . . That evening as I waited for a street car to take me home, I thought: "I'll drop around to the bank — see how things are going. Who knows what could have happened in the meantime? This is America, after all!"

"My First Deposit," by Moishe Nadir

"My First Deposit," excerpted from *Jewish Currents* magazine, July-August, 1963. Translated from the Yiddish by Lila B. Hassid. Moishe Nadir, pen name of Isaac Reiss (1885-1943), was an outstanding American Yiddish humorist and commentator.

Investment and Financial Planning: Building a "Covenanted Economy"

"**T**HE REAL JEWISH QUESTION is this," wrote Sholem Aleichem, the "Yiddish Mark Twain:" "From what can a Jew earn a living?" In 1936, the editors of *Fortune* magazine supplied an answer: Jews were making a living from junk!

Gerald Krefetz, *Jews and Money,* 1982, Ticknor and Fields, New York, pp. 1-2. Used by permission. These "rag" businesses had historically been considered undesirable and were therefore open to Jews in Europe and the U.S.

Charles Silberman notes in *A Certain People* (1985, Summit Books, New York), p. 134, that Jews are attracted to the professions becaust they can "carry their capital in their heads. . . Jewish businessmen gravitate towards fields in which capital requirements are low and turnover rapid." Silberman quotes Felix Rohatyn, the investment banker who played a major role *(Continued next page)*

American Jews: From Rags to Riches, From Junk to Junk Bonds

In that year, *Fortune* published an examination of the American Jewish community's role in the business world, partly in response to the rise of Nazism and fast-spreading anti-Semitism. Surveying the major sectors of the American economy in search of Jewish owners, directors and chief executive officers, *Fortune* concluded, according to Gerald Krefetz, that "Jews were either absent or well hidden, for none could be found in coal, rubber, chemicals, shipbuilding, railroads, bus companies, aviation, utilities, telephone and telegraph, engineering and construction, heavy machinery, lumber or dairy products. Jews were, however, prominent in scrap and waste product businesses. . . paper, cotton rag, wool rag. . ."

Half a century later, Jews control approximately 15% of the Gross National Product of the United States, according to figures developed by Gerald Bubis, the founding director of the School of Jewish Communal Service. While such unprecedented Jewish wealth was not derived in a strict sense from the *shmatteh* or rag business, neither was it derived from mainstream American "smokestack" enterprise. Rather, Jews have best performed as entrepreneurs and innovators in the experimental zones of American economic life — transforming the culture, for example, through the motion picture and television industries — or as professional "helpers" to the mainstream, as attorneys, accountants, economists, investors, teachers, social workers, and insurance and real estate agents.

Through such strivings, a whole generation of American Jews, whose life experiences included the Great Depression, the New Deal, and the post-World War II boom, achieved an upward mobility that outstripped the economic success of other American ethnic groups. Never mind the multi-million-

(Continued from previous page) in saving New York City from bankruptcy in the 1970s, vividly recalling his family's escape from Nazi-occupied France across the Pyrenees. Rohatyn spent the evening before they left opening toothpaste tubes from the bottom and stuffing them with small gold coins. "What is real to me," he told Silberman, "is what I can put in the back of a toothpaste tube, or what I carry around in my head."

Civil Rights and the Jews:
In his 1991 retirement speech, Albert Vorspan, the Reform movement's social action maven, commented that "among the chief beneficiaries of the civil rights triumphs in American life was American Jewry. Once the barriers of discrimination were knocked down, we had the cultural background, the lust for education, and the intellectual heritage which equipped us to leap from the margins of American life to the very center of American political, economic and cultural creativity."

aires: even the middle-class Jewish parents of the baby-boom generation benefitted mightily from unionization, social security, sustained post-war growth, the G.I. Bill, civil rights advances, skyrocketing urban real estate values, a democratized stock market (and hugely inflated interest rates in the late 1970s), as well as their own hard work and frugality.

But as Franklin Delano Roosevelt was the definitive figure for the first post-immigration generation, so may Ronald Reagan, with his dismantling of the New Deal, be definitive for the baby-boomers. The Reagan years of deregulation, social disinvestment and cowboy capitalism may have made overnight millionaires out of a certain stratum of the middle class, yet the long-term result of Reaganism was a fraying of the New Deal "safety net" and an economic hangover that is now producing, for many of the '60s generation, their younger siblings, and their children, an insecure sense of "downward mobility."

The Savings and Loan debacle, the tottering life insurance and banking industries, the decline of U.S. manufacturing, the decline of our urban infrastructure, the blue-collar and farm recession of the early 1980s and the white-collar recession of the early 1990s — these and other problems, coupled with our staggering federal deficit and lack of innovative busi-

> The Jewish middle class, created in large part by New Deal economics, is being seriously pressured by Reagan-era debt and economic decline. Sadly, Jews have played a highly visible role in the financial hijinx that have helped catalyze our economic ills. Yet Jewish individuals have also been quite active within the socially responsible investment movement — a movement of significant, potentially transformative, clout. Jewish financial influence, moreover, could serve as a major tool of economic and social transformation.

ness leadership, have produced deep pessimism and discouraging facts about America's economic future. Median household income in 1990, adjusted for inflation, was $1,000 less than it was in 1973, according to the *New York Times* (Louis Uchitelle, "Trapped in the Impoverished Middle Class," November 17, 1991). Income has stagnated for all but the top 20% with incomes above $80,000. "For the first time since World War II, a generation of children is leaving college without a sense of a prosperous future," Uchitelle writes. The *International Jewish Monthly* of B'nai B'rith concurs: Unemployment for college graduates rose from 5.2% to 6.9% in 1991, writes Rob Hoffman ("Help Wanted," May, 1992), and the situation is worsening. Sixty percent of college students are now worried about getting jobs in their intended fields, according to a Roper Poll, and "two-thirds," writes Hoffman, "see job security as a first job's most important feature. . . . Law firms are among those hit hardest by the economic downturn. . . starting with a 10-30% decline in recruitment by larger firms over the last two years."

SADLY, JEWS are not only suffering from this crisis, but have played a highly visible role in the financial hijinx that helped catalyze it. Ivan Boesky and Michael Milken are but two of the Jews prominently involved in financial scandal in recent years. Where our forebears dealt in junk, our contemporaries have been dealing illegally in junk bonds — or even in government bonds, as in the case of Salomon Brothers, the prestigious, Jewish-founded investment banking house that fell into scandal in 1991. "The grievous fact," said Rabbi Alexander M. Schindler, president of the (Reform) Union of American Hebrew Congregations, in 1987, "is that of late Jews are being named more often as indicted public officials and business-

"By the end of the 1980s, soon after Ronald Reagan left the White House," writes Sylvia Nasar in the *New York Times,* August 16, 1992, "wealth in this country had become more concentrated than at any time since the Roaring Twenties. The share of net worth — assets minus debts — held by the top 1 percent of households jumped from below 20% in 1979 to more than 36% in 1989, according to a new historical data series compiled by the economic historians Claudia Goldin and Bradford De Long at Harvard University and the economist Edward Wolff at New York University. . . ." This "boom," notes Nasar, was accompanied by a rising middle-class tax burden, declining union membership, and stagnating pay for the average American.

Of course, individual misdeeds on Wall Street did not single-handedly provoke the decline of the American economy. The "prolonged stagnation," writes Uchitelle in the *Times,* ". . . grew out of corporate efforts to cut labor costs to become globally competitive — an endeavor aided both by Reagan Administration policies and a decline in union militancy" — or, more to the point, the solid defeat of unionism in such struggles as those of the air-traffic controllers, the Hormel meatpackers, the UAW at

(Continued on page after next)

men than as Nobel Prize winners," while "the casual question that Jews ask about people in the news, 'Is he Jewish?' is nowadays asked more often with worry than with pride."

At the same time, however, Jewish individuals have been quite active within the social responsibility movement — a movement that seeks to affirm the profitability of ethical business practices. While less in the news than the crimes of Wall Street cheats, the constructive work of these activists deserves the attention of the Jewish community — a community of significant, potentially transformative economic clout.

65

So What *Is* the Social Responsibility Movement, Already?

In the 1920s, a consumer boycott of the Ford Motor Company, in protest of Henry Ford's anti-Semitic campaigns in *The Dearborn Independent,* forced an apology from the automobile magnate (dated June 30, 1927) to American Jewish Committee leader Louis Marshall.

In 1933 the Jewish War Veterans initiated a boycott of German goods and services in response to the rise of German Nazism. Headed by attorney Sam Untermeyer, the boycott became a mass movement with trade union backing, but was opposed as "counterproductive" by the American Jewish Committee and Anti-Defamation League.

Since 1951, American Jews have purchased billions of dollars worth of ungraded Israeli bonds — and before that, the pre-state certificates of the Palestine Building and Loan Association.

Each of these activities is an example of historical Jewish involvement in socially responsible financial activity.

The modern social responsibility movement grew out of the political unrest of the 1960s. Opposition to the Vietnam War stirred the creation of the Council on Economic Priorities (see p. 42) and the Pax World Fund (1971), founded by two Methodist ministers intent on excluding war-related industries (as well as gambling, alcohol and tobacco) from its investments. The Project on Corporate Responsibility (PCR) filed pioneering shareholder resolutions with the General Motors Company insisting that the company's board be expanded to include women, blacks, trade unionists, consumers and environmentalists (see our page box on shareholder activism, p. 92). The Interfaith Center on Corporate Responsibility (founded 1974) mobilized Protestant and Roman Catholic churches to press anti-apartheid policies on corporations through shareholder resolutions and the effective investment of their $25 billion in combined assets. Amy Domini wrote her groundbreaking book, *Ethical Investing* (1984, Addison-Wesley, Reading, MA), detailing for a broad audience how responsible investing could be profitable and politically constructive, and helped to create the Domini Social Index 400, which tracks the performance of socially responsible companies (see p. 73). Throughout the 1970s and '80s, activist groups and financial professionals, college endowments and public pension funds expanded the clout of the social responsibility movement so that, at present, some $600 billion are reported by the Social Investment Forum to be "screened," mostly on behalf of South Africa divestiture. Included are the American Jewish Committee's $10 million in endowments, the Reform Rabbinic Board's $65 million of invested pension monies, and the $20 million endowment fund of Hebrew Union College in Cincinnati, among other Jewish institutional monies.

"(B)ecause these social investors now have very respectable performance records," writes

(Continued on page after next)

(Continued from page 65) Caterpillar, etc. Uchitelle continues: "It is debatable how much these wage sacrifices have helped America's competitiveness" — particularly when they go hand-in-hand with executive salaries that are the highest in the world — typically 25 times, and ranging up to 160 times, the average wages of an American worker.

Doug Henwood, editor of the *Left Business Observer,* notes in the Philadelphia *Inquirer* (March 8, 1992) that "the real victims of Milken. . . are employees and communities wrecked by the restructuring mania of the 1980s and its heir, the downsizing mania of the 1990s. But in this Milken is one of thousands of responsible parties. . . Paul Volcker, canonized by Wall Street for slashing inflation, could have stopped the buyout mania at any time through the Federal Reserve's immense power over securities trading and the banking system. . . . (Instead) every major Wall Street house, including the blue-blooded Morgan Stanley, got into the act. Every major bank financed junk deals, as did most of our major insurance companies."

First Affirmative Financial Network, 1040 S. 8th St., Suite 200, Colorado Springs, CO 80906, 800-422-7284.

Ethical — and Profitable — Alternatives to "Business as Usual"

THE SOCIAL RESPONSIBILITY movement may actually be receiving a boost from the current crisis of confidence about America's economic well-being and the growing revulsion at the greed and ethical bankruptcy of the business world of the Reagan-era. For example, with major insurance companies facing bankruptcy and/or government takeover largely due to their junk-bond investments, alternative institutions that have consciously avoided such investments take on a new credibility.

One such institution is a new player in the life insurance business, First Affirmative Financial Network. First Affirmative is "the only nationwide financial services firm specializing in socially screened investments," according to the 1992 guide of the Social Investment Forum. Founded in 1982, the company very recently began offering life insurance coverage. "Our first concern, given the widespread public skepticism about the health of the insurance industry," says George Gay of First Affirmative, "is the safety of our investments. We invest only in government agency papers" with clearly defined social impact, such as Sallie Mae and Fannie Mae, which support education loans and home mortgages. First Affirmative's credibility is further heightened by its "venture partner" status with Co-op America, which in 1988 investigated and approved the company as Co-op America's recommended firm for investing and financial planning. Considering the company's policy of contributing the legal maximum of its profits to non-profit organizations involved in environmental, women's and community issues, and considering its products — a variety of attractive life insurance packages — First Affirmative may seem a plausible alternative to the shaky mainstream insurance giants.

67

The Social Responsibility Movement

(Continued from page 66)

John E. Schultz, Social Investment Forum president (1990-1991), "the concept of socially responsible investing enters the last decade of the 20th century as an effective, viable investment strategy. . . . No longer dominated by social activists, the (movement's) religious and progressive communities have been joined by the massive monies of the public pension funds, the private pension funds, and. . . conventional money managers. . ."

For information and resources about the social responsibility movement, contact:

- *Business Ethics* magazine — see p. 81.
- *Catalyst* — see p. 56.
- *Clean Yield* (Box 1880, Greensboro Bend, VT 05842, 802-533-7178): a monthly newsletter about social responsibility and the stock market, $85/year.
- Co-op America — see pp. 50.
- *Corporate Responsibility Monitor* (Data Center, 464 19th St., Oakland, CA 94612, 415-835-4692): a 100-page monthly clipping service from the Data Center, a user-supported library providing access to information about the corporate world and U.S. economic policy, $420/ year.
- Council on Economic Priorities — see p. 42.
- *Good Money* (P.O. Box 363, Worcester, VT 05682, 802-223-3911): a bimonthly report on socially responsible money activities, $75/year.
- First Affirmative Financial Network — see p. 67. First Affirmative has also launched a Shareholder Activism Program, aimed at connecting individual corporate shareholders with institutional investors and coalitions that are sponsoring shareholder resolutions on issues of social concern.
- Franklin Insight (711 Atlantic Ave., 5th floor, Boston, MA 02111, 800-548-5684): a monthly investment advisory service ($195/year) evaluating economic trends and companies that are both profitable and socially responsible. Franklin Insight also publishes *Investing for a Better World,* a monthly newsletter ($19.95/year).
- Interfaith Center on Corporate Responsibility (475 Riverside Dr., Rm. 566, New York, NY 10115, 212-870-2936): ICCR publishes *The Corporate Examiner* ten times annually, $35.
- Investor Responsibility Research Center (1755 Massachusetts Ave. NW, Suite 600, Washington, DC 20036, 202-234-7500: provides proxy issue reports on socially responsible shareholder resolutions and *News for Investors,* a monthly newsletter.
- Peter D. Kinder & Co. (Kinder, Lydenberg, Domini & Co., 7 Dana St., Cambridge, MA 02138, 617-547-7479): creators of the Domini Social Index 400, monitoring the performance of socially responsible companies (see p. 73); provides social analyses of over 1,000 corporations.
- The Social Investment Forum — see p. 44.

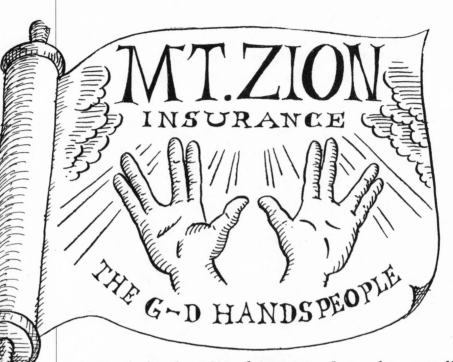

MT.ZION INSURANCE

THE G~D HANDSPEOPLE

Consumers United Health Insurance, 2100 M St., NW, Suite 207, Washington, DC 20063, 800-424-9711. CUIC's premium totals fell in 1991 from $50 million to $25 million, according to CUIC's Christine Gould, due to a sell-off of substantial assets to bring the company in line with new, tightening insurance regulations regarding capital reserves.

Similarly, the 16% of American Jews who are self-employed might be interested in knowing about the health insurance policies offered by Consumers United Insurance Company, a worker-owned, cooperatively managed company associated with Co-op America. CUIC premiums have been used to finance low-income cooperative housing in Washington, D.C., St. Louis and elsewhere, to provide red-lined neighborhoods with loans below the market rate, and to sustain many other significant projects of community uplift. The company's salary differential between its lowest- and highest-paid employees is 3:1; its work force is 80% female and 60% African-American. Meanwhile, the assets of CUIC have grown in the past decade at nearly three times the rate of the 25 largest insurance companies in the U.S.!

69

VIABLE PROGRESSIVE ALTERNATIVES do exist within each category of investment and financial planning:

- Life, health, disability and other forms of insurance;
- Checking accounts, money market funds, credit cards;
- Investments, including venture capital investments;
- Tools for estate planning (wills, trust funds, private and public foundations);
- Professional help: attorneys, accountants, money managers and investment counselors, estate planners.

However, notwithstanding the erosion of public confidence in major financial institutions, the notion of searching out "alternatives" in the realm of personal financial planning and investment can be downright nervewracking. In our culture, after all, "alternative" has usually meant idealistic but marginal, creative but unenduring — in short, not a good invest-

Viable progressive alternatives do exist within each category of investment and personal financial planning. However, notwithstanding the erosion of public confidence in major financial institutions, the notion of searching out "alternatives" can be downright nervewracking. In our culture, after all, "alternative" has usually meant idealistic but marginal, creative but unenduring — "Lots of singing, and too few noodles!" as a Yiddish proverb puts it — in short, not a good investment. But when it comes to socially responsible money activities, we're not only talking about idealism; we're talking about a good rate of return.

ment. It's one thing to buy a pint or two of Ben & Jerry's ice-cream, the profits from which help finance peace work, rather than Haägen Dazs, which helped finance Meir Kahane's Jewish Defense League some years ago (before the company was sold to another company) — but it's quite a bit more risky to entrust your financial future to unproved "alternative" institutions in the name of idealism.

"Lots of singing, and too few noodles!" says a Yiddish proverb, which might also be translated to mean, "You give a great pep talk, but what's the bottom line?"

Good question. . .

The Dollars and Sense of
Socially Responsible Investment

AMONG THE SOCIALLY responsible investment options are several mutual funds and banks that have consistently performed as well, or better than, institutions that do not consider social criteria in their decision-making. On October 19, 1987, when the New York Stock Exchange suffered tremors that dropped the Dow 22.6%, the five largest socially-responsible mutual funds at the time dropped an average of only 12.4%. The next year (1988), Lipper Analytical Services ranked the socially responsible Parnassus Fund as the fourth best performer among the 1,470 mutual funds that Lipper tracks; the fifth-place spot was held by Calvert-Ariel Growth Fund, another socially responsible fund, with a 39.97% return. (Calvert-Ariel closed its doors to new investors in April, 1990 after topping $200 million in assets and earning 69.5% since its founding in 1986 — compared to 37.9% for the Standard & Poor's 500 and 28% for the average long-term

Our information about the performance of socially responsible investment options is chiefly derived from the Council on Economic Priorities' *Better World Investment Guide* (already cited) and SIF's *Social Investment Services, A Guide to Forum Members,* January 1, 1992. For current information on which social screens are applied on mutual funds, as well as performance figures over 1,3,5 and 10-year bases, contact David B. Crocker at Shearson Lehman Brothers, 800-843-0211. Crocker works with Shearson Lehman's "Select and Suggest" manager program, which coordinates with

(Continued page after next)

Ben & Jerry's: "In Trust for the Community"

"Our bottom line," writes Ben Cohen about his premium ice cream company (in *We Gave Away a Fortune,* ed. by Christopher Mogil and Anne Slepian with Peter Woodrow, 1992, New Society Publishers, 4527 Springfield Ave., Philadelphia, PA 19143, pp. 91-94; used by permission), "consists of two equal parts. One is making a reasonable profit for shareholders, and the other is helping to improve the quality of life for the members of our communities and for all people. If we fail in either one of these areas, we have failed as a business." In addition to the "1% for Peace" project mentioned in our chapter on socially responsible consumption, the company has sponsored voter registration drives, attempted to adopt a New York City subway station (an effort foiled by the city bureaucracy and unions), and offered its stock not to the financial community but to "the mainstream Vermont community. We set a very low minimum for the stock," writes Cohen. "(F)or $126 you could become a shareholder. . . We had ads in the first section [not the financial section] of the newspaper. . . We also travelled around the state and held meetings to make it truly available to everyone. Over time, one out of every 100 people in Vermont became stockholders. I always felt like we were holding the business in trust for the community. After all, the community allows you to exist. People in the community buy your product. They provide the infrastructure; they provide all the resources that you use; they provide everything except the idea."

"At times in the history of the company," he continues, "employees have felt that we give too much to the outer community and not enough to them. . . . So as the company grew and had more money, we put more of it into the 'family.' Wages and benefits went up, the quality of the working environment improved. . . Jerry started the 'Joy Committee'. . . infusing more joy into the experience of working here." The company has a 7:1 salary ratio: Ben Cohen is paid $100,000 a year, while the lowest-paid worker receives $16,000.

(Continued from page 71)
approximately 25 socially responsible money managers to customize portfolios in the $100,000 to $2 million range.

Mutual funds are uninsured accounts in which many investors' assets are pooled to purchase stocks, bonds and other government and corporate securities.

Parnassus Fund (244 California Street, San Francisco, CA 94111, 800-999-3505) presently serves 4,000 clients. They avoid companies that manufacture weapons, alcohol or tobacco or are involved with nuclear power. In the year mentioned at right (1988), Parnassus had returns of 42.44%.

The Calvert Group (4550 Montgomery Ave., Bethesda, MD 20814, 800-368-2748), with $4.1 billion in assets, includes six funds that comprise the first and largest family of socially responsible mutual funds in the U.S., with assets of nearly $1 billion. Of these, the Calvert Social Investment Fund is most rigorous in its investment criteria. It considers a company's management-labor relations, handling of issues of sexual orientation, dealings with repressive regimes, use of alternative energy, and much more. Calvert also participates actively in proxy voting at corporate meetings and contacts management with its concerns.

growth fund.) The Domini Social Index 400, monitoring 400 companies that pass several broad-based socially responsible screens (including 255 companies that are among the S & P 500), reported a total return for the year ending March 31, 1991 of +16.75% for its stocks, compared to +14.38% for the S & P.

In socially responsible banking, the South Shore Bank of Chicago has set the pace since 1973. A full-service commercial bank, South Shore has financed housing rehabilitation, small businesses, non-profit organizations and educational projects to the tune of $115 million in loans, with cumulative loan losses of only 1.5% — less than the norm for commercial banks. South Shore Bank has meanwhile reversed the dramatic decline of several Chicago neighborhoods that were the victims of disinvestment by making loans to some 7,000 individuals.

"Our bank," said Joan Shapiro, senior vice-president at South Shore in a May, 1988 interview in *Mother Jones,* "was able to change a community that was destined to become a slum into a revitalizing, active, stabilizing neighborhood, through the synergy of *hundreds* of small-scale activities combined with a few large-scale projects. . . . Frankly," she added, "any bank in the country could do" the kind of capital reinvestment that has led Chicago's South Shore to an economic turnaround.

Some banks are doing just that: Brooklyn's Community Capital Bank, for example, which completed its initial capital drive of $6 million in July, 1990, is modeled after South Shore Bank and devotes itself to community reinvestment. Much of the $6 million came from Protestant and Catholic orders and organizations, but the Brooklyn Heights (Reform) synagogue also invested, as did the Jewish Fund for Justice as a $5,000 initial shareholder (we'll discuss JFJ's activities further in our

South Shore Bank, 71st and Jeffery Boulevard, Chicago, IL 60649-2096, 800-NOW-SSBK. The Shorebank Corporation includes the South Shore Bank, the City Lands Corporation (real estate development), the Neighborhood Fund (minority venture capital), the Neighborhood Institute (housing, economic and social non-profit programs), and Shorebank Advisory Services (technical assistance). The bank offers FDIC-insured Development Deposit™Accounts in the form of CDs, money market, savings, IRA and checking accounts; many depositors are from outside the bank's home market. According to a 1989 report in the *New Republic,* Shorebank Corporation is responsible for $160 million in new investments, the rehabilitation of 350 large apartment buildings, and the founding of hundreds of businesses.

Community Capital Bank, 111 Livingston St., Brooklyn, NY 11201, 718-802-1212.

Jewish Fund for Justice, 920 Broadway, Suite 605, New York, NY 10010, 212-677-7080.

Jewish Council on Urban Affairs, 220 South State St., Suite 1910, Chicago, IL 60604, 312-663-0960.

chapter on *tzedakah*). As CCB neared the $6 million goal that would enable it to open its doors, some private Jewish investors helped to leverage a $100,000 investment from the New York Federation/United Jewish Appeal, which brought the bank over the top. (In Chicago, the Jewish Council on Urban Affairs, which assists minority projects in the Chicago area, has been a significant booster of South Shore Bank, which has among its deposits $50,000 of JCUA's endowment funds.)

THE "BOTTOM LINE" of socially responsible investment, then, is that it makes both dollars and sense. Although long-range trends can't yet be evaluated — the movement is too young for that — some in the socially responsible investment community do argue that a company's social policies may be

---

Other socially responsible banks include:
• National Cooperative Bank (1630 Connecticut Ave., NW, Washington, D.C. 20009-1004, 202-745-4600), delivering financial services to cooperative businesses.
• Ameritrust Development Bank (1228 Euclid Ave., Cleveland, OH 44115-1831, 216-861-6964), working to rebuild or rehabilitate housing in economically struggling communities.
• Vermont National Bank, Socially Responsible Banking Fund (POB 804, Brattleboro, VT 05302, 800-544-7108), making loans for affordable housing, environmental projects, family farming, education and small business development.
• First Trade Union Savings Bank (10 Drydock Ave., Boston, MA 02205-9063, 617-482-4000), owned by the Massachusetts Carpenters Union, making loans for affordable housing.
• Development Bank of Washington (3614 12 St., NE, Washington, D.C. 20017, 202-832-2865), making small business and housing development loans.
Source: CEP's *The Better World Investment Guide,* already cited.

a strong indicator of its profitability: that enlightened employee programs, for example (flextime, health coverage, daycare, participatory decision-making, etc.), are likely to be paid back with higher productivity —

> A generous person enjoys prosperity;
> Whosoever satisfies others shall be sated.
> (*Proverbs* 11:25)

— or that a company with careful environmental practices is likely to be a tightly run ship, with minimal waste, that can endure business downturns.

> Seven times the righteous fall and get up
> While the wicked are tripped by one misfortune.
> (*Proverbs* 24:16)

Social Responsibility According to Judaism

CLEARLY, THE BOOK of *Proverbs* (attributed to King Solomon) agrees: Ethical business means profitable business! "Honor the Lord with your wealth," says *Proverbs* 3: 9-10, "With the best of all your income, And your barns will be filled with grain, Your vats will burst with new wine." In fact, the story of young King Solomon's dream (*II Kings* 3: 5-15), in which he asks God not for personal treasures but for "discernment in dispensing justice," and is awarded for his selflessness with multiple blessings of wealth and long life, could be called a biblical testimonial to the "ethical=profitable" formula.

Regardless of whether this formula is valid or naive, Judaism does demand that we consider more than profit margins in calculating our "bottom line." "(T)he achievement of economic wealth and the use thereof," writes Meir Tamari, "are

> Judaism suggests that we consider more than profit margins in calculating our "bottom line." "(T)he achievement of economic wealth," writes Meir Tamari, is ". . . very strictly limited and channeled by. . . the ethical, moral, and religous demands of the Torah, so that the individual and society can attain a state of sanctity even while carrying out the most mundane acts. . . ." While Jewish teachings do not easily boil down to CEP-style categories, certain essential principles of Judaism can be cited that link the values of the social responsibility movement and the values of our heritage.

At minimum, "the embrace of social criteria is not a financial giveaway," writes John E. Schultz in the Social Investment Forum *Guide* of January 1, 1992. "(T)he return on investment is primarily a function of the selective skill of the investment manager."

Robert Zevin, a social investment pioneer now with USTrust in Boston, writes that the financial consequence of "clean" investing is "negligible, as long as you do not exclude more than half of all possible investments. . . . However, clean investing. . . is an extremely weak way to exert effective pressure on the offending corporation. . . . Logic and experience suggest that boycotting a business' products and services provokes a more compliant response than boycotting its securities." Zevin also advocates "alternative investing. . . made directly in a political organization or community activity. . . specifically designed to achieve a social purpose. . . . However, the price of the increased social force of alternative investing is often lessened investment merit" (that is, profit). Quoted from the 1983-84 *Directory of Socially Responsible Investments* of the Funding Exchange. For discussion of the limits of socially responsible investing, see p. 90.

Meir Tamari, *"With All Your Possessions. . ."* (already cited), p. 32. Used by permission.

very strictly limited and channeled by Judaism." All Jewish actions, "including those involved in the accumulation of material goods, are to be subjected to the ethical, moral, and religous demands of the Torah, so that the individual and society can attain a state of sanctity even while carrying out the most mundane acts. . . ." Tamari further notes that of the 613 *mitzvot* derived from the Torah, over 100 are economically related, which indicates an overriding Judaic concern with creating a socially responsible "Torah of Money."

Few modern Jews, however, are interested in applying stringent *halakhic* standards to their lifestyles. A good many of the 613 commandments, moreover, pertain to Temple ritual, monarchy and other antiquated aspects of Jewish life, and are therefore largely irrelevant to contemporary times. But what about the "ethical, moral and religious demands of the Torah" to which Tamari refers? While these do not easily boil down to CEP-style categories (hence the endless reams of commentary, argument, and interpretation that comprise the Jewish Oral Tradition and are still being created and debated today), certain essential principles of Judaism can nevertheless be cited that link the values of the social responsibility movement and the fundamental values of our heritage — a linkage that can add vitality and depth to both.

The Covenant Idea: Power Made Accountable

IN OUR CHAPTER on socially responsible consumption, for example, we cited *shabbat* and the *Sh'ma* as Judaic principles with significant socio-economic implications — the former affirming human stewardship, rather than ownership, of wealth and of the earth, the latter affirming the unity of creation and the consequence of our deeds. The *Sh'ma* is, in fact, the Jewish "signature" on the "contract" or covenant affirmed at Mt. Sinai between God and the people Israel. In reciting the *Sh'ma,* Jews affirm their participation in an interdependent relation with the Divine. As the Dead Sea Scrolls scholar Theodor Gaster put it:

> Judaism has a central, unique and tremendous idea that is utterly original — the idea that God and man [sic] are partners in the world and that, for the realization of God's plan and the complete articulation of this glory upon earth, God needs a committed, dedicated group of men and women.

The Gaster quote is from *A Treasury of Jewish Quotations,* edited by Joseph L. Baron (1985, Jason Aronson, Inc., Northvale, NJ), p. 155.

Implicit in this notion of partnership is a human desire to limit or license Divine power through a contract of mutual obligation, so that the life of the people Israel can be established and maintained without fear of the kind of cosmic anarchy that reigns in pagan cosmologies. While the words of the *Sh'ma* emphasize love of God, the prayer is, in fact, rooted in an encounter with the Divine in which the fear quotient was high: "(I)f we hear the voice of the Lord our God any longer," the people tell Moses at Sinai, "we shall die" (*Deuteronomy* 5: 22). One *midrash* makes explicit this desire to delimit God's arbitrary power: "You are My witnesses. . . I am God," declares *Isaiah* 43: 12, upon which the *midrash* comments: "When you are My witnesses, I am God; when you are not my witnesses, I am, as it were, not God."

Midrash Tehillim, 123.2, as quoted in Baron's *A Treasury of Jewish Quotations,* just cited, p. 155.

The Covenanted Corporation: "Stakeholders"

THIS IDEA of making power accountable by establishing a

"The Chosen People'

A fundamental corollary to the traditional concept of the Covenant is the doctrine of Jewish "chosenness" — a doctrine that has historically given particular offense to liberal Jews. For purposes of our discussion, however, "chosenness" need not be viewed as anything more than a special sense of Jewish social responsibility that has evolved from historical and religious sources. This sense of responsibility has a prophetic role to play in the modern world, and Jews, especially, need to learn how to transmit it.

In an address to the January, 1985 meeting of the World Jewish Congress in Vienna, Rabbi Alexander M. Schindler of the Reform movement spoke of how, in the face of possible global disaster, "Our Jewish chosenness" takes on universalist meaning and "becomes the yoke of all human beings. Our Jewish consciousness becomes a global consciousness. . . . These are extraordinary times in which all of humanity is summoned to the task of human survival. These are times in which spiritual and material reality merge, in which all the faces of the human race merge. It is a merger brought about not, alas, by the hand of God, or of a messianic presence, but by the. . . shadow of death. . ."

covenant is being applied by socially responsible financial activists to the field of corporate reform. We have granted god-like powers to our corporations, these activists argue, powers over resources and human lives, over time and distance, that are exercised on a scale unimaginable to our forebears. Yet these latter-day "gods" know no obligations but to increase the wealth of their shareholders, who comprise but a tiny sector of those who are affected by corporate deeds. The corporate "covenant" thus needs enlargement, so that the "delivering hand," rather than the destructive aspects, of marketplace economics can come to the fore. John E. Schultz, president (from 1990 to 1991) of the Social Investment Forum, explains (in the SIF *Guide,* already cited):

> Nineteenth century industrial development, in a world with a population of less than one billion and an uninhabited frontier, was compatible with the dominant theory of business management, that the primary objective of management is to maximize the wealth of the shareholders. But a 21st century with more than five billion world inhabitants and no remaining habitable frontier requires a philosophical rethinking. And while the change is not a great modification of semantics, it is philosophically profound. For the dominant theory of business management in the 21st centry *must* become that the primary objective of management is to maximize the wealth of the *stakeholders.*

This stakeholder group includes "the shareholders and employees, customers and vendors, the community and the environment," Schultz notes. "(B)alancing the return to these six groups. . . requires managers to make subjective decisions as they attempt to . . . achieve a combined performance that is optimal to the group as a whole."

This expanded sense of a corporate "covenant" is not limited to the socially responsible "margins" of the business world. As

The corporate stake-holder group includes shareholders and employees, customers and vendors, the community and the environment. Under this expanded notion of a corporate "covenant," a company's impact on all of these interests must be considered in calculating success and "profitability."

Harold Williams is quoted in the Council on Economic Priorities' *20th Anniversary Annual Report.*

early as 1978, Harold Williams, then-chair of the Securities and Exchange Commission, understatedly affirmed the need for a stakeholder philosophy and a new corporate covenant: "As a society we depend on private enterprise to serve as the instrument through which to accomplish a wide variety of goals," he said.

> When viewed in light of. . . social implications, corporations must be seen as, to a degree, more than purely private institutions, and corporate profits as not entirely an end to themselves, but also as one of the resources which corporations require to discharge their responsibilities.

Such statements from the mainstream business community

79

The Valdez Principles

Protection of the Biosphere
We will try to minimize and eliminate environmental damage and will safeguard natural habitats.

Sustainable Use of Natural Resources
We will make sustainable use of natural resources and conserve nonrenewable resources.

Reduction and Disposal of Waste
We will minimize the creation of waste, recycle materials, and dispose of all wastes safely.

Wise Use of Energy
We will invest in improved energy efficiency and conservation and will maximize the efficiency of products we sell.

Risk Reduction
We will minimize environmental, health and safety risks to our employees and communities.

Marketing of Products and Services
We will sell products or services that minimize adverse environmental impacts.

Damage Compensation
We will take responsibiliity for any environmental harm we cause through restoration and compensation.

Disclosure
We will disclose to employees and the public any operations that cause environmental harm.

Environmental Directors
One member of our Board of Directors is charged with monitoring our compliance with the Valdez Principles.

Assessment and Annual Audit
We will conduct and make public an annual self-evaluation of our progress in implementing these principles.

Marjorie Kelly, "Revolution in the Marketplace," *Utne Reader,* January/ February, 1989, p. 54. Kelly is editor and publisher of the bi-monthly *Business Ethics* magazine (52 S. 10 St., Minneapolis, MN 55403-2001, 612-962-4700).

Ethical Impact Statements?

In their 1992 book, *Tough Choices* (UAHC Press, New York), Reform social action leaders Albert Vorspan and Rabbi David Saperstein apply the "covenant" idea to industry by proposing that corporations be required to issue "'ethical impact statements' for new technological developments. Before any new major technological developments could be implemented, a study would have to be done by scientists, ethicists, politicians, economists, etc. on what the ethical (including the economic, environmental, privacy, social) impact of that development would be." This proposal for an expansion on the environmental impact statement idea has also been developed by Arthur Waskow, director of The Shalom Center — see his essay in this book.

Project CERES, 711 Atlantic Ave., Boston, MA 02111, 617-451-0927. A Valdez Action Kit will be sent to you for $1 postage.

fuel the hopefulness of writer Marjorie Kelly, who describes "an emerging new paradigm. . . of what's expected of business, and what's possible. . . "

It's a picture of workplaces that are healthy for employees, of corporate citizens who are powerful yet responsive, of companies that are tools for social change, and of a corporate community that is a human presence on the earth. . . . (I)n June (1988), NCR (formerly National Cash Register) sponsored the First International Symposium on Stakeholders, inviting corporate leaders to examine questions like this one, taken verbatim from the program: "Can Marxist claims about the 'internal contradictions of capitalism' be countered with a stakeholder approach to management?"

The Covenanted Corporation: Valdez Principles

THE STAKEHOLDER concept is given further elaboration in the Valdez Principles, created in 1989 by Project CERES (the Coalition for Environmentally Responsible Economies), a coalition led by the Social Investment Forum and environmental groups including the Sierra Club, the National Audubon Society and the National Wildlife Federation. The Valdez Principles are guidelines for corporate environmental responsibility (modeled after the Sullivan Principles for U.S. corporate conduct in South Africa) that were prompted by the *Exxon Valdez* disaster of March 24, 1989, in which 11.2 million gallons of oil were spilled into Alaska's coastal waters and the lack of oil industry preparedness to deal with such accidents was starkly revealed.

The principles set a standard by which socially responsible money managers can evaluate corporate performance in the

81

environmental realm. As of January, 1992, 31 privately-held companies had signed the Valdez Principles, and six Fortune 100 corporations were negotiating with Project CERES about their participation.

A Fence for the Torah, a Fence for the Earth: No Nuclear Poisons

WIDESPREAD CORPORATE endorsement of the Valdez Principles would help create a "buffer" between business activity and the environment by ensuring policies, attitudes, and systems of accountability that would make even the accidental violation of environmental sanctity (e.g., the *Exxon Valdez* shipwreck) far less likely. An analogous notion is found in the *Pirkei Avot*, the text traditionally studied on the afternoon of *Shabbat*. In its first sentence, *Pirkei Avot* establishes the concept of *s'yag l'Torah*, making a "fence for the Torah" — that is, establishing practices that would keep us from violating Torah teachings even accidentally, unwittingly or under duress. Under this principle, certain behaviors can be judged as simply too "risky" to be tolerated, and we are urged to err on the side of caution.

The continued use of nuclear power blatantly violates this principle. As far as the social responsibility movement is concerned, the nuclear industry is "off limits," beyond the boundaries of responsible investment, for at least three reasons:

• The sheer toxicity of plutonium and the other radioactive waste products of atom-splitting, and their deadly persistence into eternity (as far as human historical time is concerned; plutonium has a radioactive half-life of 25,000+ years);

Stewardship of wealth; the Covenant of responsibility between human beings and Creation; communitarian identity ("genuine We-ness"); the creation of a "fence for the Torah" — these are but some of the Judaic concepts that can be elaborated upon in the creation of a "Torah of Money."

Chullin is a tractate in the Talmudic order *Kodeshim,* dealing with the laws of Temple service — laws compiled long after the Jerusalem Temple had been destroyed. By considering the planet Earth to be our Temple, we render the words terribly relevant: Surely the extensive radioactive pollution that has forced the shutdown even of secretive Defense Department nuclear reactors (e.g., Savannah River in South Carolina and Hanford in Washington) qualifies as hideous! Other hideous features: "The flow of capital to energy producers," writes
(Continued next page)

• The epic disaster at Chernobyl, and the near-disaster at Three Mile Island, which made clear that nuclear power's threat to Creation is by no means limited to the future;

• The key role that nuclear power plays in nuclear weapons proliferation.

However, even while extensive grassroots protest stymied the nuclear industry during the 1970s and early '80s, the organized Jewish community was less than vociferous in its opposition to nuclear power, chiefly for fear of U.S. dependency on imported (that is, Arab) oil. Nor have energy conservation and renewable sources of energy been promoted with any dedication by mainstream Jewish groups.

"Stay away from hideous things," said the sages in tractate *Chullin* (44b), "and even things that appear to be hideous." Apparently, for many Jews the hideousness of nuclear power has been obscured by the nightmare image of an Israel held hostage to Arab oil. Revelations following the Persian Gulf War about Iraq's nuclear weapons program may prod liberal sectors of American Jewry to draw the connection between nuclear power and nuclear proliferation, and on that basis of "self-interest" mount some genuine opposition to signs of revival in the nuclear industry. The leader of the Reform synagogue movement, Rabbi Alexander M. Schindler, showed such an inclination in his 1991 state-of-the-union address to his movement's biennial assembly in Baltimore:

> The spur to nuclear proliferation that nuclear power provides makes it a kind of golem run amok. . . . To entertain such a technology as viable, whether for economic or political reasons, is an arrogant blunder. . . .

Schindler even moved beyond the matter of Israeli (and global) security concerns to root his opposition in moral terms:

> The *Exxon Valdez* disaster in Alaska, or the radioactive disaster zone in Hanford, Washington, or the proliferation of

83

(Continued from previous page)
Jeffrey Dekro (*Jewish Currents,* June, 1982) "creates economic and political imbalance; the centralization of the energy industry limits investigation of other energy sources, threatens to strangle essential industry and produces unemployment. . . nuclear proliferation increases the threat of nuclear blackmail and the need for a security-conscious society. . ."

"Stay away from hideous things," said the sages in tractate *Chullin* (44b), "and even things that appear to be hideous." Apparently for many Jews the hideousness of nuclear power has been obscured by the nightmare image, real or not, of an Israel held hostage to Arab oil.

every form of cancer in our society, are not the "price of progress." They are the price of profit, the price of corporate thinking about human values, the price of a materialism so corrosive that it can rupture an oil tanker's hull or a nuclear reactor's containment vessel. . . .

The depletion of the rainforests and the daily extinction of still another species are not a function of the "human condition." It is the work. . . of a specific cattle rancher selling meat to the chains, those "fast food" spots that burgeon when a culture becomes too insanely pressured to take pause for a blessing before the meal.

Idolatry for Profit? The Complicated Choices of Socially Responsible Investing

Rabbi Schindler's words highlight the idolatrous aspects of "uncovenanted" capitalism: how it defines "progress" in profit-making terms of efficiency, speed, innovation and boundless growth, with little attention to environmental impact or impact upon the human community and the human soul; how the system encourages us to worship things (and people-as-things — as "stars," "models," or "idols"), and to view possessing them as akin to redemption. The idolatry of the system is especially revealed in its advertising, in which products are

According to Louis Ginzberg's *The Legends of the Jews* (already cited, Vol. 1, pp. 122-123, used by permission), the Jewish tradition dates the advent of idolatry to the time of Enosh, a grandson of Adam and Eve in whose era people "began to gather gold, silver, gems and pearls from all parts of the earth, and made idols thereof a thousand parasangs high [approximately 4,000 miles]. . . . (T)hey set themselves as masters over the heavenly spheres, and forced the sun, the moon, and the stars to be subservient to themselves instead of the Lord. This impelled the angels to ask God: 'What are humans, that Thou art mindful of them?'. . . God caused the sea to transgress its bounds, and a portion of the earth was flooded. . . . But there was a still more serious consequence. . . . When God drove Adam forth from Paradise, the Shekhinah remained behind, enthroned above a cherub under the tree of life. . . and Adam and his descendants sat by the gate to bask in the splendor of the Shekhinah, 65,000 times more radiant than the splendor of the sun. This brightness. . . makes all upon whom it falls exempt from disease, and neither insects nor demons can come nigh unto them to do them harm.

"Thus it was until the time of Enosh. . . [when the] Shekinah was induced to leave the earth and to ascend to heaven. . .

crassly linked with spiritual values: Coke is "the real thing," Pepsi will help us to "come alive. . . ."

"You shall have no other gods beside me," declares the God of Israel as the Covenant is being fashioned at Mount Sinai. This essential Judaic principle is given tremendous weight by traditional commentators: Not even the threat of martyrdom gives license to a Jew to perform idolatrous acts, which are variously blamed for the Deluge, the destruction of the Jerusalem Temple, and the exile of *Shekhinah,* God's intimate presence (usually considered a feminine aspect of Deity), from the earth. "Whoever professes idolatry rejects the Ten Commandments," says one *midrash,* "and whoever rejects idolatry professes the entire Torah."

Given the lack of common agreement about what constitutes idolatry in a modern context, incorporating the strict anti-idolatry prohibitions of traditional Judaism into our evolving "Torah of Money" is impossible. For most of us, "idolatrous" is simply a strange and perhaps overstated description of those aspects of the commercial culture that violate our values, strike us as tasteless, sexist, dehumanizing, exploitative of human weakness, or otherwise "wrong." Our feelings in these matters are often strong, almost instinctual, yet we usually recognize our judgments as subjective, aesthetic, "matters of taste," and only rarely trust our judgments enough to impose them on others — or even on ourselves!

Nevertheless, such a process of defining and prioritizing values is the bedrock of socially responsible investing. Rarely is a company totally "clean" in its record; it may be "good" on the environment but "bad" in its labor relations; it may be marvelously attuned to a "stakeholder" management philosophy yet manufacture a useless or harmful product. Some investors avoid having to make such judgments by pursuing only a strict, single-issue focus; this approach, however, often

The Melton Journal: "Our Earth and Our Tradition"

The Spring,1991 and Spring, 1992 issues of *The Melton Journal,* publication of the Melton Center for Jewish Education of the Jewish Theological Seminary (of Conservative Judaism) are devoted to an in-depth discussion of Judaism and ecology. Included are comments about the classic Judaic distrust of "naturalism" and rejection of "paganism" — comments of special interest to the many Jewish environmentalists and feminists who find themselves drawn to a Creation-centered spirituality.

Orthodox philosopher Michael Wyschograd writes: "It is difficult, particularly for Jews, to worship nature again. At the same time, the destruction of nature, which seems to follow to some extent from the desacralization of nature, has reached a stage that cannot continue. So we must try to combine these two themes. . . . I have long felt that the religion against which the prophets expounded so eloquently in the Hebrew Bible did not get a full hearing from them. I wonder whether the prophets gave a really fair presentation of the. . . theology of the worshipers of Baal and Ashteret. . . ."

Reconstructionist leader Arthur Green writes: "We are urgently in need of ways to increase our sense of responsibility for preserving this world and its resources. As we do this, we need a theological anchor which will serve as the basis for such a change in human attitudes. *This age cries out for a new religious language that will speak of the underlying unity of all existence, rather than the endless struggle of species against species.*"

Ismar Schorsch, Chancellor of JTS, writes: "We must. . . dare to re-examine our longstanding preference for history over nature. . . . Preoccupied with the ghosts of paganism, [Judaism] seems indifferent and unresponsive to the supreme challenge of our age: man's degradation of the environment. Our planet is under siege and we as Jews are transfixed in silence. What a monumental disservice to Judaism and human kind! . . . The awareness of God's dominion, a proprietorship anchored in creation, is the ultimate constraint erected by Judaism to stay the hand of self-destruction."

Available from the Melton Research Center, 3080 Broadway, New York, NY 10027, 212-678-8031.

Contemporary Jewish feminists have expressed pain over Judaism's unrelenting vilification and suppression of "idolatrous," including goddess-worshipping, cultures of the ancient Middle East. (See the facing page for some surprising re-evaluations of Judaism's relationship to paganism by Orthodox, Conservative and Reconstructionist thinkers.) However, the significance of the term "idolatry" within the context of a modern, secular society that worships the "Almighty Dollar" is too potent to be surrendered, and thus we are using the term, as we have many others, with an eye to modern contexts and a willingness to pare away or ignore historical contexts that might limit, bind or nullify the application of the concept to our contemporary situation.

Council on Economic Priorities, *Better World Invstment Guide*, already cited.

For most of us, "idolatrous" is simply a strange and perhaps overstated description of those aspects of the commercial culture that violate our values, strike us as tasteless, dehumanizing, exploitative of human weakness, or otherwise "wrong." Our feelings in these matters are often strong, almost instinctual, yet we would rarely trust our judgments enough to impose them upon others — or even upon ourselves!

Nevertheless, such a process of defining and prioritizing values is the bedrock work of socially responsible investing.

has us "whoring for apples to give them to the sick" (*Leviticus Rabbah* 31) — breaching our ethics in one realm in order to do good works in another.

THE McDONALD'S Corporation, for example, poses an interesting challenge to the socially responsible investor. The hamburger chain is the largest employer of minority youth in the U.S., according to the Council on Economic Priorities, with more than 5% of its restaurant franchises minority-owned and over 25% of its managers minority members (50% women). The company pursues vigorous purchasing programs for minority and women vendors; it has been responsive to criticism about the environmental impact of its packaging materials; Joan Kroc, the widow of McDonald's founder Ray Kroc, has been a generous supporter of AIDS research, peace and nuclear freeze work, and housing for the homeless. These and other features recommend McDonald's as a socially respon-

Sears Roebuck's Mixed Record — Socially Responsible but Anti-Semitic?

Sears, Roebuck and Co., the only corporation to receive the Council on Economic Priorities' highest rating in *The Better World Investment Guide* in the category of "women's advancement," and a good performer in its charitable giving and minority relations, has been charged with being anti-Semitic at management levels by Steven Slavin, co-author with Mary A. Pradt of *The Einstein Syndrome: Corporate Anti-Semitism in America Today* (1982, University Press of America, Washington, DC). "There are plenty of companies that are still *judenrein* (without Jews)," Slavin writes in a January, 1992 letter to *Jewish Currents* magazine. ". . . Morgan Guaranty, Irving Trust, Brown Brothers Harriman, Sears (founded by a Jew) [Julius Rosenwald, 1862-1932, who established the Rosenwald Fund that spent more than $100 million to aid African-American education in the American South], the oil companies (except Occidental), and the airlines." Sears is among those companies, according to Slavin, which pursue college recruitment and executive hiring practices that avoid contact with Jews. New York and its environs seem off-limits to these corporations' college recruiters, despite the existence of over 60 colleges

(Continued next page)

sible investment. As the premiere fast-food restaurant chain, however (enough burgers sold to stack to the moon and back — twice!), McDonald's has helped homogenize the American landscape. In fact, with over 11,000 restaurants in more than 50 countries, McDonald's has been homogenizing the planet. In a culture "too insanely pressured to take a pause for a blessing before the meal" (repeating Rabbi Schindler's words), might "socially responsible investment" in fast food be an oxymoron?

What about bio-technology — America's great hope for world economic leadership in the coming decades? Does genetic manipulation to create new life forms or "improved" species violate our sense of Jewish "taboo"? What about new communications technologies that quicken our already breathless pace of life? Do we accept the unfolding of such technological "advances" (many of which serve to heighten the power and indispensability of large corporations and government bodies and speed the obsolescence of small businesses) as inevitable, or withhold our support?

What about companies with socially dubious reputations that are now reforming? The Raytheon company, for example — the number five defense contractor in 1990 — is leading the trend towards diversification into the manufacture of consumer products. E.I. Du Pont De Nemours & Co., the largest U.S. chemical company, notorious for its past and present manufacture of ozone-depleting chlorofluorocarbons (CFCs) and for its oversight of the environmentally disastrous Savannah River nuclear facility, now makes an annual $1 billion investment in pollution control and has been a pioneer in corporate safety, according to CEP. (Du Pont was one of ten companies selected by *Working Mother* magazine as having the most "family-friendly" work policies in 1991.) Do we "reward" such companies for their progress by investing in them, or do

(Continued from previous page)
in commuting distance of mid-town Manhattan, according to *The Einstein Syndrome,* while corporations headquartered in New York tend to recruit less intensively on a local basis than those that are headquartered elsewhere — where there are fewer Jews, Blacks and Hispanics.

Labor historian Paul Buhle, in a January, 1993 letter to *Jewish Currents,* urges Jewish organizations to bring pressure upon Edgar Bronfman, a major Jewish philanthropist and leader of the World Jewish Congress, who sits on Du Pont's Board of Directors, to help bring an end to the company's manufacture of ozone-destroying products.

Du Pont, according to CEP, increased its number of U.S. managers and professionals who were women and minorities a hefty 38% (to 22% of the total) from 1985 to 1989. The company has a college recruitment goal of 40-50% women and minorities each year, has instituted a rape prevention program and a 24-hour hotline to report rape or sexual harassment on or off the job.

Wayne Silby in *Mother Jones,* May, 1988, "Hearts of Gold," interview by Jonathan Tasini.

Left Business Observer, 250 W. 85th St., New York, NY 10024. Reprinted in *The Utne Reader,* January/February, 1989.

do we avoid them on account of their past misdeeds or their involvement with grossly unhealthy fields of enterprise?

Those who try to pursue a "Torah of money" in the corporate world are continually confronted by such complexities. "Socially responsible investing is about self-expression," said Wayne Silby, the pioneering founder of the Calvert Social Investment Fund, in an interview in *Mother Jones.* "Much like the Buddhist concept of right livelihood, it's about extending one's values and projecting them into the world, and being able to make choices and see opportunities that are an expression of individual self-choice and awareness."

A Radical Critique of Socially Responsible Investing

SOME CRITICS of the socially responsible money movement ask, however, whether this "self-expression" that Silby describes is a force for change or merely a salve to the consciences of liberals who are making money from corporate structures that produce many inequities.

Doug Henwood, editor of *Left Business Observer,* is one such critic. "Profit," he writes, "no matter how 'ethical' the firm generating it, originates in the fact that workers are never paid the full value of what they produce; managers, bankers and investors pocket much of the difference." He continues:

> Competition requires that firms reduce their costs to the lowest possible level — not that the lower-paid workers be brought up to the higher level. But one hears little from business ethicists on such matters. . . . Sadly, ethical business practices are too often a luxury good, appropriate mainly to highly profitable firms in either rapidly growing or niche

Robert Zevin, a major authority on socially responsible investing, agrees with the critique made by Doug Henwood when he writes that "the whole approach suggests that companies are 'good' or 'bad' as a result of the social conscience of managements. While this may sometimes be the case, it is often true that differences in observed corporate behavior result from differences in the circumstances in which businesses operate. Both the acceptable and the unacceptable businesses may be doing the best they can to maximize profits under their respective conditions. In that case socially clean investing may distract attention from the real villain, which is a system that places too much emphasis on private profit and too little weight on public welfare." Quoted from the 1983-84 *Directory of Socially Responsible Investments* of the Funding Exchange. Zevin is senior vice-president of the Asset Management Division of USTrust (40 Court St., Boston, MA 02108, 617-726-7250).

markets. . . . an ethics that focuses only on micro issues of individual behavior and ignores the larger issues of the competitive marketplace and its arbiter of value, profitability, is largely cosmetic.

This classic anti-capitalist argument — that the translation of human needs into profit-making goals, and the exploitation of workers to create that profit, produce injustices no matter what the ethical intentions of participants — has perhaps been battered by the collapse of not-for-profit "planned economies" and their political bureaucracies throughout Eastern Europe. Capitalist triumphalism aside, however, the failures of modern communism merely overturn the idea that there was in the modern world an already existing, successful alternative to capitalism's reliance on the "marketplace" to satisfy human needs; it does not *ipso facto* relieve us of our own system's structural injustices.

Henwood's critique has added weight if we enlarge his notion of the significant "internal contradictions of capitalism" to go beyond the systemic tensions between wages and profits, or between private ownership and public interest, that have been mediated to some extent through government regulation, trade unionism, enlightened management philosophy and political struggle. Perhaps as significant for our time as the issue of "who owns the means of production" is the very concept of "production" itself — the tension between freedom from scarcity and unchecked materialism, between liberation from want and self-destruction from greed, which inhere in our modern technological proficiency. Balancing human progress and nature's needs, and harmonizing the relationship between rich and poor, says E. F. Schumacher, author of the pioneering work, *Small Is Beautiful*, requires the solid establishment of the principle that "enough is good and more-than-enough is evil." A Yiddish proverb assents (while avoiding

Schumacher's simplistic, good-versus-evil paradigm): "Where there is too much, something is missing." If limiting growth is a necessary component of our future well-being, can investing in growth-driven corporations be a socially responsible thing to do?

THE TALMUD provides a partial response to this question in the form of a story about Rabbi Shimon bar Yohai, who endured a 13-year exile in a cave in order to avoid the martyrdom that Rome was imposing upon many teachers and students of Judaism. Shimon had, in private conversation, expressed scorn for the "achievements" of the Roman system: "Whatever they have done, they have done for themselves: they needed streets for prostitutes, bridges for tolls, and spas for their physical welfare." Betrayed to the Romans as a malcontent by one of his conversants, and facing torture and death, Rabbi Shimon was forced to go into hiding.

Upon emerging from his 13-year exile, Rabbi Shimon sees a farmer plowing a field. Shimon is outraged: "There is so little time to devote oneself to God's words," he cries, "and you devote your time to insignificant things like the settlement of the world!" His rage is so intense that the poor farmer is reduced to a heap of ash. Nor is this the only victim of Rabbi Shimon's self-righteous anger at the sight of people participating in "the system."

Eventually a heavenly voice is heard: Has Shimon left his cave only to turn the world to chaos? Shimon is sent back to his cave for another year, during the course of which he "cools out." He emerges composed and compassionate; where before his gaze was destructive, now it heals. Elie Wiesel comments: "(I)n Rabbi Shimon's later period, we come across. . . themes

The Shimon bar Yohai story (*Berakhot* 35b) is retold in Elie Wiesel's *Sages and Dreamers,* 1991, Summit Books, New York, and in Meir Tamari's *"With All Your Possessions,"* *Jewish Ethics and Economic Life,* already cited.

Elie Wiesel translates Rabbi Shimon's exclamation as: "How can he neglect his eternal life for earthly gains?"

91

Shareholder Activism: Up Against the Boards

The March, 1990 issue of the CEP *Research Report* noted that Amoco, Chevron, Mobil, Texaco and Waste Management, Inc. had agreed to report periodically on their progress in areas covered by the Valdez Principles, in response to shareholder resolutions filed by the Interfaith Center on Corporate Responsibility with these and 19 other corporations. Such proxy resolutions have become a major tool to force corporate change; ICCR, representing over 200 Roman Catholic institutions (dioceses, pension funds, etc.) and 22 Protestant denominations, itself coordinates about 100 such resolutions annually. Of the more than 200 proxy resolutions submitted overall each season, nearly one third are withdrawn, according to CEP, after negotiated settlements such as those reported above.

The first successful effort to place a public interest shareholder resolution on a corporate proxy statement was that of the Project on Corporate Responsibility in 1970. With Ralph Nader's active endorsement, PCR filed resolutions with General Motors demanding the expansion of the board to allow representation by women, blacks, consumers and environmentalists, and the creation of a Committee for Corporate Responsibility chosen by the board, the United Auto Workers and PCR.

"PCR leaders," reports CEP (in *The Better World Investment Guide,* already cited, p. 5), "had no illusions that the resolutions would attract a large portion of the [shareholders'] votes. They knew that institutional investors routinely voted with management. But the stage was now set for full and open debate both inside and outside the annual meeting. Concerned about its public image, GM sent glowing reports to shareholders on improvements in safety and environmental records. . . . Most institutional investors did vote their shares with management, but not all: Tufts, Brown, Antioch, Boston University, Iowa State and Amherst supported one or both of PCR's resolutions." In reponse to these pressures, GM created a Public Policy Committee and appointed the Rev. Leon H. Sullivan of Philadelphia to its board — the first black to sit on the board of one of the country's largest corporations and the creator of the Sullivan Principles, which "between 1977 and 1987. . . provided a moral yardstick by which U.S. corporate treatment of black South African workers was measured."

. . . (about t)he importance of the self. . . (t)he ability, nay, the necessity, to transform curses into blessings, darkness into light."

The story argues that people must make a living — that the "settlement of the world" is both inevitable and desirable. Denouncing "Rome," or turning to ash those who participate in "the system," more often yields exile and chaos than positive political change. Would Americans be better off had Ralph Nader simply denounced the manufacture of cars, which have many inherently destructive features, rather than reforming General Motors through lawsuits, legislative lobbying, shareholder initiatives and other tools of the socially responsible money movement? Better to work to temper corporate power by establishing a new covenant that recognizes "we the people" as "stakeholders" — *including* workers whose "surplus value," according to Marxist theory, is the true source of profit.

Balancing human progress and nature's needs, and harmonizing the relationship between rich and poor, says E. F. Schumacher in *Small Is Beautiful,* requires the solid establishment of the principle that "enough is good and more-than-enough is evil." A Yiddish proverb assents: "Where there is too much, something is missing." If limiting growth is a necessary component of our future well-being, can investing in growth-driven corporations be a socially responsible thing to do?

Institute for Community Economics, 57 School St., Springfield, MA 01105-1131.
Charles Matthei now heads Equity Trust, Inc. (RFD 1, Box 430, Voluntown, CT 06384, 203-376-6174), so-named because "equity is defined both as a financial interest in property and as justice — and we believe that there must be an integral relationship between the two" (letter of November 7, 1991). The Equity Trust aims to organize community development activists on behalf of economic reform, "to enroll committed middle and upper-income people in these campaigns, not merely as charitable donors, but as people who are themselves changing property relationships;" to develop "American land reform campaigns" and "to participate in the international dialogue on property, encouraging the search for genuine alternatives to communism on the one hand and laissez-faire capitalism on the other."

Investing in Community Development Corporations

A FULLER RESPONSE to the critique of socially responsible investing is found in the strategy of "alternative" or affirmative investing — what South Shore Bank's Joan Shapiro calls "reinvestment." "Reinvestment, not just divestment, is really what it's all about," she says. "And until the dollars in the positive, reinvestment side of this equation even begin to equal what we've got now on the disinvestment side, we're really not making any significant change." In the same *Mother Jones* interview, Charles Matthei, former director of the Institute for Community Economics (ICE), a national, non-profit community development corporation, notes that he has encouraged many investors to move out of stocks and bonds entirely. "As a social investor," Matthei says, "you're going to consider what issue you want to address. . . [and examine] companies that have a bearing on that issue. But you may choose an issue, like the crisis in affordable housing or the problem of the homeless, and conclude that none of the companies with stock for sale on the exchange are meaningfully addressing that issue. And then you may decide that you can't effectively make a clear, personal response to that particular social crisis in the conventional markets."

For investors able to accept a below-market rate of return on their money, the outstanding vehicle for what Joan Shapiro calls "reinvesting" is the community development corporation (CDC). ICE itself, for example, runs a revolving loan fund with a capitalization of $10 million that makes low-interest loans to support rural and urban community land trusts, limited-equity housing cooperatives, affordable rental housing, worker-owned businesses and other projects that help stabilize communities and ward off real-estate speculators. ICE's capital comes from lenders, 80% of them individual, who negotiate interest rates and terms on an individual basis, from 0% to slightly below market rate. The lower the interest rate required by the lender ($1,000 is the minimum amount that ICE seeks), the greater the social impact of his or her investment, as the "subsidy" is passed on to borrowers. ICE has made over 270 loans in 26 states, totalling over $18 million, with a loan loss of only $11,000 (.06%) — and no loss to investors.

Most community development loan funds, like that run by ICE, are not insured and therefore not risk-free. Most do maintain reserve funds to protect investors against bad loans, however. Loans are frequently collateralized, and are always carefully underwritten. Most important, as providers of technical assistance as well as capital, community development loan funds tend to be "skilled evaluators of borrowers, able to accurately assess their needs and capacities," writes Susan Meeker-Lowry in her *Economics as if the Earth Really Mattered* (already cited). The "working relationship [between lender and borrower] often extends through the whole loan period" — which greatly contributes to the low default rate.

The hallmark of community development corporations is that they are run by and for the community members themselves, with the CDC activists/professionals providing skills and leadership training, legal assistance and managerial expertise. CDCs have been remarkably successful at sustaining grassroots community projects at a time when governmental social disinvestment and bank and insurance company "redlining" (excluding poor neighborhoods as a whole from receiving loans and insurance, regardless of the worthiness of individual loan applicants) have prevented poor and working-class communities from developing their local resources. CDC involvement often leverages loans and investment monies from mainstream businesses; the New Community Corporation of

There are now 65 community land trusts located in 18 states, for which ICE acts as a national information clearinghouse.

See Maggie Garb's article, "Saving the Inner Cities," in *In These Times,* Aug. 5-18, 1992, for a useful portrait of the New Community Corporation and other CDCs that are investing in business enterprises.

Seeking Jewish Monies
for Community Development Corporations

The National Association of Community Development Loan Funds (NACDLF, 924 Cherry Street, Philadelphia, PA 19107-2405, 215-923-4754), founded in 1985, now has some 40 member funds and approximately $80 million under management (up from only 18 funds managing $19 million in 1986). These community development loan funds (CDLFs) lend capital, borrowed at the lowest possible interest rates from progressive investors, to support development projects in communities that have been historically excluded from control over investment capital and over their own resources. Since the first community loan fund was established in 1969, over 3,100 loans totalling $88 million have been made nationwide, creating at least 14,000 affordable housing units and 3,700 jobs, according to NACDLF. Loans have ranged from $500 to $350,000. The overall default rate has amounted to only 1.3%.

In addition to loan-making by CDLFs, community development corporations serve as developers of housing and business projects, often in partnership with government, business and philanthropic institutions. Two key players in launching such partnerships are The Local Initiatives Support Corporation (733 3rd Ave., New York, NY 10017, 212-455-9800) and the Corporation for Enterprise Development (1725 K St. NW, Suite 1401, Washington, DC 20006, 202-293-7963).

Religious sources have provided 23% (nearly $18 million) of the investment capital in NACDLF's member funds. Catholic and Protestant churches, denominations and orders have provided virtually all this money, with almost no investment capital (or operating funds) coming from Jewish institutional sources. Yet nationwide, Jewish family foundations have assets amounting to billions of dollars. Many of these foundations were endowed from the fortunes of urban-based businesses, real estate developers, attorneys, etc. In addition, several billion dollars are now held in Jewish institutional endowments such as Federation community foundations. These monies represent an abundant source of potential investment capital for community development loan funds in cities across the country.

The Shefa Fund has launched a "*Tzedek* (Justice) Economic Development Campaign" that includes among its goals the raising of new community investment capita from Jewish sources. For information, see p. 191.

96

Newark, NJ, for example, has moved beyond housing by developing a shopping center that includes a supermarket co-owned by the CDC (two-thirds) and Pathmark Supermarkets (one-third). The shopping center employs 300 people. New Community's share of the profits are funneled into other community development efforts.

Other examples of these high-impact, affirmative investment opportunities include:

• The National Federation of Community Development Credit Unions (59 John Street, 8th floor, New York, NY 10038, 212-513-7191)), a coalition of federally insured credit unions that serve low-income communities. The typical community development credit union has assets of less than $1 million and serves between 500 and 1,000 members (with household incomes averaging less than $20,000).

• Womenventure (formerly the Women's Economic Development Corp., 2324 University Avenue West, St. Paul, MN 55114, 612-646-3808), which makes loans ranging from $200 to $10,000 to women business owners, acts as a guarantor for bank loans to women-owned businesses, and provides extensive technical assistance to help low-income women develop and run their own companies.

• The Industrial Cooperative Association (58 Day Street, Suite 203, Somerville, MA 02144, 617-629-2700), which has a revolving loan fund that has provided nearly $2 million in capital and equipment financing, long-term debt and member equity loans to worker-owned companies and other enterprises across the country. The loan fund offers investors the Community Jobs Certificate of Deposit, an FDIC-insured account with a maximum interest rate of 4% (offered through the South Shore Bank), and accepts unsecured loans of at least $5,000 for a minimum of three years, with interest of 3-5%.

• First Nations Development Institute (69 Kelley Road, Fal-

For a complete list of funds committed to women's economic and political empowerment, contact the National Network of Women's Funds, Suite 409-N, 1821 University Ave. West, St. Paul, MN 55104, 612-641-0742.

Women's Workplace Inequality

Excepting women-owned businesses, which are expanding in number but remain few and far between, the corporate world has excluded women from significant decision-making positions and discriminated on the basis of sex in matters of pay equity and advancement. In 60% of large corporations, fewer than 5% of senior managers are women, according to Catalyst, Inc., a corporate-sponsored research organization promoting women's leadership. (Catalyst, founded in 1962 and located at 250 Park Ave. South, New York, NY 10003-1459, 212-777-8900, states that its "mission will be achieved when gender is no longer a determinant in the career advancement of women or men, and when companies fully respond to employees' need to balance their work and family responsibilities.") The reality is reflected in Council on Economic Priorities' ratings for corporate conduct in the "women's advancement" category: CEP gives high approval ratings to companies that have merely two or more women on their boards, and of the 100 companies profiled (in *The Better World Investment Guide,* already cited), only 37 met that standard, while four (Gannett, Philip Morris, Campbell Soup and Houghton Mifflin) had the largest total of four women on their boards (out of 15, 22, 16 and 15 members, respectively)!

The status of women in business has nevertheless been improving over the past two decades — a progress forced by sex discrimination lawsuits, among other social pressures. The damage done to American women, however, and *to the American economy as a whole,* as the result of economic sex discrimination, has been vast. Clifford Adelman, a senior researcher at the U.S. Department of Education, writes of this in his June, 1991 report, "Women at Thirtysomething: Paradoxes of Attainment." Adelman points to the gap between American women's educational attainments and their employment attainments with these words of warning:

The United States will enter the next century with a remarkable edge over its global competitors. U.S. women, of all races, are the best educated and trained in the world and will constitute 64% of the new entrants to the work force over the next 10 years. . . . Labor market equity, sadly, is another issue.

"Americans are missing something," said Kerstin Keen of Volvo. . . "you're not utilizing (women) as well as you have prepared them. . . . in most of Europe, the problem is precisely the opposite."

In addition, Adelman notes, to income discrepancies between men and women, which are acute at all levels of educational attainment, there is a substantially higher percentage of women than men from the class of 1972 who have experienced "genuine unemployment," and a disproportionate number of women holding bachelor's degrees found in lower-paying and traditionally female jobs

(Continued on page after next)

Essential to the vision of community development corporations and related institutions is the recognition that (in Gar Alperovitz' words) "the community as a whole plays an historical and fundamental role in the creation of wealth and of new technologies, and in the overall development of education and skills." This recognition of community provides striking contrast to the "rugged individualism" and extreme privatization of wealth, property, and achievement that are articles of faith within American capitalism. Here again the vision of social responsibility movement dovetails nicely with Judaism, which views community as a core part of Jewish existence.

mouth, VA 22405, 703-371-5615), which assists three Native American reservation-based loan funds and has brought over $2 million in loan capital to aid in tribal land consolidation, housing development and other reservation needs.

• YACHAD, the Jewish Community Housing Development Corporation of Greater Washington, D.C. (2025 I St., NW, Suite 715, Washington, DC 20006, 202-466-8048), with a $35,000 capital pool from which to make loans and grants. That capital has directly helped to produce 62 units of affordable housing in the District of Columbia. YACHAD has also attracted more than 20 congregations to join its program, which includes participation in the Coalition for Non-Profit Housing Development and its technical assistance service network.

• The Community Ventures Program (CVP) of the Chicago Jewish Council on Urban Affairs (220 South State St., Chicago, IL 60604, 312-663-0960), which has attracted over $1.5 million in development grants and low-interest loans that have been used to leverage some $45 million for more than 1,200 housing units in five low-income minority neighborhoods. In conducting the CVP, the Jewish Council on Urban Affairs plays a comprehensive role as broker and technical assistant for both investors and community organizations.

• Manna, Inc. (POB 26049, Washington, DC 20001, 202-232-2844), a not-for-profit developer of low and moderate-income housing in Washington, D.C. Manna has a revolving loan fund (the Capstone Fund) that finances acquisitions and construction costs on some projects.

• The Corporation for Independent Living (30 Jordan Lane, Wethersfield, CT 06109, 203-563-6011), specializing in the development and management of community-based homes for people with special needs.

• The National Rural Development and Finance Corporation (1818 N Street NW, Suite 410, Washington, DC 20036,

Women in the Workplace *(Continued from page 98)*

(e.g., nursing, teaching, and office work). "In only 7 of 33 major occupations," Adelman reports, "did women achieve pay equity with men." Yet he also points to "a pattern of evidence suggesting that women are more enthusiastic and potentially productive workplace participants at the same time they are underrewarded."

>*This is where the rubber hits the road for the nation. Who do we want setting the tone and conditions of our economy? . . . (R)ecent work on women's psychological development may hold economic significance. Those who. . . integrate self-knowledge and external "procedural knowledge," who have a high tolerance for ambiguity, who are challenged by complexity, and who learn and work in ways that connect the human environment to the knowledge environment can affect the workplace in powerful ways. . . .*
>
>*Perceptive employers agree. . . "Women come into the workplace like immigrants," says Harold Tragash, vice president for human resources at Rorer Pharmaceuticals, "determined to succeed on the basis of what they know, not who they know." Tragash thus sees women more likely than men to "influence co-workers from a technical knowledge base.". . . Changing the knowledge content of work is critical to innovation in manufacturing, services and public administration. Innovations stemming from this supply side of knowledge that women in particular bring to the job can make the difference in our economy in the 21st century.*

The Jewish stake in this matter is high, even in narrow terms of self-interest, as Jewish women achieve high levels of education in disproportionate numbers and therefore are more numerous among the frustrated corps whose educations are betrayed by their careers. In addition, the Jewish historic experience of "outsider" entrepreneurial success (which benefitted and transformed the U.S. economy) gives potent support to Harold Tragash's predictions of transformative success for women "immigrants" in the workplace.

Tragash is hardly alone, in fact, in his perceptions of women's potential in the workplace. A recent survey conducted by Catalyst of chief executive officers and human resources officers in *Fortune 500* and *Service 500* corporations revealed that "Not one CEO responding to the survey cited a shortage of qualified males as a motivation for his company to increase its representation of women in management. . . . CEOs most frequently cited the increased presence of talented women and the need to use the most talented human resources." Yet these attitudes are not backed by action: "The most critical barrier. . . is management's aversion to taking risks with women in line responsibility" (i.e., production or sales, as opposed to personnel or staff-support) ". . . even though CEOs cited line

(Continued on page after next)

For more complete lists of community development loan funds, venture capital firms, banks and other agencies involved in affirmative investment activities, contact the Social Investment Forum, 430 First Ave., North, Suite 290, Minneapolis, MN 55401, 612-333-8338.

"(W)hatever the shifting realities of Judaism in a history spanning nearly four millennia," writes Emil Fackenheim in *What Is Judaism?* (1987, Summit Books, New York), p. 44, "'God, Torah and Israel,' in however changing constellations, are the lasting components. They are, as it were, the ever-presupposed past."

800-233-3518), an economic development loan fund that has since 1981 leveraged loans totalling $7 million to 80 projects in 20 states. NRD&FC focuses on locally owned small businesses, the key players in most rural economies. The organization pays a near-market annual return on secured, 7-10 year investments of $500,000 to $1 million.

"Genuine We-ness": The Centrality of Community in Jewish Thought

THESE COMMUNITY development corporations and related institutions are involved in what Gar Alperovitz calls (in the Spring, 1992 issue of *Israel Horizons*) "the slow, steady elaboration of [economic] alternative(s)" that "embrace many aspects of community life, and which provide the possibility of an evolving social environment and culture different from the dominant culture." Essential to this alternative vision is the recognition "that the community as a whole plays an historical and fundamental role in the creation of wealth and of new technologies, and in the overall development of education and skills" — a recognition that provides striking contrast to the "rugged individualism" and extreme privatization of wealth, property, and achievement that are articles of faith within American capitalism.

Here again the vision of the social responsibility movement dovetails well with the essential principles of Judaism, for of the three pillars of Judaism that were linked and consecrated at Mount Sinai — God, Torah and the people Israel — it is peoplehood, that multi-faceted sense of belonging to an internationally interdependent people, that is most universally em-

101

Women in the Workplace *(Continued from page 100)*

experience as . . . necessary. . . to move up to senior positions. . . "

Relative to the very weak corporate performance in the realm of women's empowerment, several corporations have superior records (according to *Business Week,* August 6, 1990), including:

• Avon Products, with women occupying 25% of its highest paid positions and 44% of its managerial spots. "Perhaps this is so," notes the Council on Economic Priorities, "because so many of its employees are not full-time."

• Dayton-Hudson (the originator, in 1956, of the enclosed shopping mall), with 20% of its corporate officers women, up from 7% in 1981.

• Gannett, the newspaper corporation, with four women directors and 27% of its top jobs held by women, and a policy of linking 10% of managers' bonus pay to managers' records on promoting women and minorities.

• U.S. West Communications, with women making up 21% of the top 1% of employees who earn $68,000 or more.

• Sears, Roebuck and Co., with over 40% female officials and managers and 62% female professionals. (The entire Sears workforce is 55% female). CEP notes, however, that Sears also has a history of sex discrimination litigation, including a suit that "noted that while 60% of applicants for sales jobs at Sears from 1973 to 1980 were women," according to the *Better World Investment Guide* (already cited), "only 27% of those hired were women." The suit belatedly came to trial during the Reagan years and was heard by a Reagan appointee who ruled in favor of Sears. In addition, in 1985 a former Sears employee won $1 million in what was at the time the largest sex-discrimination award for one person in California.

That the patriarchally oriented Bible repeatedly "affirms a male community" to which women have a "submerged and non-normative" relationship is the critical point of Plaskow's book, which bids Jews to expand the Jewish definition of community by exploring the tradition anew from a feminist perspective.

Buber's words are derived from *The Way of Response: Martin Buber* (already cited), p. 86. Used by permission.

braced by Jews of every persuasion, religious or secular. "Jewish memory is communal memory," affirms Judith Plaskow in *Standing Again at Sinai* (already cited), "and centers on community even as it forms and is formed by community. . . .The Jew stands before God" — and, we might add, before History — "not as an individual but as a member of a people."

That people, moreover, is meant to serve as "a light of nations. . . That My salvation may reach the ends of the earth" (*Isaiah* 49: 6). Jewish communitarian consciousness is thus a dress rehearsal ("come-unity") meant to demonstrate the redemptive potential of human unity. "To form unity out of the world is our never-ending work," wrote Martin Buber, calling this the task of "responsible personal existence." In a passage that implicitly rendered the Jewish covenant into a mandate for all humanity, he bemoaned the "typical man [sic] of today" and his "flight from responsible existence. . ."

> Since he is not willing to answer for the genuineness of his existence, he flees either into the general collective which takes from him his responsibility or into an attitude of a self who has to account to no one. . .
> In our age, in which the true meaning of every word is encompassed by delusion and falsehood, and the original intent of the human glance is stifled by tenacious mistrust, it is of decisive importance to find again the genuineness of speech and existence as We. *This is no longer a matter which concerns the small circles that have been so important in the essential history of man [sic]; this is a matter of leavening the human races in all places with genuine We-ness.* We will not persist in existence if we do not learn anew to persist in it as a genuine We. (Italics added.)

The "we-ness" that Judaism proposes, however, is not merely attitudinal or spiritual. It is, rather, a foundation-stone of the "Torah of Money." "People may be classified in

Tzedakah as Social Investment

American Jews often refer proudly to the Hebrew root of the word *tzedakah,* which means "justice" or "righteousness." Their intention is to indicate that *tzedakah* is not merely charity, the expression of an individual's kindness, but more accurately translates to mean "investment," an investment in social justice that profits the donor and the entire community.

Close review of Maimonides' eight levels of *tzedakah* (in his *Laws of Gifts to the Poor*) deepens this understanding of *tzedakah* as social investment. The seven lesser types of giving that he cites deal with various forms of relief and intervention; the highest, most laudable degree of *tzedakah* is not about relief but investment: about taking a position *with,* not over, against or apart from the intended beneficiary. In the greatest acts of *tzedakah* the entire community gains, beginning with the investor and the investee who each have a stake in the ultimately "profitable" outcome of the *tzedakah* deed. For a discussion of the implications of this concept for our actual deeds of giving, see pages 125-129.

three ways," affirms the Talmud (*Avot deRabbi Natan*): "May blessing come upon the one who provides relief. Better is one who makes loans. But the one who provides a share for the poor *and holds a stake in their success* transcends them both" (italics added). Twelve years of Reaganomics, of the rich getting richer (see our top sidebar note, p. 65) and the poor getting poorer and more desperate, did not disprove this Talmudic insight into economic "we-ness;" indeed, the low educational achievement, high crime, and social disintegration that swelled at the bottom as rapidly as the wealth at the top during those twelve years are now threatening the revitalization of the entire U.S. economy and the sense of well-being throughout American society. The reality of interdependence thus stands revealed, as so often, through mass malaise and suffering, rather than through the shared rewards of social investment.

Why Have Jewish Institutions Not Participated in the Social Responsibility Movement?

IN LIGHT of the communitarian vision at the core of the Jewish tradition, and given the direct link that most Jews perceive between self-interest — our safety and well-being — and general economic and social justice, the lack of Jewish organizational involvement in such social investment projects as community development loan funds is surprising. The fact is, however, that of the approximately $18 million in investment capital raised from religious institutions by the National Association of Community Development Loan Funds (see p. 96), *less than one tenth of one percent* has come from Jewish

Jewish Credit Networks

An historical precedent for the latter-day community development loan fund was the Jewish loan society, which provided a vital source of credit for Jews during the 1920s, '30s and '40s. According to Henry L. Feingold's *A Time for Searching,* Vol. 4 of Johns Hopkins University's five-volume *The Jewish People in America* (1992), before 1925 "only one bank in all of New England and one in the Middle Atlantic extended credit to Jews, and 85% of the Jewish population was in any case too poor in collateral to qualify for bank loans. . . . By 1927" this credit gap was filled by some 509 Jewish loan societies and 2,367 mutual benefit societies. "Credit unions could spring up anywhere, from synagogues to *landsmanshaftn*" (fraternal organizations of Jews from the same European towns), notes Feingold (p. 142), and were "important in helping Jews establish themselves in business and improve their skills."

institutions. Similarly, of the $3 million raised from religious institutions as capital for the Community Capital Bank in Brooklyn (in a city with the largest Jewish population of any city in the world), only five Jewishly identified investments were forthcoming — this following a prodigious effort to recruit Jewish community investment from New York and elsewhere, involving meetings, letters, personal briefings and solicitations. Of the bank's $13.6 million in deposits, Jewish institutional deposits amount to only $160,000.

Several small Jewish organizations do keep their monies with socially responsible mutual funds, but no major Jewish group that we know of is rigorously applying any screens but South Africa divestiture to its investments. None to our knowledge even has a well-defined and consistently implemented guideline about withholding investments from corporations that participate in the Arab boycott of Israel — though several report that their finance committees and/or boards are developing such policies.

Why has the organized Jewish community shied away from

Agitating loudly for reform in a corporate world that has only recently been cleared of charges of boardroom anti-Semitism would not be a natural course of action for most Jewish organizations. "(A) visceral distrust remains," writes Charles Silberman in *A Certain People*, "even among Jews whose achievements have catapulted them into the ranks of the American elite." This wariness about sparking anti-Semitic backlash also makes Jews guarded about publicly and forthrightly using money as a tool of political influence.

105

Barry A. Kosmin and Paul
Ritterband, eds., *Contemporary
Jewish Philanthropy in America,*
1991, Rowman and Littlefield
Publishers, Savage, MD.

the socially responsible movement? We tentatively offer the following, all-too-brief explanations:

1) Despite the scope of American Jewish wealth detailed in this book, few Jewish organizations have historically had substantial monies available at the national level for investment. Most operate on cash-flow budgets, and the building of endowment funds is a relatively new development in Jewish organizational life. Nevertheless, during the past two decades, substantial capital has been accumulated in the form of Federation and private family foundation endowments. According to Barry A. Kosmin, 7% of the more than 5,000 now-existing U.S. foundations with over $1 million in assets are identifiably Jewish. This philanthropic capital could be a powerful tool to advance Jewish goals of social justice and coalition-building if it were used affirmatively for community development and corporate reform.

2) The Jewish community is highly decentralized. Within each Jewish community, and from one locale to the next, diverse interests compete for the allegiance and resources of individual donors. Few opportunities exist to explore and develop policy, including philanthropic and investment policy, on issues other than those of direct and exclusive Jewish communal concern. Those "direct and exclusive" Jewish concerns, moreover, are daunting. They include protection of Jews worldwide from anti-Semitism and physical threat; economic and political support for Israel; Jewish immigration and social welfare needs in Israel and the U.S.; promotion of Jewish education and culture; and maintenance of Jewish institutional networks — all this on the shoulders of fewer than six million Jews, a large plurality of whom are not even organizationally affiliated with the community.

3) For all its vaunted clout, the Jewish community has a cautious and wary mindset. Agitating loudly for reform in a

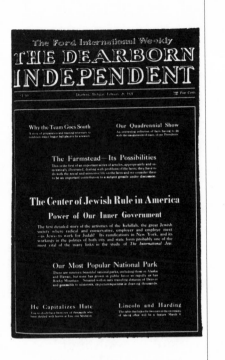

The *Dearborn Independent*, newspaper published and circulated by industrialist Henry Ford, conducted a vicious anti-Semitic campaign from 1920 until 1928, when protests and a boycott campaign led by the American Jewish Committee forced an apology from Ford to Louis Marshall, head of the AJC, on June 30, 1927. Among the publications circulated by Ford's newspaper was *The Protocols of the Elders of Zion*, a forgery created in Tsarist Russia that nevertheless persists today as a widely-read tract in the Middle East, the U.S. and elsewhere. Graphic from the American Jewish Committee's 75th anniversary commemoration brochure, 1981.

corporate world that only recently has been cleared of charges of boardroom anti-Semitism would not be a natural course of action for most Jewish organizations. "(A) visceral distrust remains," writes Charles Silberman in *A Certain People* (already cited), "even among Jews whose achievements have catapulted them into the ranks of the American elite." Silberman refers, as illustration, to a 1981 study that found 75% of Jews believing that the majority of non-Jews think "Jews have too much power in the business world" — a view actually expressed by one in three non-Jews. Similarly, 55% of Jews thought that non-Jews viewed them as trying to "push in where they are not wanted," a view held by only 16% of non-Jews. This extreme sensitivity to anti-Semitism makes Jews particularly guarded about using money, publicly and forthrightly, as a tool of political influence — though the tool is available and is used.

4) Israel's historical alliance with the U.S. military-industrial complex has muted Jewish opposition to the bloated U.S. military industry, whereas the social responsibility movement has deep roots in the opposition to that industry that arose during the Vietnam War. Though many Jews and some Jewish organizations (notably the Reform movement) actively opposed that war, there remains a Jewish fear that disinvestment in military-related corporations may threaten Israel's security. Thus a certain distance has been established between the Jewish community and the social responsibility community.

5) Alienation has also grown up between Jews and African-Americans, fed by harsh black anti-Semitism, which has driven Jews away from many of the community-empowerment activities with which the social responsibility movement is directly involved. Feeding this anger between blacks and Jews are such factors as: Jewish organizational opposition to affirmative action quotas; black intolerance for Jewish claims to oppression "status;" Jesse Jackson's "Hymietown" utterance

While black anti-Semitism has been a distressing reality in recent years, the extreme sensitivity of Jews to it is viewed by some as an effort, in part, to "duck responsibility." "Why is it," asks Albert Vorspan, the recently retired social action leader of Reform Judaism, "that we Jews, who were not panicked by George Wallace, [neo-Nazi leader] George Lincoln Rockwell. . . or the Ku Klux Klan, can be panicked by anti-Semitism coming from blacks? And why is it that. . . we talk about *black* anti-Semitism almost exclusively?. . . For many Jews, this is an excuse to . . . justify disengagement and withdrawal from the social scene." (Excerpted from *The Jesse Jackson Phenomenon* by Adolph L. Reed, 1986, Yale University Press). Yet black anti-Semitism *is* on the rise (fueled by black-Jewish economic and political competition, as well as by Christian and Muslim influences within African-American life), and it resonates deeply within a Jewish community that has historically been persecuted "from below" in the name of populism.

Black-Jewish cooperation nevertheless remains a potent political force. See the Religious Action Center of Reform Judaism's recent publication, *Common Road to Justice* (co-published with the NAACP), for over 200 examples of cooperation between synagogues and black churches (2027 Mass. Ave., NW, Washington, D.C. 20036).

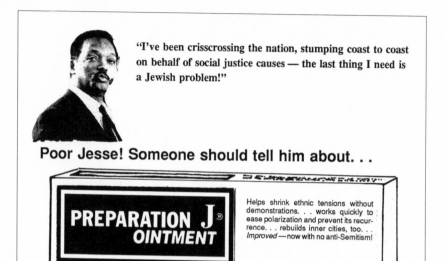

"I've been crisscrossing the nation, stumping coast to coast on behalf of social justice causes — the last thing I need is a Jewish problem!"

Poor Jesse! Someone should tell him about. . .

PREPARATION J® OINTMENT

Helps shrink ethnic tensions without demonstrations. . . works quickly to ease polarization and prevent its recurrence. . . rebuilds inner cities, too. . . *Improved*—now with no anti-Semitism!

Approved by the National Conference of Christians and Jews for temporary relief of minor ethnic flareups.

(and black anger at the Jewish refusal to forgive Jackson, despite his diligent efforts at reconciliation); Jewish indulgence of neoconservative stereotypes of a hopelessly mired black "underclass" with problems that are impervious to social programs or community development monies; black indulgence of anti-Semitic "leaders" in the name of unity; etc. Jewish migration from the cities to the suburbs during the past three decades has also lessened the Jewish sense of "stake" in urban black economic and political advancement, as has the very successful passage of many Jews into the ranks of the economically and culturally privileged.

DESPITE THESE OBSTACLES, there is still substantial agreement among American Jews about the need to overcome

racism and ameliorate the poverty that torments poor families and communities and undermines the well-being of the United States as a whole. Jewish philanthropy still serves as a progressive, humanizing force in our society, and individual Jews remain unceasingly involved in projects seeking economic and social justice. Over the past decade, organizations such as The Shalom Center and Shomrei Adamah, periodicals such as *Tikkun* magazine, and public foundations such as The New Israel Fund, the American Jewish World Service, and the Jewish Fund for Justice (all three to be discussed in more detail in our next chapter) have created new channels of Jewishly identified social activism. The Shefa Fund has been working with Jewish donors to cultivate an expanding role for Jewish philanthropy as a force for social change. Established liberal Jewish institutions such as the Religious Action Center of Reform Judaism, the American Jewish Congress, the National Council of Jewish Women, and others remain important centers of legislative lobbying, education and leadership training. Building an alliance between the social responsibility movement and the organized Jewish community does not, therefore, necessitate "converting" American Jews to a liberal political agenda. Jewish individuals and institutions, rather, need simply to be emboldened to "put their money where their values are."

To help achieve this, Jewish social responsibility activists need to cultivate a positive enough identification with Judaism and the Jewish community to speak as "insiders" and help engender the cross-fertilization of Judaism and socially responsible politics. (For that matter, many more activists must learn to deal comfortably with issues of money, investment, banking, and so on, rather than indulging an anti-corporate, "eat the rich" politics that damns the "marketplace" instead of engaging with it as a forum for social change.)

Jewish "insiders," for their part, need to overcome their embarrassment and distress about money (see our discussion about money and anti-Semitism on pages 159-164) and start applying their high ideals to their financial dealings — and their finances to the furtherance of their ideals.

Our critical time cries out for this, for every stakeholder in the twin enterprises of American and Jewish renewal to participate: as thinkers who can bring the most fruitful aspects of Judaism to bear upon the many issues of economic decline, social disempowerment and environmental degradation facing our country; as leaders who can move beyond the inoffensive but uninspiring statements typical of mainstream Jewish organizations to address social and environmental problems with the urgency they require; as energetic activists equipped with the Jewish commitment and vocabulary needed to bring the Jewish community once again into coalition with other concerned constituencies; and as funders ready to put the "Torah of Money" to work.

Questions to Consider and Discuss

How do you feel about the relative economic success of American Jews? How confident do you feel about that success continuing in the future?

What hesitations do you feel about applying a "Torah of Money" to your most significant financial activities? Which of your values would you simply not compromise in the name of profit? What measures might you, your social networks, your Jewish community or your society undertake to help you commit to a "covenanted" economic life?

How might you apply the "stakeholder" concept in evaluating your own sense of worth?

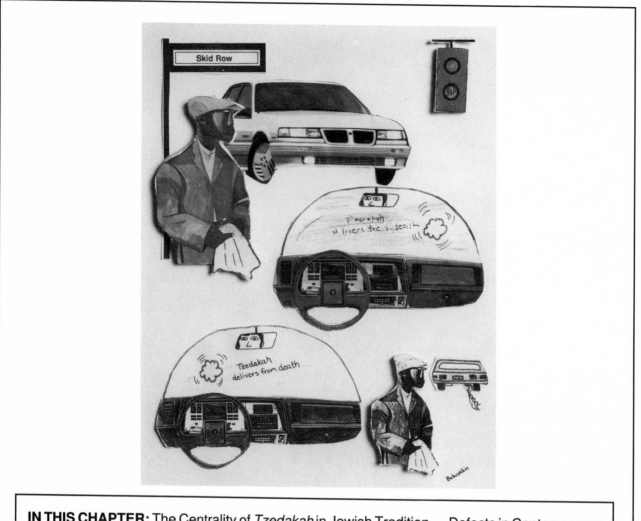

IN THIS CHAPTER: The Centrality of *Tzedakah* in Jewish Tradition. . . Defects in Contemporary Jewish Philanthropy. . . A Pathway of Righteousness through the Minefield of Power Relations . . . Defining Standards for Individual *Tzedakah*. . . Giving as a Group: The *Tzedakah* Collective . . . Organizational *Tzedakah:* Seeking a Unity of Means and Ends. . . Community Makes All the Difference. . . Creating a Will: *Tzedakah* at the End of Life.

Rabbi Yehudah used to say:
Ten strong things were created in the world—
A mountain is strong, but iron cuts through it.
Iron is strong, but fire causes it to bubble.
Fire is strong, but water extinguishes it.
Water is strong, but clouds contain it.
Clouds are strong, but the wind *(ruach)* scatters them.
Breath *(ruach)* is strong, but the body holds it in.
The body is strong, but fear breaks it.
Fear is strong, but wine dissipates its effects.
Wine is strong, but sleep overcomes its power.
Death is harder than all of them.
But *tzedakah* saves from death, as it is written,
"And *tzedakah* saves from death" (*Proverbs* 10: 2)
Bava Batra 10a

Derived from Danny Siegel's *Where Heaven and Earth Touch,* already cited.

Tzedakah: Giving and Receiving Without Shame

"**P**OVERTY," TEACHES THE TALMUD (*Nedarim* 7b), "is like death." Certainly it is immobilizing, in the restrictions it imposes on the health, time, and choices available to poor people. Poverty devours the body and spirit; it brings tears of stress and sorrow to loving relationships; it devours the present and obliterates the future. It buries the poor in a coffin of invisibility, removing them from our sight and consciousness — except, perhaps, when the wraiths of poverty make their criminal appearance on our very doorstep.

Poverty is like death.

It breeds despair in the hearts of its victims, as well as in the hearts of the rest of us who, seemingly lacking the means to "do something" about homelessness, hunger, AIDS, crime and other poverty-related problems, resort instead to shunning the poor, counting our blessings and building moats around our good fortune. The Talmudic tractate *Avodah Zarah* likens the poor person to the leper, the blind person and the childless person: "four kinds of people who are regarded as if dead." Outmoded views of disability and childlessness aside, the Talmud is speaking of isolation, of being shunned and dehumanized.

Poverty is like death.

YET *TZEDAKAH,* says the Jewish tradition, "saves from death." This salvation is gained not only by recipients of *tzedakah,* but by solicitors and donors as well. "It was taught in the name of Rabbi Yehoshua: The poor person does more for the householder than the householder does for the poor person" (*Leviticus Rabbah* 34: 8). The poor person permits the "householder" to gain life by participating in partnership with God in the reconstruction of the world; to gain life by participating in the community; to gain life by releasing his or her heart from the clench of selfishness and self-involvement — as in the story of the wealthy Rabbi Tarfon, who was known not to give sufficiently to the poor:

> Rabbi Akiba once found him and said: "My teacher, would you like me to purchase a city or two for you?" Rabbi Tarfon replied yes, and immediately gave Rabbi Akiba 4,000 gold

Adapted from Danny Siegel, *Where Heaven and Earth Touch* (already cited), pp. 63-64.

dinars. Rabbi Akiba took the money and distributed it to the poor.

A while later, Rabbi Tarfon found him and said: "Where are the cities you purchased for me?"

Akiba took him by the hand and brought him to the house of Torah-study. He took a copy of the Book of Psalms and placed it in front of them. They read and read, until they came to the verse, "If a person gives freely to the poor, his *tzedakah* deeds will stand him in good stead forever" (Psalm 112: 9). Rabbi Akiba said to him: "This is the city I bought for you!"

Rabbi Tarfon rose and kissed him on the head and said: "My teacher, my hero! My teacher in wisdom! My hero in the essences of life!" He then gave him more money to give away.

The Centrality of Tzedakah in Jewish Tradition

THIS IS THE SAME Rabbi Tarfon who is quoted in *Pirkei Avot* as declaring: "It is not incumbent upon you to complete the work, but neither are you free to desist from it." Nowhere does this sense of must-do obligation more obtain, in the judgment of the Jewish tradition, than in the realm of *tzedakah*. In the days when Jewish communities were ruled by rabbinic authority and *halakhic* principles, the rendering of funds and other resources to sustain the poor was akin to taxation: "Every city which has Jews," wrote Maimonides, "is obligated to appoint officials who are well known and trustworthy, who will go among the people during the weekdays and collect from each one what is appropriate and what has been assessed of him. . . . We have never seen or heard of a Jewish community which does not have such a fund for charity." The parameters of the community's *tzedakah* obligation included the providing

Maimonides, *Mishneh Torah, Hilkhot Mat'not Aniyim,* chapter 9, *Halakhot* 1-3 as quoted in Meir Tamari's *"With All Your Possessions,"* already cited. Maimonides (Rabbi Moses Ben Maimon, or Rambam, 1135-1204) was the greatest legal and philosophical thinker of
(Continued next page)

115

(Continued from previous page) medieval Judaism. He was author of the *Mishneh Torah,* the first great post-Talmudic *halakhic* compilation, and *The Guide to the Perplexed,* an effort to harmonize Jewish religious thought and the scientific and philosophical knowledge of his day. Through these works, Maimonides served as Judaism's great systematizer and coordinator.

Reuven Kimelman, *Tzedakah and Us,* published by CLAL, the National Jewish Center for Learning and Leadership, 99 Park Ave., New York, NY 10016, 212-867-8888. Kimelman is associate professor of Talmud and Midrash at Brandeis University.

"He who says, 'Mine is yours and yours is mine' is an ignoramus," says *Pirkei Avot.*

of food, clothing, shelter, household utensils and the means to be married; of care for the elderly, for orphans and for widows; of assistance to travelers (a tradition that played no small role in the development of Jewish mercantilism); of a religious education for all Jewish males; and of ransom for captives (*pidyon sh'vuyim,* "the characteristic *mitzvah* of this century," writes Rabbi Reuven Kimelman, "which has witnessed the Holocaust" as well as the rescue of Jews from Syria, Iran, Argentina, Ethiopia, Yemen and the Soviet Union). In addition to participating in this communal *tzedakah,* individual Jews were expected to respond with alms and assistance to needy people as the occasion arose. "I gave at the office" was no excuse for ducking an opportunity to give *tzedakah.*

Poverty was viewed as a communal problem requiring a public solution lest it cause society-wide degradation. Wealth was seen as a God-given form of custodianship that imposes responsibilities. Communal *tzedakah* "taxation" was levied upon every individual and was enforceable by sanctions. The tithe was customarily set at 10% of annual income. The goal of this system was not economic equality but balance, relief from dire poverty, and the development of a binding Jewish communal consciousness.

This Judaism would have judged as intolerable the contemporary situation in the United States, in which some 32 million Americans, including at least 10% of American Jews, live in nearly inescapable poverty while the upper crust of the population controls a vast amount of wealth. While the Jewish tradition by no means advocates the forced equalization of wealth, it does look askance upon power relations that stigmatize, trap or discriminate against the poor:

> The inhabitants of Sodom and Gomorrah and the three other cities of the plain were sinful and godless. . . . The cause of their cruelty was their exceeding great wealth. Their soil

The Sodom and Gomorrah material is from Louis Ginzberg's *The Legends of the Jews,* Vol. 1 (1989, Jewish Publication Society, Philadelphia, 15th printing), pp. 245-249.

This version of the Talmudic story of Nahum Gimso is quoted from William B. Silverman's *The Sages Speak* (already cited), pp. 79-80.

was gold, and in their miserliness and their greed for more and more gold, they wanted to prevent strangers from enjoying aught of their riches. . . . Their laws were calculated to do injury to the poor. The richer a man, the more he was favored before the law. . . .

Likewise would the fact that America has wearied of its homeless citizens rather than addressing their misery — the fact that many municipalities expend as much energy to remove the poor from public places as to house them — be intolerable in the traditional Jewish view:

> Nahum Gimso was blind in both eyes, both his hands were crippled, his feet were both cut off, and the whole of his body was covered with leprosy. He lay stretched out in a tottering house, and his legs were thrust into pots of water, so that the ants might not be able to get to him.

Amazingly enough, this grotesque description is not of an impoverished wretch, but of a sage of some means who one day failed to perform the *mitzvah* of *tzedakah.*

> One day his pupils. . . said, "If you are so just a man, why do all these evil things overtake you?" "My children," he answered, "I have brought them all on myself; for one day, as I was going to the house of my father-in-law, leading with me three donkeys — one laden with provisions, one with wine, and one with rare fruits — I chanced upon a poor man who stopped me and said: 'Master, give me something to eat.' 'Wait,' I said, 'until I have unladen my donkey.' But I had not ended unlading the beast before the man died. Then I went and threw myself upon him, saying: 'May my eyes, which had no pity on your eyes, lose their sight; may my hands, which had no pity on your hands, be crippled; may my feet, which had no pity on your feet, be cut off.' And my spirit was not at rest until I had said, 'May my whole body be covered with leprosy.'"
>
> His pupils replied: "Woe to us, that we see you in this condition." But he said: "Woe to me if you were not to see me thus."

117

The Reagan Administration's notorious ruling about federally subsidized school lunches, which sought to save money by declaring ketchup to be a vegetable, would have been roundly condemned by the sages:

> "Do not rob from the poor because he [sic] is poor" (*Proverbs* 22: 22). Our rabbis have taught: What is this verse really about? If the person is poor, what could he possibly be robbing him of? Rather, the verse must be speaking of the Gifts to the Poor that the Torah requires the person to give — the gleanings, forgotten sheaves of grain (*shikh'chah*), and the corners of the field (*pe'ah*), and the poor person's tithe (*ma'aser ani*). The Holy One, blessed be, issued a warning that a person should not rob him [sic] of these gifts which are rightfully his because he is poor. His poverty is as much as he can handle. Is it not enough that the wealthy person is comfortable, and the poor person is in pain — and yet he would steal from him, what the Holy One, blessed be, gave?
> —*Numbers Rabbah* 5: 2

Our welfare system's guiding philosophy of "deterrence," which promotes indignities so as not to "encourage" people to seek assistance; which has us spending millions of dollars on miserable and dangerous welfare hotels rather than providing the means for permanent, secure housing with some form of equity for the poor; which refuses to prevent homelessness with single or short-term payments to hard-pressed families, but rather waits for disaster to overtake them; which refuses medical, nursing home and other benefits until one's personal resources are utterly depleted — such mean and means-testing policies would be anathema to the traditional teachings about *tzedakah:*

> "And if your brother becomes poor and his means fail him with you, then you shall strengthen him, be he a stranger or a settler, he shall live with you" (*Leviticus* 25: 35). Rashi's commentary on this verse (paraphrasing the midrash in

Our welfare system's philosophy of "deterrence," which promotes indignities so as not to "encourage" people to seek assistance; which has us spending millions on miserable welfare hotels rather than providing the means for permanent, secure housing with some form of equity for the poor; which refuses to prevent homelessness with single or short-term payments to hard-pressed families, but rather waits for disaster to overtake them; which refuses medical, nursing home and other benefits until one's personal resources are utterly depleted — such mean and means-testing policies would be anathema to the traditional teachings about *tzedakah*.

From "Charity," by David Hartman and Tzvi Marx, in *Contemporary Jewish Religious Thought* (already cited), p. 48. Meir Tamari notes that *halakhic* definitions of poverty allowed for "temporary distress, or for difficulties caused by serious problems of liquidity. For instance, a person who had assets over the poverty line but would have suffered great loss if they were sold at a bad time in the market" was entitled to a portion of *tzedakah* (up to half the value of the assets) until a more propitious season arrived.

Torat Kohanim, Behar, 5:1) focuses on the clause, "you shall strengthen him": "Do not let him slip down until he falls completely, for then it will be difficult to raise him; rather strengthen him as he begins to fall.

Yet neither would the Jewish tradition absolve the poor of responsibility for overcoming poverty — or of participating in the giving, as well as the receiving, of *tzedakah:*

The Homeless Look

Doubleweight plastic footwear, $300
Matching shoulder bag, $175
Two-legged trousers, $225
Collarless half-stitched shirt, $90

Available at
the income
gap

119

Even a poor person who is kept alive by *tzedakah* funds must give *tzedakah* from what he receives.
Shulchan Aruch, Yoreh De'ah 251: 12

The greatest of our scholars were hewers of wood, porters, drawers of water for gardens, and workers in iron and coal. They did not ask anything of the public and when offered did not accept. A person who deserves to be helped but who refrains from public assistance even at the expense of dying in poverty and difficulty will merit that he will be able to support others. In this respect it is written, "Blessed be the man who trusted in God" (*Jeremiah* 17: 8).

Maimonides, *Mishneh Torah, Hilkhot Mat'not Aniyim,* chapter 10, *Halakhot* 18, 19, derived from Meir Tamari, as cited, pp. 247-248.

Defects in Contemporary Jewish Philanthropy

CERTAIN TRAITS of modern *tzedakah* within organized Jewish life deserve criticism as well, from the perspective of the Jewish tradition. The much-touted ability of the American Jewish community to raise money certainly has deep roots in traditional *tzedakah* discipline, and the preeminent focus on Israel as recipient for these funds is consistent with traditional prioritizations — yet the grandiosity and pomposity that often accompanies modern Jewish philanthropy has more kinship with the traditions of American glamour than with Judaism. For example, the general popularity of building funds and other "naming opportunities" in Jewish philanthropic life evince a tendency to use *tzedakah* to erect personal monuments — a practice decried by the Jerusalem Talmud (*Shekalim* 5:4):

Rabbi Abun erected two grand gates for the House of Study, and he showed them to Rabbi Mina. Rabbi Mina

Israel as the #1 Priority
Reuven Kimelman notes that "obtaining jobs for immigrants fleeing persecution" — in which Israel is an unparalleled achiever — "combines the priority of *pidyon sh'vuyim* (redemption of captives) with the eighth degree of charity" (as per Maimonides, whose discussion of *tzedakah* we will exam-
(Continued next page)

quoted *Hosea* 8: 14, "Israel builds temples, and forgets its Creator," and went on to say, "Had you spent this money more piously, would there not have been more people studying Torah?"

The "glamourization" of *tzedakah* is, in fact, a dangerous strategy for Jewish philanthropies to pursue, according to Paul Ritterband's essay in *Contemporary Jewish Philanthropy in America.* "When it comes to large gifts, the Jewish community has to compete with the powerful public relations apparatus of the concert hall, the opera house, the university, the research library. . . . What can the Jewish community offer by way of distinctions and honors comparable to those offered by the venerable cultural institutions?. . . The ubiquitous annual dinners mounted by Jewish causes with their distinguished 'honorees' are poor competition for the elegant occasions sponsored by the major secular cultural institutions." Thus the appeal to Jewish religious and historical values, rather than the appeal to what Ritterband calls "the socially useful sublimation of egocentricity," deserves greater emphasis in Jewish fundraising circles, for it is Jewish values that can give Jewish philanthropy its unique appeal.

ALSO PROBLEMATIC in modern Jewish philanthropy has been the occasional acceptance as *tzedakah* of "tainted" money, money from unrighteous sources, and even the bestowing of honors upon the donors, by decision-makers in the Jewish community. The significant contributions to Jewish communal institutions by Ivan Boesky and Michael Milken immediately come to mind (though several Jewish organizations were reported to have spurned charitable offerings from both men following their Wall Street indictments). On a more local scale,

---

(Continued from previous page) ine shortly), "making for the supreme act of *tzedakah.*"

Support for the poor in the Land of Israel is traditionally viewed as taking higher priority than support for Jews in foreign lands. Israel, moreover, certainly has its share of poverty: more, reports the *Forward* of January 10, 1992, "than in any other country in the Western world, except for America," according to a report issued in Jerusalem by the National Insurance Institute. "Were it not for social welfare payments, no less than 34% of Israeli families would be situated below the poverty line. In the past decade, the number of poor has quadrupled." These statistics *exclude* the 400,000 new immigrants who came to Israel during the past two years. Israel's governmental "safety net," however, is under attack by advocates of privatization who are critical of the "socialist" trappings of the Israeli economy.

The Jerusalem Talmud (actually compiled in Tiberias) is the "lesser" of the two Talmuds created through discussion, correspondence and compilation between 200 and 600 C.E. The longer and generally more authoritative Talmud is the Babylonian.

Paul Ritterband, "The Determinants of Jewish Charitable Giving in the Last Part of the 20th Century," in *Contemporary Jewish Philanthropy* (already cited), p. 70. Used by permission. Ritterband points to two trends in Jewish philanthropy that are helping preserve its uniqueness: the creation of philanthropies that "have a particularist base of givers (Jewish) with recipients chosen on universalist grounds: the poor" (e.g., the Jewish Fund for Justice, Mazon, and the American Jewish World Service, all to be discussed in this chapter), and philanthropy in which "their contributors are likely to be their clientele" (e.g., adult education programs).

it has been rare for a Jewish institution to deny *koved* (honor, dignity) to donors because of their unscrupulous business dealings, or to use the occasions of their gifts to raise consciousness about the "Torah of Money."

Yet the sins of exploiting the poor and the weak, or of cheating workers or customers (defined by the *halakha* as theft, irrespective of whether the victims be Jewish or gentile, children or adults), are not neutralized by the redepositing with the community of some portion of the purloined wealth. Were such gifts acknowledged to be a form of penance — were the donors dragged before a *bet din* (rabbinic court) rather than a chicken dinner! — and were the monies then translated into programs of recompense for the actual victims, justice would perhaps be achieved by Judaic standards. Accepting and honoring gifts without regard for their source, however, may be akin to buying stolen goods, or to laundering stolen money. "Not the mouse, but the hole, is the thief," says Rabbi Joseph ben Hiyya in the Talmud *(Gittin* 45a). "A benediction over stolen things is a blasphemy," says Rabbi Eliezer ben Jacob (*Baba Kamma* 94a).

MOST AT VARIANCE with the traditional pathway of *tzedakah* in contemporary Jewish philanthropy is simply the non-involvement of a large plurality of American Jews in Jewishly-aware giving. In addition to sociological factors of assimilation, non-affiliation, intermarriage, etc., which contribute to this lack of involvement but are beyond the scope of our discussion, there are aspects of the prevailing culture of Jewish philanthropy that constrict participation. For example, of the $750 million or so now being annually raised by the Jewish Federations/United Jewish Appeal (the major American vehicle of Jewish communal philanthropy), nearly 60% comes

American Jewish philanthropy has been overly privatized, with power devolving upon wealthy donors and fundraising technocrats. The problem is not the inclusion or even the centrality of people of wealth ("All the prophets were wealthy," said Rabbi Yochanan), but rather the exclusion from the *tzedakah* process of the non-wealthy and of other groups at the margins of Jewish life. Modern Jewish philanthropy is operating largely as a trickle-down system of *tzedakah,* which fails to enlarge the sense of participation and obligation of the whole community. One outcome of this failure is the increasing involvement of Jewish women and others with non-Jewish philanthropic activities that address their concerns and do not carry the baggage of contemporary Jewish philanthropy.

Contemporary Jewish Philanthropy in America (already cited), p. 64.

from donors of $10,000 or more, who comprise little more than 1% of the donors. "Less than half of the lowest income Jewish households report having been asked to give to the Federated Jewish campaign," writes Paul Ritterband, "while in contrast four-fifths or more of the higher income households report having been solicited. . ." Partly as a result, only 30% of the lowest-income Jewish households give, compared with 81% of the top-income group. "By contrast, in. . . non-Jewish [charitable] campaigns, 51% of the lowest income group [among Jews] report having given a gift as compared with 79% of the highest income group." Ritterband concludes that "a significant difference between the Federated Jewish campaign and non-Jewish philanthropies is based upon [the former's] stra-

123

tegic decision to be 'efficient,' to go after the potential big givers, and to largely ignore or at least invest relatively little in a broad-based campaign that would include housholds of modest means."

American Jewish philanthropy has thus been privatized, with power devolving upon wealthy donors and fundraising technocrats. The problem is not the inclusion or even the centrality of people of wealth ("All the prophets were wealthy," said Rabbi Yochanan [*Nedarim* 38a]), but rather the exclusion from the *tzedakah* process of the non-wealthy and of other groups at the margins of Jewish life — an exclusion that lessens the relevance of Federation activities to a great number of American Jewish households.

Despite the advances of women in gaining leadership within Federation organizational life, for example, "data indicate that even in the volunteer sector, women's role is confined mostly to the traditional [enabling rather than decision-making] realm," according to Barry A. Kosmin and Madeleine Tress. This exclusion is, in part, the result of a system in which "the term 'leader' is used. . . as a synonym for large donor" — a formula not easily embraced by women, who "on average. . . take their roles more seriously, asking more questions, and 'hanging around' the office much more. . . . (T)hey see their roles as active participants in the Federation decision-making process."

It is only fair here to emphasize that the status of women within the Federation world is changing; Kosmin and Tress, for example, point to the significant growth in recent years of Federation-sponsored daycare as a sign of increasing women's influence (though this should hardly be considered only a "women's" issue). It is also worth affirming that, oligarchically structured or not, the Jewish Federations exemplify a tradition of American Jewish *tzedakah,* self-help, self-reliance and generosity that should be an example and inspiration to any

---

Gary Ferdman, formerly a fund-raiser with the American Jewish Committee, observes that an unofficial membership requirement of Jewish country clubs across the land seems to be a sizable donation to the Jewish Federations. This practice, says Ferdman, has caught on in non-Jewish country clubs, which require that donations be made to the United Way.

Barry A. Kosmin and Madeleine Tress, "Tradition and Transition," in *Contemporary Jewish Philanthropy in America* (already cited), pp. 75-92. Kosmin and Tress note that 20% of Federation presidents are now women, a three-fold increase since 1975, and 25% of Federation treasurers are now women, an eight-fold increase since 1975.

Gay and lesbian Jews have made no such progress within the Federations. "Despite the existence of gay and lesbian congregations in most major cities," write Kosmin and Tress, "as well as Jewish gay and lesbian societies on most major

(Continued next page)

124

(Continued from previous page)
college campuses," Federation "Women's Division lesbians are still 'in the closet,' that is, they simply do not exist."

The rise of Jewish family foundations in recent years has intensified the trend toward philanthropic elitism. Today, a relatively small number of trustees from approximately 5,000 family foundations have disproportionate power to influence Jewish communal policy through their allocations, without even the accountability of local federation representatives.

"Contemporary Jewish life is united behind four core concerns," writes Reuben Kimelman in *Tzedakah and Us* (already cited). "1. Support of Israel. 2. Support of Judaism. 3. Support of World Jewry. 4. Support of Jewish needs. The changing nature of Jewish life requires a leadership growing Jewishly to represent adequately these concerns. Leadership succeeds by interpreting the agenda of the community, and by getting Jews to act on it. The more leaders serve as role-models, the greater the potential for success. To further their commitment to Jewish growth, leadership programs should afford their members the opportunity, e.g., at annual meetings, of

(Continued next page)

immigrant or downpressed minority in the U.S. Nevertheless, the Federations also exemplify how modern Jewish philanthropy is operating largely as a trickle-down system of *tzedakah*, which fails to enlarge the sense of participation and obligation of the whole community. One outcome of this failure is the increasing involvement of Jewish women and others with non-Jewish philanthropic and volunteer activities that address their concerns and do not carry the baggage of contemporary Jewish philanthropy. Another symptom is the somewhat slow response of institutions like the Jewish Federations to the changing circumstances and needs of American Jewish life.

Of course, oligarchical leadership is not new to Jewish life, nor are democratic principles intrinsic to traditional Judaism. One might even cynically argue that the system of obligatory *tzedakah* was designed to sustain the oligarchical alliance between the rabbis and the wealthy by establishing the means of support for the former and the claim to piety for the latter, all the while defusing the rage of the poor. The ideal of Jewish *tzedakah*, however, is the empowerment of both the donor and the recipient as partners rendering justice in this world. The bond sought between them is one of kinship, identification and truly mutual obligation. Thus there is no word for "beggar" in the Hebrew Bible: the only term used is "your brother."

To achieve this bond within the context of the unequal power relations that unequal wealth fosters, the tradition imposed upon donors strictures of obligation and, wherever possible, measures to ensure anonymity for both donors and recipients ("Charity must be given in secret," says the Talmud, in a variety of teachings). In our modern, sprawling, uncovenanted economic system, however — ruled by the "Almighty Dollar" rather than by spiritual values — these strictures of traditional *tzedakah*, even if enforced, might not serve adequately to offset the power gap between rich and poor and fulfill the spiritual

(Continued from previous page) taking voluntary self-grading appraisals to mark their growth from year to year." Kimelman's booklet deals hardly at all, however, with the issue of democratization of leadership with which the Jewish community needs to grapple, that is, the development of leadership, beyond the traditional model of double oligarchy (Jewish scholars allied with Jewish wealth), that will succeed not only by "interpreting the agenda of the community, and by getting Jews to act on it," but by empowering more and more Jews to help establish that agenda and thus have a dynamic relationship to Jewish life.

purpose of the *tzedakah* partnership. *Democratization of tzedakah, including a certain degree of "self-determination" for recipients, are necessary "additives" if we want to preserve the humanizing mission of the mitzvah in a contemporary context.*

Ideally, for example, recipients should participate in decision-making about the allocation of *tzedakah* monies (as when a foundation is governed by a community board), to help assure the appropriateness and effectiveness of funding efforts within their particular communities. Funding agencies should establish and use channels of communication and mutual accountability among themselves, their contributors and their recipients, to help prevent the kind of damaging scandal that beset the United Way early in 1992, the fallout of which is cynicism and apathy on the part of the contributing public. While such anti-oligarchic measures have not been proposed within Jewish lore, their justification can, in fact, be found within Maimonides' famous proclamation (in his *Laws of Gifts to the Poor*) that "the highest degree [of *tzedakah*]. . . is where one strengthens the hand of an Israelite who faces poverty" by providing a loan, gift, business partnership or job. Maimonides urges us to help the recipient acquire the tools of independence rather than maintain a relationship of dependency and benevolence, shame and honor, uncertainty and control, between recipient and donor.

A Pathway of Righteousness through the Minefield of Power Relations

THE VERY ROOT of the Hebrew word, *tzedakah*, from *tzedek* — meaning "righteousness" or "justice" — gives indication of the centrality of this *mitzvah* in the Jewish ethical structure *as a means of establishing a covenantal community despite inevitable differences in ability, power, wealth and privilege among people.* "To feel the obligation of *tzedakah* is to. . . experience the emotion of communal identity," write David Hartman and Tzvi Marx.

Hartman and Marx, *Contemporary Jewish Religious Thought* (already cited), pp. 47-48. Used by permission.

According to the Talmud and Maimonides, the disposition to be responsive to human beings in need is a *conditio sine qua non* of membership in the covenantal community of Israel. . . . Through personal moral training in the very specific issues involved in *tzedakah*. . . the foundation is laid for the reformation of society in its juridicial and political dimensions. Efforts to solve the dilemmas and frustrations in the microcosm of charity are expected to bear fruit in the macrocosm of righteousness. . . . Thus Maimonides can claim, on the authority of Rabbi Assi. . . that "we are duty bound to observe the *mitzvah* of *tzedakah* more than all other positive commandments.'. . . It is because of the overreaching effect that *tzedakah* works upon the character of man [sic] that such a claim can be made."

Maimonides' description of the "eight degrees of *tzedakah*, one higher than the other," in his *Laws of Gifts to the Poor*, is perhaps the best known discourse on *tzedakah* that takes into account the human dynamics that are displayed, tested and advanced in the course of fulfilling this *mitzvah*. Highest-ranking on Rambam's scale, as we have noted, is *tzedakah* that "strengthens the hands" of the poor person unto self-sufficiency. Next highest is the "double-blind" method of giving, in which "neither the giver nor the receiver knows of the other, for in this case the duty of giving *tzedakah* for its own sake has been carried out. . . . "

A lesser degree is where the givers know to whom they have given but the poor do not know to whom they are indebted.

New Israel Fund: Participatory Funding for a Participatory Democracy

While it has by no means "broken the mold" on donor/technocrat-controlled philanthropy, the New Israel Fund, which has grown from revenues of $80,000 from 80 donors in 1980 to $6.4 million from over 10,000 supporters a decade later, does try to pursue an approach to philanthropy that reflects two key perceptions about the nature of *tzedakah:* first, that it is a reciprocal relationship of involvement and accountability, and second, that successful *tzedakah* should create more *tzedakah.*

"From our inception," writes NIF in its 1991 handbook, *Strengthening Democracy,* "we have insisted that the Fund be managed. . . as a genuine partnership. Our North Americans bring a set of particular insights and experiences to our work, but it is not their intention to impose their understandings on the Israelis. Instead — and this is reflected in the composition of our Board of Directors (which includes North Americans and Israelis) — we work as a joint enterprise, with responsibility fully shared by both parties.

"The application process is extensive, usually lasting about six months and involving multiple contacts between the applicant and NIF. . . . Each grantee is ensured not only funds, but also priority for assistance from SHATIL [the Support Group for Voluntary Organizations, an NIF technical assistance arm], and regular contacts with NIF staff.

"The same commitment to accountability. . . informs [NIF's] relationship to its donors. NIF enables donors to choose to give general support, core funding for a particular program area. . . or, if desired, donor-advised funding to a specific organization. . . . NIF is committed to providing full and accurate reports to its donors about the use of their contributions. . . . In short, our grantees are not fleshless file folders, nor are our donors disembodied check-signers. We seek intimate and ongoing contact with both. . ." For the last few years, NIF has also been raising money in Israel from Israeli Jews and Arabs, as well as from North American Jews.

The commitment to *tzedakah* that creates more *tzedakah* is reflected in the roster of NIF grantees, which includes scores of Israeli grassroots groups that are themselves performing *tzedakah* deeds of the highest order, giving time, skills and heart to projects of empowerment in any of five fields: civil and human rights, Jewish-Arab coexistence, the status of Israeli women, bridging economic and social gaps, and the encouragement of pluralism and tolerance.

Writing in *Contemporary Jewish Philanthropy in America* (already cited), pp. 205-216, the late Ira Silverman notes that while new Jewish philanthropies such as the New Israel Fund represent in both their external and internal politics "a reaction against the thrust and style of the mainstream, established Jewish charities" (though neither "their founders [n]or a majority of their current supporters voiced any of these specific criticisms"), the gap between the "mainstream" and the "alternative" has shrunk. "These new philanthropies are direct descendants of the late 1960s counterculture that challenged the. . . General Assemblies of the Council of Jewish Federations, calling for more emphasis on education, [and] led to significant community change. . . . Jewish education *has* been accorded a much higher priority [by Federations]. . .young leadership groups have flourished, academics and Jewish organizational professionals have been given more visible platforms, religious rituals have been incorporated into previously "secular" meeting agendas, and informal groups such as *havurot* have been encouraged." At the same time, NIF's growth has forced a "depth of [NIF donor] involvement [that] is necessarily less uniformly intense. . . ." (NIF, 1101 15 St. NW, Suite 304, Washington, DC 20005, 202-223-3333.)

Maimonides

At this writing, *Hesed* is not an actively functioning organization.

. . . Less than this is where the poor know to whom they are indebted but the givers do not know to whom they gave. . . . Less than this is when the givers give money directly to the poor without having to be asked for it. . . . Less than this is when they give after the poor have asked. . . . Less than this is when they give the poor less than they should but with a cheerful countenance. . . . Less than this is when the givers are glum.

Contemporary Jews striving to think with similar complexity and sensitivity about the impact of both organizational and individual *tzedakah* upon power relations might dissent from Maimonides' particular prioritization. Rabbi Marc Gopin, for instance, the co-founder of *Hesed* International, a Jewish project to relieve world hunger, believes that the "double-blind" method of *tzedakah*, which served as a social "equalizer" between rich and poor in the intimate Jewish communities of eras past, today too easily boils down to "checkbook *tzedakah*," in which the donor can give without encountering the humanity of the recipients. The *mitzvah* is thus incomplete, its transformative influence upon the donor truncated. Gopin therefore advocates hands-on *tzedakah* wherever possible, so that the invisibility of the poor, and the protective shields that the non-poor place over their hearts, can be shattered.

Defining Standards for Individual Tzedakah

EXPLORATION OF *tzedakah* values is perhaps most commonly prompted on an individual basis by encounters with panhandlers or by direct mail solicitations. Arthur Kurzweil, senior editor at Jason Aronson Publishers and director of the

129

Anonymity vs. Community Decision-Making

A further difficulty arises from the acceptance of Maimonides' elevation of anonymity as a value in *tzedakah:* It gives inordinate support to the principle of privacy, both regarding the ownership of resources and the establishing of public policy and priorities. In fact, donors often give anonymously out of a feeling of fear or shame. Anonymity enables them to avoid accountability and preserve private control over wealth and policy-making — necessary assurances where the "Torah of Money" is not practiced. If, however, we assume 1) that "the earth is the Lord's," 2) that we are all stewards of the world's resources, including money, 3) that everyone will give to their maximum capacity, and 4) that we all have a role to play in deciding how communal needs should be met, the need to contribute anonymously is significantly reduced. Our goal might well be to make our communities open to honoring everyone who contributes time, money, goods, services and energy, so that the dignity of every contributor is guaranteed as a consequence of the act of giving, not as a result of the amount donated. When giving takes place in this way, *tzedakah* becomes a continuing process, not a climactic gift of charity.

Jewish Book Club, wrote eloquently in 1981 about how his study of Judaic teachings on *tzedakah* helped him figure out how to handle the perturbing number of beggars on the streets of New York City. His quest — predating the rapid rise of homelessness in New York, which has made his dilemma terribly commonplace — provides an exciting example of an individual Jew's exploration of the tradition as a source of guidance and inspiration.

John D. Rockefeller, Sr. was known during his final years to distribute dimes to poor people on the street, along with financial advice.

"Don't spend it all in one place!"

Arthur Kurzweil, "Brother Can You Spare a Dime? The Treatment of Beggars According to Jewish Tradition," *Moment* magazine, November, 1981, Vol. 56, No. 10; reprinted as a pamphlet by the *Tikkun Olam* Program of United Synagogue Youth (Conservative). Kurzweil relies on English-language renderings of traditional Jewish sources for his scholarship; he suffers from a language-learning disability that has prevented him from mastering Hebrew or Aramaic. His article displays an unabashed desire to convince Jews with comparably deficient literacy nevertheless to undertake Jewish studies: "I can't read Hebrew," he writes, "I can't read much Aramaic, I never went to yeshiva, but I study Talmud every chance I get."

Should UJA Influence Israeli Policy?

The United Jewish Appeal has played an indispensable role in galvanizing American Jewish support for Israel and for *(Continued next page)*

Kurzweil noted that his behavior with "beggars" was thoroughly inconsistent, dependent upon his own mood and the demeanor of the person asking for help. He developed 15 questions about responding to the poor, many of which reflect concerns that are common to us all:

"What if they are fakes or frauds?" (Or, expanding on Kurzweil's notion, what if there are no obvious obstacles to their being employed? What if their begging seems motivated more by temperament than need?) "Rabbi Eleazar said: We must be grateful to the deceivers, for were it not for them, we might sin every day" (*Ketubot* 68a). "In other words," writes Kurzweil, "the fakers keep us in the habit of giving."

But what if they are obviously alcoholics or drug addicts? "When a poor man asks you for aid," Kurzweil quotes Rabbi Shmelke of Nicholsburg, "do not use his faults as an excuse for not helping him. . . . " Yet wouldn't such souls be better served, Kurzweil continues, were he to control the donation by buying them food (or a cup of coffee or a subway token) rather than give money? "Don't decide what is best for the beggar," he concludes, citing a story from the Jerusalem Talmud (*Pe'ah* VIII: 9, 21b) about Nehemiah of Sihin, who gives a beggar money instead of what he asks for — the chicken that Nehemiah is carrying. "The man went and bought some meat and ate it and died. Then Nehemiah said, 'Come and bemoan the man whom Nehemiah has killed." Kurzweil's dilemma is reversed here; the person asking Nehemiah for *tzedakah* wants the food rather than the money. The essential point of the tale, however, is that we should not dictate how our *tzedakah* shall be used in contradiction to the recipient's wishes. The Jewish tradition is deeply concerned about preserving the self-esteem and dignity of the *tzedakah* recipient, something that cannot be easily sustained in the face of a stranger's judgmental attitude. (Means-testing — evaluating the legitimacy of a person's claim

(Continued from previous page) endangered Jewish communities around the world. Critics have emerged, however, who are angered by the fact that UJA does not hold the main recipient of its *tzedakah* — Israel's Jewish Agency — accountable for how it spends UJA monies. Donors to the UJA can only object, for example, to expenditures on behalf of the right-wing religious parties by "voting with their feet," withholding *tzedakah* from the UJA. This, in turn, means they are withholding support from local Jewish communal projects, since Federation and UJA fundraising drives are combined.

Writing in *Tikkun* (Vol. 2, No. 4, p. 27), Prof. Eliezer Jaffe of the Hebrew University argues that "since the creation of the State of Israel there has never been a serious general discussion regarding new roles for Diaspora charity in Israel, new options for distributing these funds, accountability for them, and relative needs in both Israel and the Diaspora. Layers of jobs, institutions, and premises that were valid more than 50 years ago at the [Jewish] Agency still thrive today, due to inertia, self-interest, and lack of will and imagination. . ."

Rabbi Bruce E. Kahn, a former activist within the UJA, responded to what he describes as "gross fraud, waste and abuse among the *tzedakah* giants" by founding Amcha for Tzedakah (10801 Lockwood

(Continued next page)

132

of entitlement to community funds — is permitted by the Jewish tradition, but such probing is kept within bounds and would not pertain to the one-to-one encounters with which Kurzweil is concerned.)

He continues: "Shouldn't official or private organizations be supporting these people?" (Former Mayor of New York Ed Koch, towards the end of his tenure in office, argued this by urging citizens *not* to give alms to the homeless, as it would lead them to shun the city's social service agencies.) Kurzweil quotes a rabbinic responsa: Although "the poor are everywhere supported from the communal chest, if they wish in addition to beg from door to door they may do so, and each should give according to his understanding and desire."

"The message [of Judaism] seems clear," Kurzweil concludes after framing and answering his 15 questions. "(D)on't ignore the beggar, don't treat him [sic] with anything but kindness, don't find excuses as to why not to give. Rather give to everyone, regardless of who he or she is, but just give a little." He continues:

> For me, the texts represent an ideal, and one which I confess I do not live up to regularly. Yet this research was not just an academic exercise for me. . . . the exploration of the text moved me — literally — to avoid passing up the opportunity of observing the *mitzvah* of *tzedakah* each day in the neighborhood. I often fail at seizing each opportunity offered to me, but I struggle to come closer to the ideal — and this is, in my opinion, the purpose of the teachings.

									Total
IDEALISTS	0	0	0	0	0	0	0	0	1
REALISTS	3	1	0	2	2	1	0	5	1	0

(Continued from previous page)
Drive, Silver Spring, MD 20901, 800-488-5115), whose Israeli recipients have included In-terns for Peace, Israel National Council for the Child, Rabbinic Human Rights Watch, and many others. "We were blessed," writes Kahn, "with a bequest that pays for all administrative costs so that every cent we receive in regular contributions gets sent to accredited recipients. Every contributor may designate for what purposes or to what organization one's gift is to go. About half our givers take advantage of this opportunity." Kahn is particularly critical of the UJA's "inability. . . to adequately address what I see as a. . . vast increase in Jews hating Jews and Jews hating non-Jews. . . The purveyors of what I think of as destructive Judaism are too often supported through our *tzedakah* process or ignored by it. . . . the network of leadership is. . . closely tied to the political and religious figures most responsible for the problem. . ."

On the other hand, Ira Silverman notes (in *Contemporary Jewish Philanthropy,* already cited, p. 213) that "the extremely broad base of donors who voluntarily continue to give what they do [to UJA] provides a tolerably good reflection of their preferences," which is a manifestation of the "democratic" way of defining the Jewish "community interest. . . . Plainly," Silverman adds, "these big

(Continued next page)

ARTHUR KURZWEIL'S teacher in matters of text and *tzedakah* has been Danny Siegel, a prolific poet and writer who has for a dozen years been pursuing the *mitzvah* of *tzedakah* not merely as a thoughtful individual but as a creative activist. Siegel is founder and chair of the Ziv Tzedakah Fund, Inc., founded in 1980. Through the Fund ("Ziv," which means "aura" or, in Siegel's words, "a reflection of God's immediate presence"), Siegel has raised and distributed, principally in Israel and the U.S., nearly one million *tzedakah* dollars from several thousand donors. In 1990-'91 Ziv supported four special projects and "*mitzvah* heroes" (who collectively received nearly $74,000), including Hadassah Levi, an Israeli woman who has, for a dozen years, been raising some 40 Down's Syndrome children, all of whom were abandoned as infants in hospitals. Ziv also supports Jewish refugee projects (almost $17,500 in '90-'91); projects for individuals with special needs (nearly $35,000); projects for elderly people ($8,000); three American doctors serving valiantly in poor neighborhoods ($250 each); individuals and families in dire need (over $8,000); and a miscellany of good works, both Jewish and non-sectarian ($5,330). Ziv does not accept grant applications or earmarked funds; most of the recipients have simply crossed paths with Danny Siegel in his role as a thoughtful and earnest distributor of *tzedakah*.

"There are no secrets to good *tzedakah* work," he writes in Book Two of his *tzedakah* handbook, *Gym Shoes and Irises:*

The good will of good people — and people who want to be good people — can bring about grand and glorious changes in the world, and these changes can be far more dazzling and extensive than we would normally think possible. In that sense — the extent of what *tzedakah* can achieve — there is something mysterious and magical, but the actual doing of the *mitzvah* is the simplest-of-simple things: we just do it, and marvelous things happen. . . .

133

(Continued from previous page)
organizations do suffer from the
endemic institutional reluctance to modify, diversify, de-
centralize, and innovate. . . .
Whether a degree of new
philanthropy competition and
duplication with the mainstream
groups is really the best outcome, however, is another matter."

Ziv Tzedakah Fund, Inc., Bena
Siegel, treasurer, 263 Con-
gressional Lane, #708, Rock-
ville, MD 20852, 301-468-0060.

Danny Siegel, *Gym Shoes and
Irises: Personalized Tzedakah,*
Book Two, 1988, the Town
House Press (552 Weathers-
field Rd., Fearrington Post,
Pittsboro, NC 2731, 800-525-
5470), pp. 14, 20. Used by
permission. Book One, published in 1982, includes Arthur
Kurzweil's essay on encountering beggars; Book Two establishes the fact that an individual
can "make a difference" with
the following, on its opening
page: "In 23 years of collecting
money in a blue-and-white tin
can in front of Canter's Deli on
Fairfax Avenue [Los Angeles],
Sylvia Orzoff, 76, has netted
more than $2 million for the
Jewish National Fund."

Siegel considers the *mitzvah* of *tzedakah* to be a therapeutic experience for the doer:

I would invite researchers to conduct an appropriate study to confirm the following assumptions: the more that people are involved in *mitzvah* work, the less depression, despair, sense of defeat and failure, alcoholism, drug abuse, anorexia, bulimia and suicide. It would be important to ascertain just how much less, and to develop suggestions for integrating *mitzvah* work into therapy programs of all kinds. . . .

Tzedakah is really just another form of *Teshuvah* — changing, turning, repentance. [It] serves as a reminder of who we are in essence, human beings with awesome power to act, move, make changes in the world. *Tzedakah* allows us to re-establish our balance and our sense of meaning and value.

Giving as a Group: The Tzedakah Collective

WHILE DANNY SIEGEL'S *tzedakah* is highly personalized, he affirms that "*tzedakah* acts gain more significance when performed in intimate contact with friends, and the richness of the friendship grows through the *mitzvah* acts done together. . . . The idea of *chevra* — your associates, your friends . . . is paramount to intensified *tzedakah* work. . . . The rabbis praise again and again the idea of *chevra*-for-the-sake-of-*tzedakah*. . . . Rabbi Akiba says, 'Whoever attaches himself [sic] to mitzvah doers — even though he did not do as much as they did — even so, he still receives a similar reward' (*Avot deRabbi Natan* A: 30)."

In this spirit, during the mid-1970s, participants in the burgeoning *havurah* movement organized *tzedakah* collectives in Boston, Los Angeles, New York, Philadelphia, Washington, D.C. and other cities. Together, members of these collectives confronted questions about levels of giving (considering income and need disparities within each group), about how to decide cooperatively on disbursement of funds, about whether to give to non-Jewish recipients, about how to incorporate Jewish teachings into decision-making processes, about how to preserve individual privacy while building group intimacy, about how to build trust about money matters that are, indeed, so very privatized in our lives.

Despite the graying of participants and factors of geography and career-crunch, a score of these *tzedakah* collectives have maintained themselves to the present day. One survivor is the Havurat Ha-emek Tzedakah Collective in Northampton, Massachusetts, founded in 1979. The collective is a project of Havurat Ha-Emek, which meets twice a month for *davenning* (prayer) on *shabbat*. Martha Ackelsberg, serving as clerk for the collective, writes to The Shefa Fund: "For the first few years, most, but not all, members of the *havurah* joined. Since then, most of those people have left the *havurah*, and not that many of the new people have joined the collective. We now have about 10 members. . ."

> We agreed to meet twice a year (around Rosh Hashanah and Pesach) to collect and disburse funds. . . . We would each contribute 1-2% of our annual income, spread over those two sessions. . . . establish a bank account in the name of the collective, and agree jointly on how to disburse the funds. Initially, contributions were anonymous. We each wrote down on a piece of paper how much money we'd be putting in, and put them into a bag. Someone totalled up the amounts and announced to the group how much money we had to disburse. Each person was then able to name one "cause" to which he/she wanted to contribute funds. We kept going until everyone had all the groups they wanted in

Cost-Sharing: "Sanctifying the Money Part of Life"

Writing in the Spring/Summer, 1992 issue of *Bridges* (Vol. 3, No. 1), Felice Yeskel, co-director of Diversity Works, Inc., a group of social change educators, tells of the efforts of her Jewish feminist spiritual community, *Achyot Or* (Sisters of Light), to pursue a "Torah of Money" through a process of cost-sharing at their annual gathering. This process involves discussion of one's class background and current financial situation, with the goal of developing equitable assessments that reflect both one's ability to pay and one's psychological needs. The ground rules, Yeskel writes, include: "All disclosures, emotional sharing and financial pledges are *voluntary. . .* we. . . keep each other's stories *confidential. . .* we. . . speak from *our own experience and not. . . for others; any question or feeling is o.k.*"

After preliminary discussions aimed at building trust, the *Achyot Or* women formed "class identity groups" of four, within which they discussed their backgrounds, feelings and dealings with money, reviewed the overall costs of the gathering (about $250 per head) and made initial pledges towards covering those costs. Next, the women arranged themselves into groups by amount pledged, ranging from $0-$100 to over $450. Discussion continued within these groups, and then the "class identity" groups reconvened and adjusted initial pledges. (Throughout the process, each woman had a "buddy" for intensive sharing and support.)

Participants finally committed their pledges to paper and placed them in "open" or "confidential" files (pledgor's choice). The open file was reviewed by other women, discussed and sometimes adjusted; then the pledges were tallied. "We raised more than we needed," Yeskel writes, "so women met with their identity groups and discussed whether to revise their pledges." In the end "we still had more than we needed so we decided to give the surplus to *tzedakah.*"

"We ended. . . by discussing. . . how the cost-sharing process related to Judaism, feminism and spirituality. Cost sharing. . . allows us to bring integrity and connection to dealing with money issues. . . it is a practice that helps us to sanctify the money part of life." (*Bridges* is $15/year, $10/ low income; P.O. Box 18437, Seattle, WA 98118.)

The 1-2% of income given as *tzedakah* by the Havurat Ha-emek Collective is within the average household range for the U.S. population but below the giving rate for the 300,000 or so Jewish households that comprise the major donor pool for the Jewish Federations and other mainstream Jewish philanthropies (Barry A. Kosmin's estimate, from *Contemporary Jewish Philanthropy in America,* already cited). Generally, however, within the *havurah* subculture "there appears to be a strong and serious commitment to *tzedakah*," writes Bethamie Horowitz in the same book (pp. 187-204). Most *havurah* households also labor under the financial burden of synagogue affiliation ("an affiliated young family with an income of $50,000," writes Kosmin, "in 1983 would be unable to make a significant philanthropic contribution after paying for the costs of religious and communal services, tuition, and fees in addition to maintaining a normal suburban standard of living").

the "running." Then, people would speak briefly to the merits of each, and others could ask questions. At this point, we allowed a "veto" — if anyone felt he/she could not remain a member of the group if funds were donated to a particular organization or cause, the group would not donate funds there. In practice, the veto was used only on issues of abortion, which caused some considerable conflict in the group.

We would vote our preferences and come up with a rank-ordered list of groups to which we wanted to give money. Then we would decide how much money to give to each. After the meeting, we had a certain amount of time to deposit our pledged amounts into the collective account, and then the clerk would draw checks and send them to the groups.

Over the years, we developed a number of variations on this scheme. For a while, we sorted potential recipients into categories, and voted amounts to categories. At another point, we switched to agreeing as a group on the recipients, but allowing each member to divide his/her contribution among the groups as he/she wished. This system was less anonymous, but we kept with it for about two years, since people seemed to feel better about it.

Non-monetary *tzedakah* has also been undertaken by the Havurat Ha-emek Collective, including sponsorship of a Cambodian refugee family of four who settled in Northampton. "We brought them here, settled them, guided them through the vagaries of social security, Medicaid, food stamps, child care, abortions, job hunting, etc.," Ackelsberg writes. "It was an enormous commitment for us, over the course of a number of years. And it was very satisfying. The family is now fully on its own, very much a part of a Cambodian community in the area."

Recently the collective reduced the individual contribution to one-half of 1% of annual income, "to decrease people's sense of frustration if their pet project was rejected by setting a level that would not cut too severely into the total amount of *tzedakah* a person might be giving for the year. We agreed, at the

Secular *tzedakah:* Another pattern of *tzedakah* is displayed by the 275-member Sholem Aleichem Club in Philadelphia, a secular, *Yiddishkeit*-oriented organization that gives approximately $2,000 a year, or 20% of the Club's revenues: 50% to Jewish-related causes (e.g., the National Yiddish Book Center, the New Israel Fund, the Philadelphia Jewish Children's Folkshule), and 50% to groups working on behalf of peace, African-American empowerment and civil liberties. Allocation decisions are made by the 25-30-member Executive Board. "We have several criteria for our contributions," writes Jack Rosenfeld, an officer of the Club. "It must have some affinity to the work of the Club, it should lead to some interaction with the recipient group or organization, and it should be an indication of our involvement with the Jewish community or the larger community." Over the years, he adds, "we have evolved a concentration on local agencies rather than the large national organizations."

US/Israel Women to Women, 1501 Broadway, Suite 1613, New York, NY 10036, 212-768-0477.

same time, to limit ourselves to three or four recipients, so that the amount of money to go to any one source would not be too small." Ackelsberg concludes: "In addition to our initial and intermediary discussions about *tzedakah* in general, we have also had more recent discussions, involving the entire Havurah, about *tzedakah* and its place in Jewish life, and about *tzedakah* and spirituality. These conversations, initiated by members of the collective, have been very well received."

The Shefa Fund is currently engaged in helping to inspire and organize *tzedakah* collectives across the United States. Our aim is to increase the number of Jews involved with *tzedakah* as a public Jewish activity, which in turn would increase the Jewish community's vitality and increase the amount of money available for progressive projects both in and outside the Jewish community.

Organizational Tzedakah: Seeking A Unity of Means and Ends

CERTAIN *TZEDAKAH* collectives have evolved into full-blown organizations that bring the transformative benefits of *tzedakah* to thousands of people, donors and beneficiaries alike. US/Israel Women to Women, for example, began in 1979 when Virginia Snitow, now an octogenarian who is former chair of the National Conference of Jewish Women's Organizations, learned of a battered women's shelter in Israel that was about to close for lack of $200 for rent. Snitow called a few friends together, and the needed funds were sent. The group then began to send money to nascent shelters in Haifa, Herzliya and Jerusalem (three of only four such shelters in

Israel, though it is estimated that a minimum of 100,000 Israeli women, of all social classes, suffer from domestic violence). "These shelters," writes Snitow to The Shefa Fund, "were the achievement of a handful of dedicated Israeli women, but not yet of a women's movement." As such a feminist movement began to evolve in Israel, however — focusing on issues of divorce law and legal discrimination, reproductive choice, violence and rape, political empowerment and peace issues — US/Israel Women to Women became a steady, expanding, source of support. "There is no other organization in the U.S. devoted exclusively to the overall progress of the women of Israel," Snitow notes. "That is what we continue to do." After a decade of *tzedakah* work, the organization opened a small office in 1990 and launched a men's auxiliary.

For up-to-date information about the women's movement in Israel, the Israel Women's Network can be reached at P.O. Box 3171, 91031, Jerusalem (Tel. 02435976).

LIKE U.S./ISRAEL Women to Women, the Jewish Fund for Justice (JFJ) began with a small group of donors who organized themselves in common cause: to provide a Jewish source of *tzedakah* for, and involvement with, grassroots American groups working with low-income populations to promote community self-sufficiency. In seven years, JFJ has grown to include over 7,000 donors. Jews-in-need and Jewish activists have been among the recipients of JFJ funds — Project Ezra in New York (aiding impoverished elderly Jews — $500), the Jewish Council on Urban Affairs in Chicago ($15,500), the Dallas Jewish Coalition ($5,000) and the San Francisco Jewish Sanctuary Coalition ($6,960) have all been funded — yet the Jewish Fund for Justice is unabashedly unconcerned about the Jewishness of grant recipients.

JFJ's Jewish consciousness is reflected, rather, in its commitment to prophetic and historical Jewish social values,

Jewish Fund for Justice, 920 Broadway, Suite 605, New York, NY 10010, 212-677-7080.

Other New Jewish Philanthropies:
Mazon, the American Jewish World Service, The Abraham Fund

***Mazon*: A Jewish Response to Hunger** (2940 Westwood Blvd., Suite 7, Los Angeles, CA 90064, 213-470-7769; 47 W. 34 St., New York, NY 10001, 212-268-0212): Founded in 1985 as the brainchild of Leonard Fein, then-editor of *Moment* magazine, *Mazon* (Hebrew for "food") asks Jews to contribute a tax-deductible amount of 3% of the costs of private celebrations such as bar and bat mitzvahs, weddings, and birthdays (it is estimated that American Jews annually spend half a billion dollars on such celebrations). Mazon also conducts annual Passover and Yom Kippur appeals among its 700 "partner synagogues" nationwide. From these and other efforts, *Mazon* is able to distribute over $1 million a year to hunger-relief projects such as Jewish Family Services of San Diego, the New York Coalition for the Homeless, Prairie Fire Rural Action in Iowa, the Jewish Foundation for Christian [Holocaust] Rescuers, the Jewish Community Center of Greater Minneapolis, Navajo Nation Agricultural Project (at Ben-Gurion University of the Negev in Israel), and the North American Conference on Ethiopian Jewry, among many others. *Mazon*'s *tzedakah* is notable for its inclusion of the broadest possible sector of the American Jewish community as donors.

The American Jewish World Service (15 West 26 St., 9th floor, New York, NY 10010, 212-683-1161): AJWS was founded in 1985 by a group of rabbis, scholars, business and communal leaders organized by Lawrence Phillips, the chief executive officer of the Phillips-Van Heusen Company. The organization's goal is to provide Jewish economic development aid as well as disaster relief to Third World countries, "in collaboration with local, non-governmental organizations active at the grassroots level, who design and implement projects with our assistance" (quoted from the 1990 Annual Report). The programs focus on two basic themes: sustainable agricultural production and the promotion of "micro-entrepreneurial activities" ("alternative income-generating opportunities outside of the agricultural sector") through "modest loans, particularly to women, to initiate a small enterprise or expand an existing one." Over $1.5 million is being distributed annually. Recipients have included projects in Armenia, Ethiopia, Haiti, Honduras, India, Iran, Israel, Jordan (to assist refugees from the Iraqi invasion of Kuwait), Mexico, Nicaragua, Phillipines, Tanzania, and Zimbabwe. AJWS's *tzedakah* is notable for its emphasis on self-reliance and community development.

The Abraham Fund (477 Madison Ave., 8th floor, New York, NY 10022, 212-303-9421): Begun in 1989 by Alan B. Slifka, a businessman and philanthropist in New York, and Eugene Weiner of Haifa University in Israel, the Fund's objective is to support projects "that foster cooperation and coexistence between Israel's Jews and Arabs." It does this by maintaining the *Abraham Fund Directory,* a thick compendium of joint Jewish-Arab programs (within Israel's pre-1967 borders), and by accepting contributions earmarked for one of four funding options: the Abraham General Fund, the Designated Area option (focusing on one of the 22 areas constituting a chapter in the directory), the Adopt-a-Project option, and the Abraham Educational Project option.

Jewish Fund for Justice, *Seeking Justice for All. . .,* 1989. JFJ also sponsors a "Youth Endowment Fund," which enables *b'nai mitzvah*-age children to mark their passage to adulthood with "a personal commitment to thoughtful philanthropy. . . . Annually honorees are asked to choose which of several groups researched by the Fund they wish to suport with the earnings from their endowments. Groups supported by the Youth Endowment Fund promote leadership development, skills training, and other opportunities for disadvantaged young people."

"Charity begins at home, justice begins next door," writes Reuven Kimelman, as previously cited. "Judaism is the training ground for creating the consciousness of a mega-family which will ultimately incorporate all of humanity."

its dedication to "safeguarding. . . the conditions of democratic pluralism that have enabled American Jews to flourish in the United States," and its educative role in helping to heighten American Jewish awareness about *tzedakah* and social justice. "In creating the Jewish Fund for Justice," the organization writes in its annual report, "its architects sought to challenge the notion that the Jewish community has turned inward. . . . *While most American Jewish families have journeyed from disadvantage to economic security, the Fund assures that Jews do not become estranged from the daily realities of poverty that once affected us so directly.*"

The JFJ grants to Project Ezra and the Jewish Council on Urban Affairs, for example, came from JFJ's "Synagogue Challenge Program," a matching-fund program in which congregations select and help support community organizations (mostly non-Jewish) that meet JFJ's guidelines. Members of synagogue social action committees often end up sitting on the boards of these organizations "and contribute to their long-term stability and growth," writes JFJ. A second program, the "Purim Fund," "heightens awareness among Jews of the special problems that confront poor women. . . whose struggles recall how our grandmothers and mothers fought with dignity to build lives for themselves and their communities. . . . In a number of community gatherings, low-income women have shared their experiences and organizing efforts with local Jewish women. Sermons and studies led by women rabbis have made Jews more aware of the feminization of poverty, and have involved many in grassroots efforts to combat this alarming trend."

"I would rather be a *tzedakah* collector," the Talmud cites Rabbi Yossi as saying (*Shabbat* 118b), "than a *tzedakah* disdistributor." Yet the Jewish Fund for Justice and other new Jewish philanthropies undertake to do both the collecting and distributing with thoughtful care, recognizing that the "means" of collecting and the "ends" of distributing are, in fact, a single transformative unity from which all involved — funders, solicitors, and recipients — should emerge with a heightened sense of *mentshlikhkeit* (humanity). Indeed, in *all* aspects of what we at The Shefa Fund call "organizing money," opportunities exist to implement the important *tzedakah* principles touched upon in these pages: reciprocity, accountability, empowerment, and the encouragement of Jewish communal consciousness.

Community Makes All the Difference

TZEDAKAH IS SO central in the Jewish worldview that it is, according to some, the definitive trait even of the hereafter. One tale tells about a righteous human being who is granted foreknowledge of the "world to come" and sees two identical banquet rooms, each set with delicious food and drink. In the first, the souls of the unrighteous are wallowing in hunger and misery, for their arms, bound in splints, are unable to bend at the elbows and bring food to their mouths. In the second room, the souls of the righteous are well-fed and joyous — yet they, too, have their arms in splints. These righteous ones, however, are feeding one another, and from this flows all the difference.

Creating a Will: Tzedakah at the End of Life

DOWN HERE ON EARTH, meanwhile, *tzedakah* obliga-

From Danny Siegel's *Where Heaven and Earth Touch* (already cited), p. 171.

Danny Siegel, p. 75.

tions extend to, and perhaps even expand at, the very end of your life.

> When a person is dying. . .
> he brings his money and says to it,
> "I have worked hard for you — night and day —
> please redeem me from this death and save me."
> And the money replies,
> "But haven't you heard—
>   'Wealth is of no avail on the day of wrath'" (Proverbs 11:4).
>   *Pirkei DeRabbi Eliezer 34*

> When Mar Ukba was dying, he said:
>   Bring me my *tzedakah* records.
>   When he discovered that his accounts showed that he given away seven thousand gold. . . dinars, he said: These are meager provisions for such a long journey. He then gave away half his money to *tzedakah*.
>   But how could he do this? Did not Rabbi Ila'i say in Usha: A person should not spend more than a fifth [of his estate] on *tzedakah*?
>   That rule only applies during a person's lifetime, in order to prevent the person from becoming poor himself, but since death makes this issue irrelevant, we have no objection. . .
>   *Ketubot 67b*

The creation of a will is one of the most difficult and vital acts of *tzedakah* to be undertaken: difficult, obviously, because it demands that we look the Angel of Death in the face, which is nearly as hard at looking at God's face. Nathan Ausubel (in *A Treasury of Jewish Folklore*) tells of a weary Jewish worker carrying a heavy load on his back, who lets his burden fall and bitterly proclaims his wish to die. At once the Angel of Death appears and asks, "Why do you call me?" The fearful man humbly asks for help in remounting the burden on his shoulders.

Creating a will is difficult also because the emotional en-

143

tanglements of money matters, the ways in which money mediates relationships within families and within other circles of intimacy, must be brought to the surface and confronted. Danny Siegel's insight that *tzedakah* is but another form of *teshuvah* becomes at no time more apparent than when you create your will in anticipation of your own death.

Yet this act of creation is the tool by which you can preserve whatever aspects of "covenant" you have applied to your wealth, the tool by which you can expand your money's justice-making power beyond your lifespan, the tool by which you can fulfill the true meaning of work: to preserve and enlarge the wealth delivered into your hands by Divine Goodness and through the collective achievement of past generations, for the sake of future generations. Psalm 116 asks, "How can I repay the Lord for all the bounties to me?" Rabbi Abraham Joshua Heschel responds:

> The greatest problem is not how to continue but how to return. . . . The world to come is not only a hereafter but also a herenow. . . .
> The aspiration is to obtain; the perfection is to dispense . . . . this act of giving away is reciprocity on our part for God's gift of life.

In planning for that repayment by preparing (and reviewing and revising) your will, you have the opportunity to put into play the virtues of holistic *tzedakah* described in this essay. Whether you have the means only to make small charitable contributions, or the means to establish a private family foundation (or endow an existing non-profit organization), your legacy is likely to pass into a greater number of hands, each of which will have the potential for multiplying or diminishing the *tzedakah* power of your money. Keep this in mind as you select your executors, trustees and beneficiaries. (Instructing and

One very stimulating resource is *So that Your Values Live On: Ethical Wills and How to Prepare Them*, edited and annotated by Jack Riemer and Nathaniel Stampfer, 1991, Jewish Lights Publishing, Woodstock, VT. Another very practical resource is *A Time to Prepare*, by Richard F. Address, "A Practical Guide for Individuals and Families in Determining One's Wishes for Extraordinary Treatment and Financial Arrangements," published by the Bio-Medical Ethics Commitee of the Union of American Hebrew Congregations (838 Fifth Avenue, New York, NY 10021).

Abraham Joshua Heschel, "Death as Homecoming," from *Jewish Reflections on Death*, edited by Jack Riemer, 1974, Schocken Books, New York, p. 73.

inspiring those around you with a Jewish ethical will is a time-honored tradition that has been renewed among thoughtful American Jews in recent years.)

There can be a profound therapeutic effect in the writing of a will. "When you have made plans for what is to happen to your money after your death," write the authors of *Robin Hood Was Right*, the Vanguard Public Foundation's 1977 "Guide to Giving Your Money for Social Change" (already cited), "we guarantee that you'll have an easier time dealing with it in the here and now. For many wealthy people we've observed, making a will which embodies a strong commitment to social justice has often been a major, morale-raising step on the road to dealing successfully (that is, creatively and happily) with money."

A "strong commitment to social justice" might conflict, however, with your strong commitment to loved ones and your hope of ensuring their well-being in the future. We have no glib preachments to make about this very complicated and personal judgment, only a prayerful thought to offer: that the rectification of the world through *tzedakah* is, in fact, a vital part of ensuring your loved ones' well-being in the future — a future in which human interdependence will become ever-more apparent, whether in our common redemption or our common suffering. "(A) person (who) says, 'I am giving this coin to *tzedakah* so that my child will live'. . . that is an act of complete *tzedakah*," says the Talmud (*Pesachim* 8a-b).

Danny Siegel, p. 76.

IN SUMMARY, perhaps it is helpful to view money and wealth as the blood within the body of the human race. If it circulates, bringing nutrients to all parts, the body prospers and, indeed, produces more blood. If, on the other hand, wealth fails to circulate, but accumulates and clots, the results are potentially fatal.

145

Tzedakah is the heart that keeps the blood circulating.
Tzedakah saves from death.

Questions to Consider and Discuss

When have you given tzedakah and felt that you were making a "sacrifice?" When have you given and felt that you were making an "investment?"

To what extent do you consider people to be at fault for their poverty or other problems? To what extent do you hold society ("the system") responsible for poverty and other problems? How do these considerations influence your giving?

Do you tend to associate wealth with blessedness or corruptedness? Do you see your own abundance in the same terms, or differently?

Why do you think there are so many stereotypes about Jewish fundraising and other public money activities? What do you like best about the Jewish culture vis-a-vis money? What do you like least about it?

Conclusion:
Judaism and Response-ability

"**W**HO IS A JEW?" asks one midrash, replying: "One who testifies against idols." As we have noted earlier in this essay, the Talmud stresses this as a defining quality of Judaism several times. More than one commentator has pointed to the Second Commandment — "You shall have no other gods beside Me. . . . You shall not bow down to them or serve them" — as the single greatest innovation of the Decalogue, the commandment that broke precedent with other ancient law codes and propelled the Jewish people towards their unique destiny as a folk united not only by the usual forces of national identity — land, language, ethnicity, history — but by the quest for holiness and wholeness in all aspects of life. The Sinaitic call to monotheism, to the unification of the many pieces of reality into one whole fabric, was a call to full consciousness, to full *mentshlikhkeit*, to changing the world not through ritualistic manipulation, not through intensification of this or that rite, but through the cleansing awareness of ourselves as covenanted to our Creator.

Despite the Jewish tradition's emphasis on opposing idolatry, most modern Jews have little relation to the concept. Idolatry is an antiquated notion that refers, we believe, only to the religious worship of statues representing alien deities. In fact, for many Jews the most irrelevant or objectionable parts of Torah are precisely those bloodthirsty passages describing the Hebrew people's "holy wars" of conquest under their war-god, Yahweh, against the pagan peoples surrounding them.

There are, however, Jewish thinkers who have imbued the concept of idolatry with painfully relevant modern meaning. Erich Fromm, for instance, in his 1950 study of humanistic religion, *Psychoanalysis and Religion* (Yale University Press, New Haven and London), described idolatry as "the deification of things. . . and man's [sic] submission to such things, in contrast to an attitude in which his life is devoted to the realization of the highest principles of life, those of love and reason, to the aim of becoming what he potentially is, a being made in the likeness of God."

> It is not only pictures in stone and wood that are idols. Words can become idols, and machines can become idols; leaders, the state, power, and political groups may also serve. Science and the opinion of one's neighbors can become idols, and God has become an idol for many.

To aspire to our potential as beings made in the likeness of God — this, says Fromm, is the key value of the religious life. Rabbi Arthur Green elaborates on this idea in his profound theological work, *Seek My Face, Speak My Name:* "The very core of our self-understanding as Jews and as persons calls upon us to see each man and woman as a lens through which the Divine is reflected. . . ."

Arthur Green, *Seek My Face, Speak My Name, A Contemporary Jewish Theology,* 1992, Jason Aronson, Inc., pp. 79-81. Used by permission.

(W)e constantly face the question, "Am I treating human beings — myself as well as others — as the image of God?" This demand will shape and restrict our actions rather clearly in attempts at the "use" of other human beings — whether as sexual objects, as tools to help us gain money or political power, or as fulfillment of some other need we have. . . . it will restrict both those activities that harm the human body, and those that lead us into situations of personal degradation. It is the basis of that hard-to-define term *mentshlikhkeit,* or decent humanity, that sets the agenda for the instinctive ethics of many Jews, even those cut off from the theological moorings of their own values.

"To take seriously our faith that each person is God's image," Green concludes, "is to treat every person with a spiritual dignity and caring that would transform all of our lives." Not to strive to do so, we would add, means capitulating to the siren song of idolatry.

If Isaiah Were Alive Today:
The "America Pronouncement"

THAT SONG surrounds us in America. It is sung by the purveyors of a commercial culture that urges us to think of artists and performers as "superstars" and "idols" — words that reveal devotion not to *tselem Elohim* — seeing humans as God's image — but to seeing people as receptacles for our fantasies. It is sung by the purveyors of a political culture that offers only opportunistic, fragmentary social policy and ritualistic manipulation of public passion and pain.

Consider, for example, how the prison population of the U.S. doubled during the Reagan-Bush years to exceed South Africa's as the largest in the world on a percentage basis — while job-training and employment programs have been cut to the bone (amidst a major restructuring of the U.S. economy that brought about a huge decline in manufacturing jobs). Is our society's eagerness to dehumanize criminals, to lock them in cages without responding to the grim social conditions that desensitize them and help breed their criminality, not a manifestation of idolatry?

> They do not care for the way of integrity,
> There is no justice on their paths.
>
> *Isaiah* 59: 8

Or consider the criminals themselves, whether or not they wind up in prison: the inner-city kid who will risk everything and injure anyone in order to buy a pair of three-hundred-

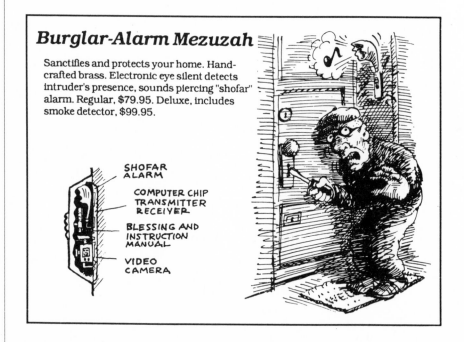

Burglar-Alarm Mezuzah

Sanctifies and protects your home. Hand-crafted brass. Electronic eye silent detects intruder's presence, sounds piercing "shofar" alarm. Regular, $79.95. Deluxe, includes smoke detector, $99.95.

SHOFAR ALARM

COMPUTER CHIP TRANSMITTER RECEIVER

BLESSING AND INSTRUCTION MANUAL

VIDEO CAMERA

dollar sneakers, or the Nike executive who will pay starvation wages in the Third World in order to hold the manufacturing costs of those three-hundred dollar sneakers down to less than a couple of bucks. Isn't their common notion of "making it" a manifestation of idolatry?

> Why do you spend money for what is not bread,
> Your earnings for what does not satisfy?
> *Isaiah* 55: 2

Consider how the private realm of sexuality is endlessly exposed, distorted and exploited for profit in the marketplace, while that which should be publicly discussed about sexuality — including sexually-linked disease, rape and abuse — is only grudgingly acknowledged.

> You who inflame yourselves. . .
> Who slaughter children in the wadis,
> Among the clefts of the rocks. . .
> To them you have poured out libations,
> Presented offerings.
> *Isaiah* 57: 5-6

1987, 60 minute VHS video
SEXY GIRLS AND SEXY GUNS

Consider how *punishing* the poor for their failure to overcome the unjust barriers of race and class and age and gender seems to be our society's social policy goal; how the mythical "welfare queen" is so much more despised than the defense contractor who steals billions from the taxpayer through cost overruns and outright theft; how most voters, and certainly most politicians, would rather cling to feel-good preachments about America's stature as "Number One," or create bogus scapegoats to explain our country's ills, than truly reckon with the realities of poverty, unemployment, violence, addiction and widespread misery.

153

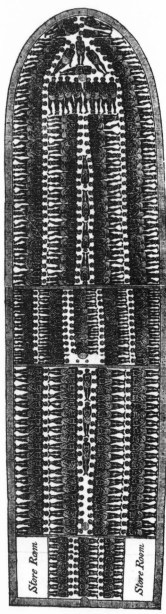

Slave Ship

No, this is the fast I desire:
To unlock the fetters of wickedness,
And untie the cords of the yoke
To let the oppressed go free;
To break off every yoke.
It is to share your bread with the hungry,
And to take the wretched poor into your home;
When you see the naked, to clothe him,
And not to ignore your own kin.
Isaiah 58: 6-7

Consider the lack of wholeness in our vision of the future and the lack of atonement in our vision of the past — atonement for the historic crimes of slavery and slaughter that still haunt our culture. Consider the prideful American mystique of "rugged individualism," which lends an egotistical perspective to every success and every failure and renders Martin Buber's concept of "genuine We-ness" inconceivable or highly subversive. Consider how even the vocabulary of pluralism, never mind community, is falling into disuse; how racism, anti-gay prejudice, and unreal "family values" have become the main selling points of a dominant political conservatism that seems more and more incapable of coping with the tremendous historical changes and opportunities of the past few years.

The inner-city kid who will risk everything and injure anyone in order to buy a pair of three-hundred-dollar sneakers, or the Nike executive who will pay starvation wages in the Third World in order to hold the manufacturing costs of those three-hundred dollar sneakers down to less than a couple of bucks — isn't their common notion of "making it" a manifestation of idolatry?

We hope for redress, and there is none. . .
For our many sins are before You. . .
Planning fraud and treachery,
Conceiving lies and uttering them from the throat.
And so redress is turned back
And vindication stays afar,
Because honesty stumbles in the public square
And uprightness cannot enter.

Isaiah 59: 11-15

"O America," Isaiah might prophesy today, "your leaders are like the Pharaoh of Egypt, who was unable to acknowledge his nation's plagues as real and beyond the power of his magicians to repair. Violence is spreading through your streets like the frogs that swarmed across Egypt — and you sacrifice to the god of Law and Order. Cancer and other environmentally-linked diseases spread like boils through the population — and you invoke the name of Industrial Progress. Greed and irresponsibility consume your prosperity like locusts — and you decry the demon of Government Regulation. Drug abuse and domestic violence darken the very atmosphere — and you chant 'Just Say No.'

"But the Almighty Dollar cannot hear your prayers. The Cult of the Individual cannot assure your well-being. Star Worship cannot bring light to the dark corners of your unhappiness. Your false gods shall fail you time and again!"

Response-ability Versus the Class System

WHAT, THEN does it mean for modern American Jews to "testify against idols," as the Talmud bids us? In this essay, we

155

> In this essay, we have suggested lifestyle choices and creative uses of money that defy the competitive mystique of American capitalism. As people imbued, however, with individualism, class, race and gender bias, and complex fears about money, all of us are blocked from easily embracing notions of "community" and "social responsibility," because our very "ability to respond" has been damaged, our very *mentshlikhkeit* diminished. Social "response-ability" thus means healing ourselves, peeling away from the class-linked values and cultures in which we are trapped, and restoring our wholeness by participating in a *tikkun* of the soul.

have suggested lifestyle choices and creative uses of money that defy the dog-eat-dog, competitive mystique of American capitalism. As people imbued, however, with individualism, class, race and gender bias, and complex fears about money, *all* of us are blocked from easily embracing notions of "community" and "social responsibility," because our very "ability to respond" has been damaged, our very *mentshlikhkeit* diminished. We have *all* become inured to the human suffering that surrounds us, and the great majority of us have ducked out of any sense of covenantal obligation or religious mandate, such as the Jewish system of obligatory *tzedakah,* that might discipline us to respond to suffering despite our alienation, even when we are "not in the mood." We have *all* yielded ourselves, moreover, to ways of thinking that legitimate and perpetuate the unjust distribution of money and power by fostering a false ranking system of human "worthiness" — a ranking system that is idolatrous to its core. Social "response-ability" thus means healing ourselves, peeling ourselves away from the class-linked values and cultures in which we are trapped, and restoring our wholeness by participating in a *tikkun* of the soul.

This need for healing sweeps across class lines. Whether we are rich, poor, middle-class or somewhere in between, our class status imposes on us its own forms of soul-disorder and thought-distortion, what we might commonly call "class traits." Most obvious, perhaps, are the traits forced upon poor people — as described, for example, by Oscar Lewis in his classic essay, "The Culture of Poverty." Lewis sees the class traits of the poor as

> . . . both an adaptation and a reaction. . . to their marginal position. . . . an effort to cope with feelings of hopelessness and despair which develop from the realization of the im-

probability of achieving success in terms of the values and goals of the larger society. . . . Once it [the "culture of poverty"] comes into existence it tends to perpetuate itself from generation to generation. . . . Low wages, chronic unemployment and underemployment lead to low income, lack of property ownership, absence of savings, absence of food reserves in the home, and a chronic shortage of cash. These conditions reduce the possibility of effective participation in the larger economic system. . . . On the family level, the major traits of the culture of poverty are the absence of childhood as a specially prolonged and protected stage in the life cycle, early initiation into sex, free unions of consensual marriages. . . a sense of resignation and fatalism, a widespread belief in male superiority. . .

Many have argued with the particulars of Lewis' description, and all should be forewarned about generalizing and thus stereotyping *any* group of people; nevertheless, it takes only minimal empathy to recognize how the restrictions imposed by poverty upon people's autonomy and wholeness can create, by way of "adaptation and reaction," a "culture of poverty."

It probably takes *greater* empathy, in fact, to realize that wealth, too, creates a restrictive "culture." ("It's not as good with money," one Yiddish proverb has it, "as it is bad without it"). In her 1987 doctoral dissertation, *The Experience of Inherited Wealth: A Social-Psychological Perspective,* Joanie Bronfman sums up her findings, based on interviews with over 100 wealthy people, by noting that "contrary to common expectations, wealth also brings many psychological injuries. . ."

Wealthy people are taught many attitudes that are personally injurious but useful for the maintenance of the system. . . wealthy people are taught to "maintain appearances" at all times, regardless of the often tremendous cost of isolation and self-denial. This leads to a disconnection from one's self and from others that precludes empathy and

---

Lewis cites the "Jews of Eastern Europe" as being "very poor, but they did not have many of the traits of the culture of poverty because of their tradition of literacy, the great value placed upon learning, the organization of the community around the rabbi, the proliferation of local voluntary associations, and their religion which taught that they were the chosen people."

Joanie Bronfman, *Inherited Wealth: A Social-Psychological Perspective,* 1987, Brandeis University, pp. 385-393. Used by permission of the author.

157

intimacy. . . . upper-class people are expected to control their feelings. By appearing unemotional, they seem to be in charge and invulnerable. . . The denial of their own pain inhibits many upper-class people's abilities to be sympathetic to the plight of others. . . . isolation is systematically instilled, though generally unconsciously, through a lack of familial intimacy and scant contact with people of different backgrounds. Wealthy people's isolation leaves them uncomfortable with intimacy in general and afraid of anyone whom they perceive as different. . . . The same disconnection leads wealthy people to dissociate their actions from their effects on the fate of the world. . .

The middle/working class, meanwhile, looks "up" in envy, "down" in fear, and develops a stiff neck: tense with ambition and dread, dissatisfaction and guilt. "Both families and schools," writes Martha Ackelsberg, "tend to foster a sense of independence and autonomy for middle-class people, although many jobs increasingly deny it. This emphasis on autonomy. . . creates considerable confusion about the role and importance of community and support. It becomes difficult for those who are born and brought up middle-class to ask for help from others — or, sometimes, even to give it — because, ideally, each of us is supposed to be able to manage on our own. To ask for help seems to call into question one's autonomy — and, therefore, one's dignity as a person."

This constellation also leads to guilt and paralysis in a social/political context. Middle-class people do not, after all, have enough money either to change things dramatically in the society as a whole, or to feel completely secure in their own position. They are also aware of the arbitrariness of it all. Consequently, they may feel guilty for their own success, even at the same time that they are unable to take full responsibility for it. Thus, middle-class people, too, suffer from a sense of alienation, isolation and powerlessness. . . feelings that probably help explain why so many middle-class people

---

"The greatest pain," says a Yiddish proverb, "is the one you can't tell others about." For wealthy people, one form of class oppression is their inability to have their problems taken seriously and sympathetically, due to the mythicization of money as the solution to all ills and the general envy and resentment felt towards those with wealth. This communication gap drives people of wealth to repress their feelings and isolate themselves within their class, lest they be belittled by the classic, classist response, "I should have such problems!"

Martha Ackelsberg, "Money and Class: Dealing with Difference in the Jewish Renewal Movement," paper for The Shefa Fund retreat, March 31-April 2, 1989.

The Disadvantages of Living in a Mansion

One of the most startling passages in Joanie Bronfman's dissertation is the testimony of a woman about the disadvantages of growing up in a mansion (pp. 83-84), in particular the lack of intimacy: "The ordinary child sleeps in a room next door to his [sic] parents or nearby. He can practically hear his parents breathing through the walls. But I remember being locked in my room for some reason. . . . I really needed my parents. . . for some urgent thing and I called and I called and no answer. I cried and no answer, and finally I just lost control and I had a tantrum. I threw my piggy bank at the door until the door was all bruised and splintered. I must have gone like that for a half hour and thinking that I'm sure people are going to hear me and come in and punish me, at least I would get attention. . . . Nobody came. . . I finally came to the end of the tantrum because I had no more strength. When I got the strength together, I crept out through my window and wandered downstairs. My mother was having cocktails with my father and some guests and she had no idea that anything was wrong. She said, 'Hello, what brings you down here?' It just made me feel terrible. I had absolutely pulled out everything in my arsenal and they didn't even know that I had any trouble at all.

"'. . . Having money made it very easy for my parents to ignore me.'"

prefer not to have to think about class, or about their monetary situation, at all.

These and other constraints of class culture are experienced in deeply personal ways, enmeshed with our family dramas, yet their common scar is a sense of isolation, fragmentation, lack of wholeness. "This feeling," Martha Ackelsberg sums up, "has an important connection with spirituality, or wholeness—which, as I understand it, means being in touch with the sources of power, integrity and capacity within each of us, and in connection with each other. . . . (I)f we are divided from one another — and even from ourselves — by class differences, then we are unable to experience that wholeness. Further, if those same divisions block our ability to act — and, in particular, to act in concert with others — then they disempower us and undermine our ability to do the work of *tikkun olam*."

Jewish Fears about Money and Class

FOR THE UPWARDLY MOBILE American Jewish middle-class mainstream, class tensions have been particularly acute. Due to the disproportionate numbers of Jewish teachers, social workers, attorneys, shopkeepers and property owners, the encounter between the poor and the Jewish middle class has been intimate, conflicted and marred by anti-Semitism. Relations between the wealthy and the Jewish middle class, on the other hand, have been marked by anti-Semitic policies of exclusion or, at least, assimilationist pressures — pressures that produced a generation of de-Judaizing name changes, nose jobs, and deculturation.

159

Charles Silberman, in *A Certain People* (already cited), argues convincingly that the exclusion of Jews from the elite structures of our society is the practice of a bygone era. Yet "many of the norms of American upper-class culture," notes Joanie Bronfman (p. 91 of her dissertation), "have been significantly affected" by "Northern European heritage. Wealthy people from other ethnic groups who want acceptance into this upper-class society may therefore often conform to those norms" — in particular the deadening norm of "emotional management," what Arlie Russel Hochschild calls "feeling rules."

Chaia Lehrer, "Those Old Working Class Values," *Bridges*, Vol. 2, No. 1, Spring, 1991. See also Myron Perlman's "Work, Study, Get Ahead" in *Chutzpah, A Jewish Liberation Anthology* (1977, New Glide Publications, San Francisco), p. 75. "Most of my life," Perlman begins, "I've been trapped by two myths. The first is that all Jews are rich, or at least middle class. Hearing it over and over again made me believe that I was middle class, since I knew I wasn't rich. . ."

Within the Jewish community itself, the presumption of middle-class status or "better" as normative for American Jews has created a certain degree of oppressive invisibility and shame for poor and working-class Jews. Writing in *Bridges* magazine, Chaia Lehrer, a Jewish lesbian mother, postal worker and community activist, describes how in "Jewish community organizations, I felt the pressure to be articulate, plus a great deal of classism expressed around respect for professionals and people with money. . . ."

> Middle-class people think that all working-class people want to be like them. But it's not true. More than that, we want to be proud to be working class. Proud of a set of values that says people don't have to prove themselves in order to be respected. . . that we are grateful for everything we have, and that the ability to survive comes from our inner strength and our natural tendency to care for one another. Upward mobility destroyed those values in my mother's family. I live with a deep wound left by their loss and I struggle every day to regain and live by those old, working-class values.

What Lehrer calls "working-class values" are also essential Jewish values: respect for human dignity, thankfulness for our blessings, mutual responsibility within our community, and emphasis on the depth of soul, rather than the depth of pocket, of a human being. The extent to which such values have been overwhelmed in American Jewish life by the successful quest for upward mobility is another measurement of our assimilation and loss.

Jewish Success=Jewish Survival

YET MANY ASPECTS of the American Jewish success story

Many aspects of the American Jewish success story are rooted in historical Jewish habits of survival and adaptation. Ours is chiefly neither a "culture of poverty" nor a "culture of wealth," but a culture of resilience that views achievement as survival gear.

"Perspective of abundance. . . peculiar faith. . ." quoted from Andrew R. Heinze's *Adapting to Abundance, Jewish Immigrants, Mass Consumption and the Search for American Identity,* 1990, Columbia University Press, New York, p. 3. Reprinted by permission of the publisher.

are profoundly Jewish, rooted in historical habits of survival and adaptation. Ours is chiefly neither a "culture of poverty" nor a "culture of wealth," but a culture of resilience that views achievement as survival gear. "For Jews," writes Gerald Krefetz in *Jews and Money,* "money has stood between life and death" and "had an existential reality. . . for it gave them substantiality in alien eyes. Without their financial usefulness, they would have been obliterated long ago. . . . It has been incumbent upon them to succeed."

"Incumbent upon them to succeed" — and in America, *permitted.* Here was a spacious, fast-growing industrialized land with tremendous economic opportunity. Here were democratic protections afforded by a stable political system (and expanded through grassroots activism). Here was a "perspective of abundance" — America's "peculiar faith in the principle of a rising standard of living." All of this combined to enable Ashkenazic Jewish immigrants to convert long-acquired survival skills and religiously-based disciplines into money-making tools:

• The communal self-sufficiency, innovativeness and skills-diversification that enabled European Jewish communities to survive the chaos and arbitrary persecutions of feudal Europe became the basis, in America, for the kind of entrepreneurial innovativeness that was responsible, in good part, for the film and television industries, mass-market retailing, and other mainstays of the American consumer culture.

• The urban quality of Jewish life — often imposed in Europe by ghetto walls — gave rise in America to real estate fortunes and other business opportunities that took advantage of this country's rush to urbanization and suburbanization in the 20th century.

• The orientation towards scholarship and professionalism that had shielded Jewish self-esteem and extended Jewish

Charles Silberman notes, in *A Certain People* (already cited), that some 40% of New York City's real estate developers in the 1920s (at the close of the great wave of Eastern European Jewish immigration to the U.S.) were Jews, in part because the field was not closed to Jews by the discriminatory barriers that existed in other industries; real estate dealings required only a phone and a desk, rather than an elaborate corporate structure.

Nathan Glazer is quoted by Silberman in *A Certain People*, p. 132.

American-Jewish acquisitiveness was perhaps best spoofed by *Mad* magazine's Frank Jacobs and Mort Drucker in a 1973 satire, "Antenna on the Roof," which portrays a modern Tevya (from *Fiddler on the Roof*) singing not about "Tradition!" but about "Possessions!"

survivability in days of marginality, exile and persecution was converted in America into an ability, in Nathan Glazer's words, to "turn their minds to ways and means of improving themselves that were quite beyond the imagination of their fellow workers. . . They, or their friends or relatives, had the necessary experience or knowledge."

• The frugality and non-ostentation bred by the fear of lower-class violence in pogrom-ridden Europe translated to the ability to get ahead in America, to postpone gratification, raise capital and class climb.

American Jewish success, in other words, is based on skills that were forged through suffering — a legacy of suffering that remains an active ingredient in our psyches and complicates our attitudes towards money and class.

For some Jews, especially of the second and third generations, "living well is the best revenge" has been the response to this legacy, and ostentatious consumption has become a lifestyle. The Jewish parvenu has been parodied endlessly (and to the suspect delight of gentile America) and requires no description here. Instead, we offer a less mocking perspective: that Jewish acquisitiveness be seen as an affirmation of American citizenship, an expression of hope (and insecurity) about Jewish well-being in America, and a nose-thumbing at anti-Semitism (in particular the anti-Semitism of the "WASP" establishment, which has used accusations of vulgarity and pushiness to defend the bastions of privilege from Jewish encroachment — the modern "Jewish American Princess" appellation being the latest variant).

Andrew R. Heinze argues, in fact (in *Adapting to Abundance,* cited on p. 161), that for Jews "consumption was central to American acculturation." Jews have been keenly aware, he writes (pp. 4-5), "that items of consumption in general constitute. . . important building blocks of American identity."

Heinze's analysis even links the rise of Jewish consumerism with elements of Judaism — and with the decline of Jewish religiosity in America:

> A fundamental part of traditional Jewish culture was engaged, both positively and negatively, by the immigrants' pursuit of the American standard of living. For centuries, Jews had used items of luxury in the celebration of the Sabbath and holidays in order to deepen their distinction between the holy and the mundane spheres of life. During those special times, the humblest Jew was thought to be blessed with a foretaste of God's splendor, which was signified by prized things reserved exclusively for the occasion. The distinction between the holy and the mundane was bound to collapse in the American city, where luxuries were routinely converted into necessities. Not only did the holy days lose the support of material luxury, but, signaling the eminent decline of traditional Judaism in America, the Sabbath, the proverbial "queen" of pious Jews, became a shopping day.

Heinze does not bemoan this process by which "the secular American environment refocused the [Jewish] awareness. . . of luxuries as a type of instrument for dignifying the individual." Jews, he writes (p. 6), benefitted by being "quick to detect the democratic symbolism of mass-marketed luxuries in America. Their traditional culture thus helped them realize that Americans sought, in the realm of consumption, a parity with each other that was unattainable in the world of capital and labor." Indeed, many Jewish fortunes were built upon that very insight. However, the phenomenon of Jewish "conspicuous consumption" has had so many costly accompaniments, for individual Jewish families and for the community as a whole — a high mortality rate for overstressed men, bodily self-abuse and low self-esteem for women, a religious and spiritual emptiness that has young Jews fleeing from the synagogue, widespread Jewish illiteracy and self-hatred rooted in carica-

Writing a full generation before Heinze, Judith R. Kramer and Seymour Leventman, authors of *Children of the Gilded Ghetto*, a 1961 study of a Midwestern Jewish community (Yale University Press, New Haven and London), attribute Jewish acquisitiveness in part to the first and second generations' lack of "occupational variety and economic *yichus* (the prestige of old and respected family businesses)," so that money became substituted as the measure of success and status. The third generation (the "young Philistines," in the authors' words), restored occupational status by joining the salaried professions, but with this came "an escape from any ethnic uniqueness fostered by traditional economic specialization." "The style of life of the second generation rests largely on what it can afford to buy. But like other young people, the third generation adopts more general occupational determinants of lifestyles. . . shaped less by income than by interests. . . . The young Philistines of the third generation are contemptuous of paternal preoccupation with money at the same time that they profit from the fruits of their fathers' [sic] labors. They affect a rationale of refined sensitivity in contrast to the vulgar, mink-clad tastes of their fathers."

163

ture and stereotype, etc. — as to suggest that the obtaining of American "citizenship" via consumerism has had its price.

"Living well is the best revenge" has lost moral legitimacy as a philosophy, moreover, thanks, in part, to the successful civil rights activism of a sector of the Jewish community, which won true political and economic citizenship for Jews in the U.S. and made anachronistic the need for conspicuous symbols of "belonging." Rather than confront the challenges of socially responsible citizenship, however, some American Jews prefer to persist in a victim mentality, to numb their "response-ability" and live as consumption junkies, "safe" within their walls, "safe" within their wealth. Still others have graduated to a neo-conservative political perspective, advocating a Jewish political agenda of narrow "self-interest" ("moral autism," Amos Oz calls it) and a fawning, Disneyland view of America as a perfected democracy plagued only by a few noisy malcontents.

Happily, these Jews are far from the majority. "When Ronald Reagan asked and George Bush echoed, 'Are you better off today than you were eight years ago," said Michael Pelavin, then-chair of NJCRAC, in a 1989 address, "the Jewish community answered not individually but collectively. While many of us may indeed be better off financially today than in 1980, we dispute the premise of the question. We ask today, 'What is the state of America today as compared to eight years ago?'. . . *The strength of the Jewish community and its ability to survive in freedom bears a direct relationship to the quality of life of those around us. . .*" (italics added).

Pelavin's words testify to the remarkably well-preserved prophetic and empathetic sensibility that has made Jews into tenacious advocates of democracy, generosity and open-mindedness in America. Nevertheless, the increased presence and influence of what Earl Shorris calls "Jews without mercy" ("the elegance of the Jewish love of mercy. . . replaced by the desire for power; the beauty of. . . belief in social justice. . . replaced by the vulgarity of self-interest") have somewhat neutralized the dynamic liberalism that the Jewish community displayed throughout this century in opposing worker exploitation, legal segregation, sexist discrimination, and other idolatrous aspects of American society. While right-wing anti-Semitism, fundamentalist Christian triumphalism, and other quirky aspects of the conservative movement have kept Jews from committing themselves to alliances with the right, Jewish liberal activism is on the defensive and needs resuscitation.

Earl Shorris, *Jews Without Mercy, A Lament,* 1982, Anchor Press/Doubleday, New York.

Building an Alliance with the Social Responsibility Movement

THIS ESSAY has been an effort to inspire some of that resuscitation by introducing the Jewish community to the social responsibility movement. *We believe this movement to be a likely home for Jews and a likely coalition partner for Jewish organizations for the following reasons:*

1) The "old" modes of grassroots political activism that engaged Jews as trade unionists, students and community residents have become less and less relevant to the daily lives of professional, suburbanized Jewish Americans today. Jewish liberal instincts, therefore, have found expression in recent years in a narrowing scope, chiefly the ballot box and the *pushka* (charity box). By defining an activist role for the consumer, investor and contributor, the socially responsible

---

The "old" modes of grassroots political activism that engaged Jews as trade unionists, students and community residents have become less and less relevant to the daily lives of professional, suburbanized Jewish Americans today. Jewish liberal instincts, therefore, have found expression in recent years in a narrowing scope, chiefly the ballot box and the *pushka* (charity box). By defining an activist role for the consumer, investor and contributor, the socially responsible money movement expands the landscape of "politics" to include spheres in which Jews of every class can easily and naturally participate.

money movement expands the landscape of "politics" to include spheres in which Jews of every class can easily and naturally participate.

2) While addressing the major social ills of our society, the social responsibility movement nevertheless affirms the blessings and potentialities of the free market system — to which the American Jewish "success story" is a testimonial. The movement demands no renunciation of the material abundance that, for Jews, is a real as well as psychological safeguard against persecution; rather, the movement encourages the use of that abundance to help create social conditions that would permit Jews, along with the rest of the population, a reasonable measure of peace of mind. It poses not a dualistic, good-versus-evil, "either-or" political view ("If you're not part of the solution, you're part of the problem"), but a more holistic, Jewishly resonant "and-therefore" ("We're all part of the problem *and* the solution, *therefore. . .*") There are no membership requirements or vanguard groups within the social responsibility movement, no utopian schemes or reductionist assumptions about human beings. Rather, there is a trust expressed — a trust perhaps innocent, yet effective in its optimism — that human beings, including those in powerful positions within amoral institutions, can be moved to perform acts of conscience — to contribute to the creation of the Tabernacle rather than the Golden Calf. At the same time, the social responsibility movement is as profoundly practical as the arena in which it operates: Justice, it simply affirms, has a market value that must be calculated to ensure the worth of our commodities and our nation.

THIS ESSAY has also attempted to summon readers to Judaism, to urge Jewish activists to root their social action commitments in the idioms and insights of the Jewish tradition. Just as Judaism and Jewish survival skills equipped Jews in America with "great resourcefulness" (in Andrew Heinze's words) "in overcoming the barrier of alienation that initially faced all immigrants," so can Judaism, we believe, now help overcome the barriers of alienation that confront us as established American citizens: the disease of consumption, the worship of the Almighty Dollar, the exaltation of the individual, the adoration of wealth, the addiction to violence, the denial of pain, and the distorting influences of classism, racism and sexism, all of which threaten to atrophy our response-ability.

Judaism has market value! Judaism's perception of each human act as having consequence, of each human life as constituting a universe, and of the entire universe as ours to preserve with daily, constructive deeds and disciplines, deserves to be "bought" by a world that is in ideological limbo. Judaism's "liberation theology" — emphasizing the *soul* of the human being more than social *role* of the human being, *healing* more than conflict, *awe* and *humility* more than anger and righteousness — deserves "investment" from caring people for whom the "ism's" of the past century have exhausted their theoretical and prescriptive power.

"All the calculated dates of redemption have passed," declares the Talmud (*Exodus Rabbah* 5: 19), in a prophetic passage that might well serve as the credo of the social responsibilty movement, "and now the matter depends on repentance and good deeds." Indeed, with the Cold War ended, with doomsday nuclear madness somewhat abated, with triumphalist power politics somewhat neutralized by binding global realities, the crises of our species that transcend economic systems, political dogmas and national boundaries are gaining the international attention they have too long been denied. The search for solutions to such monumental problems as mass starvation,

"Economic labor, prayer and contemplation, and service to people," writes Jeffrey Dekro, "all of this is focused in Judaism into one word — *avodah* . *Avodah* is a noun based on a verb root that intimates an ongoing process. This shows the deep-structure wisdom of the Hebrew language and the Jewish religious sensibility."

or the international AIDS crisis, or the global impoverishment of women and children, or the degradation of our biosphere, brings us all face-to-face with questions about self-restraint and self-preservation, personal and communal responsibility, particularism and universalism, moral authority and political power — questions that are at the very core of the Jewish religious tradition.

For the politics of "repentance and good deeds" to be embraced on the scale necessary for environmental repair and social progress, however, the wisdom and moral insights of Judaism must be conserved, reconstructed and reformed — puns intended! — into accessible, humanistic and compelling forms. Jewish leaders must learn to translate their faith into meaningful terms for generations that have, indeed, allowed the sabbath to become a shopping day. The psycho-dynamics of modern Jewish life must be discussed openly, without censurious cries, so that the persecuted Jew hiding in each of us can be assured safe passage into daylight. Circles of community and leadership must be democratized and enlarged across lines of class, gender, sexual orientation and age, so that the many who feel marginalized in Jewish life can have access and lend their wisdom to our process of renewal. Finally, we must bring our Judaism and our Jewish selves into fruitful contact with issues of universal concern — issues with which many Jewish activists who make their home outside the organized Jewish community are already dynamically involved.

In short, we must build alliances with our heritage, with ourselves and with others. Only then will this Judaism of ours, this uniquely practical-yet-visionary religion, gain the "market share" it deserves in the ongoing enterprise of human liberation.

Questions to Consider and Discuss

When does the ancient notion of "idolatry" take on modern meaning for you, if at all? How is it related to your notion of "holiness," if at all?

How was "class culture" manifested in your family when you were young? How does "class culture" influence your present family and community?

To what extent are your identities as a Jew and as an American harmonized? To what extent are they in conflict? Do you consider it an advantage, a handicap, or neither, to be Jewish in America?

Do you think of Jewish values as "liberal" or "conservative" or both? To what extent do you think the social responsibility movement's goals threaten to undermine Jewish security, and to what extent do you think those goals support the health and strength of the Jewish community?

Supplementary Materials

"Women and Philanthropy"
by Letty Cottin Pogrebin

"Toward an Eco-Kosher Life-Path"
by Arthur Waskow

Bibliography and Recommended Resources

About the Shefa Fund

Women and Philanthropy

by Letty Cottin Pogrebin

I'M NEVER SURE how I get roped into it, but several times a year I find myself engaged in what Gloria Steinem calls the world's second oldest profession: fundraising.

I hate asking people for money; who doesn't? Nevertheless, I grit my teeth, get on the phone, or shill from the lecture stage trying to build financial support for the causes I care most about. In the process, I've discovered that fundraising is consciousness-raising, especially for women.

When I was growing up, my mother warned me always to wear clean underwear in case I got hit by a truck. Today, I use the same corny hypothetical to raise money.

"Suppose you get hit by a truck and someone finds your checkbook," I say. "What would the check stubs reveal about your giving habits? How recently did you make your last contribution and how generous was it relative to your means? Who were the beneficiaries of your giving and why did you choose those causes? If your husband handles philanthropy, does he give to causes *you* believe in?"

By this time, most of the women in my audience are suppressing guilty smiles. It's a safe bet they will write a few checks that night — and watch out for trucks on their way home.

Women's philanthropy may sound like an agenda item for the rich, yet it concerns all but the poorest of the poor. The average American household gave $790 to charitable organizations in 1987. Surprisingly, the less people make the more they give. Those earning between $50,000 and $75,000 a year give an average of 1.5% of their income, while people who make less than $10,000 donate 2.8%.

The problem is not that women don't give. The problem is that the whole philanthropic process makes many of us uncomfortable, for understandable reasons.

Women who are employed are in no hurry to part with their hard-won wages, which average only 69¢ to a man's dollar. The very fact of earning money in their own names may be a new experience and they may be unsure it will last.

As for the younger generation, many of whom earn as much or more than their husbands and have equal power over the couple's financial resources, my experience mirrors that of the alumni fundraiser who had trouble persuading

LETTY COTTIN POGREBIN, a founding editor of *Ms.* magazine, is the author of seven books, including, most recently, *Deborah, Golda and Me.* This article is reprinted by permission of the author. © 1990 by Letty Cottin Pogrebin. Published originally in the *New York Times Magazine* of April 22, 1990.

a wealthy classmate to give $500 to Vassar the same year that woman's husband made a $10,000 gift to Yale. I find it's the women who tend to think small: to many who can afford to give in the thousands, a hundred dollars still sounds like a lot of money. Often, women I ask agonize over the amount of their contribution; they need time to think about it, or they're offended that anyone might suppose they can afford a large donation, or they say they want to discuss it with their husbands. The men usually commit (or refuse) on the spot. They seem flattered when you assume they can afford a large donation and no man has ever told me he wants to consult with his wife.

Often a homemaker restrains her giving in the belief that she is not entitled to "give away my husband's money." Only when she values her housework and child-rearing as an in-kind contribution to the couple's net worth will she grant herself permission to do her own charitable decision-making.

But what about the woman who *does* control the family spending and still doesn't give philanthropic dollars easily? I suspect statistics have made her cautious. High rates of divorce and widowhood remind her that wives who seem financially secure may be only one man away from welfare. Her preeminent concern is to conserve disposable money for the worst contingency — being left alone.

Many women compensate for not giving money by donating time, the commodity in shortest supply for career women and mothers of young children, but the one resource they feel

is theirs to give. Overall, 45% of American women compared to 38% of all men did volunteer work in 1989. I'm not sure how those respondents defined "volunteer work," but after 20 years of activism, I can testify that women are the quintessential givers when it comes to effort, energy, comfort and service.

Perhaps money isn't as forthcoming because of a woman's unconscious belief that she herself is the most worthy cause she knows. In return for all her nurturing, she may secretly feel it is

Even though women still suffer sex discrimination and sexual harassment in the workplace, are victims of rape and incest, hold the lowest-paying jobs, head the poorest families, and with their children are the fastest-growing segment of the homeless, it has been a real struggle raising money for women's health, safety or empowerment projects.

her turn to receive — or at least keep what she's got.

If women have trouble giving money because we are already giving everything else, I wonder whether men give partly to relieve their guilt at not nurturing enough, or to neutralize the masculinization of wealth. I'm grateful for male generosity, but I know that those who give also

173

Less than 4% of foundation funding and 0.3% of corporate contributions goes to the needs of women and girls.

get. They get seats on the boards of prestigious universities and medical centers. They get testimonial dinners and rooms named for them. Obviously, many big givers become community leaders. I wish more of our savvy, high-achieving women would wake up to the fact that power and status accrue to those who write large checks to worthy causes.

Which brings up the question: What is a "worthy cause?" Whatever speaks to us; whatever inspires our feelings of concern, empathy, urgency and even passion — whether the cause is the library, the symphony, a university, cancer or AIDS. However, like a mother favoring her runt, what worries me are causes that are less publicized and harder to "sell" — for instance, projects that *directly* benefit disadvantaged females. Even though women still suffer sex discrimination and sexual harassment in the workplace, are victims of rape and incest, hold the lowest-paying jobs, head the poorest families, and with their children are the fastest-growing segment of the homeless, it has been a real struggle raising money for women's health, safety or empowerment projects.

If I were a conspiracy theorist, I'd suspect that this is due to some unexamined misogyny, a resistance to helping women become strong, independent and self-sufficient. But talking with potential givers taught me that the reluctance has other roots: some people resented causes that benefit one gender; several women thought giving money only to women would mark them as selfish. Others found certain issues too threatening to support openly: one woman contributed anonymously rather than have her name appear on a list of donors supporting a lesbian mother's custody suit.

As long as most people are comfortable giving or raising money for, say, an Ivy League university than for rape counseling, and as long as less than 4% of foundation funding and 0.3% of corporate contributions goes to the needs of women and girls, I choose to support cutting-edge women's issues, currently the runts of the litter. Moreover, I subject my giving to a feminist litmus test: *Will this money empower women and their children or will it just reinforce dependency?* I want to fund change, not charity. I want to enable, not just help.

By deciding what causes she cares about, and then supporting them enthusiastically, every woman can further her moral and ethical world view. Whether her donations run in the thousands or the low three-figures as mine usually do, the act of giving money is itself a rejection of the feminine stereotype. It involves risk-taking, decision-making and putting our money where our values are. For me, the badge of feminist courage is visionary philanthropy.

Toward an Eco-Kosher Life Path

by Arthur Waskow

ACCORDING TO the Jewish tradition, the violation of a special Divine code of kosher food was the first act of human history.

God said there was one fruit that was not kosher. Chava and Adam ate it anyway — and thereby shattered the primordial Garden of Delight. What followed was struggle between Adam and Adamah, between earthlings and the earth, human beings and the humus. In pain and sweat the humans would toil to bring forth food, and in hostility the humus would bring forth thorns and thistles.

Eating — not killing, making fire, learning of sex — was the Jewish metaphor for making trouble. (Note that making trouble with God turns out to mean having trouble with the earth.) One aspect of the wisdom at the heart of this legend is that since eating is a crucial nexus between human beings and the earth, a flaw in the eating process — consuming in some crucially incorrect way what comes from the earth — should indeed lead to trouble between earth and earthling.

The first possibility of reversing this disaster is also connected in Jewish tradition with food. Shortly after the great liberation of the Israelites from dreadful toil and slavery in Egypt, they received the great symbol and actuality of freedom in human society and of peace between humans and the earth: *shabbat*. This learning came directly from food, for in the wilderness came manna, a food the Israelites had only to gather, not to sow or cultivate. A double portion came on the sixth day and none on *shabbat* — and this is how the Israelites were first (even before the Revelation at Sinai) taught about *shabbat*, the foretaste of a messianic time when human beings would no longer have to toil and sweat in order to eat.

This retelling of what might be called the sacred history of food went along with the great celebrations of food at the heart of the Temple's sacrificial system. How to praise the God Who was the Life-Source from which sprang the whole interrelated economy/ecology of the Land of Israel? By two rhythms that echoed the seasonal rhythms of the earth. In one of these

ARTHUR WASKOW is director of The Shalom Center, a Fellow of the Institute for Jewish Renewal and initiator of its Eco-Kosher Project, and founder and co-editor of *New Menorah*, the P'nai Or journal of Jewish renewal. Among his books are *Godwrestling, Seasons of Our Joy*, and *Down-to-Earth Judaism: Food, Money, Sex and the Rest of Life.*

rhythms, the people gathered the products of that single land to a single place, there to consecrate grain and meat and bread and wine and water. And in the other rhythm, the land and the social-agricultural hierarchy were to be given sacred rest every seventh and every fiftieth year — in order to reaffirm that the productive land belonged to no owner but God.

When the destruction of the Temple and the dispersion of the Jewish community necessitated some new approach to hallowing food, the Talmud described each family's dinner table as

---

Our technology has transformed the medium of the relationship between earth and human earthling. Originally, food was the great connection. That is no longer so. We may, in our generation, need to apply Jewish teachings about food to other "consumables" that come from the earth, and also to the money that connects us with them.

---

a holy altar, and *kashrut* was elaborated far beyond its Biblical simplicity. Without a separate food-producing land to make them distinctive, the Jews made their diaspora dinner tables so distinctive that at every meal their separate peoplehood was reaffirmed.

The content of kashrut has puzzled many

analysts. Some have argued that the entire system of elaborate distinctions concerning food was an integral part of a culture that focused on distinctions. Still others have argued that *kashrut* was grounded in ethical considerations — that the prohibition of certain meats was the compromise that a deeply vegetarian ethic made reluctantly with inveterate eaters of meat, and that the method of ritual slaughter minimizes the animals' pain. Still others saw the separation of milk (the first life-giving food of mammals) from meat (the product of their death) as a way of teaching people to distinguish life-nurturance from death and killing.

For many Jews in our generation, the question of *kashrut* is still problematic. Some affirm *kashrut* because it is commanded by Torah. Others affirm it for the sake of Jewish peoplehood — precisely because it is a banner of differentiation from other cultures.

On the other hand, many Jews today resist the external imposition of black-and-white distinctions upon their lives: this you *must* and this you must *not* — and see this as an unpleasant characteristic of *kashrut*.

There are also some Jews who have concluded that pure individualism leads to the death of ethics and community, and who believe that accepting communal standards for what to eat might make sense — but who do not see the Jewish community as the relevant one for this issue. Many who feel comfortable with communal discussions and decisions about vegetarianism, macrobiotic diets, or boycotts of foods grown by oppressed workers, feel much less comfortable about choosing a diet that is distinctive according to a uniquely Jewish pattern — perhaps seeing no ethical reason for separating ourselves from others with whom we share many political, cultural and spiritual values.

Is there any way to reshape this ungainly bundle of our partly contradictory values so that it makes a coherent whole, affirming and strengthening our lives as Jews?

IN OUR own generation, the triumphs of technology have made the foretaste of manna and the promise of the Prophets — that all of us could eat in plenty under our own vines and fig trees — practically possible, though obviously not yet politically achieved. But the very technological progress that has made that possible has also befouled the earth and air and water, poisoned them so that they poison us. It is not clear that the planetary biosphere can survive a long continuation of the treatment we are now giving it. So we have made the gift of food from the earth even more problematic, in some ways, than it was before.

Our technology has also transformed the medium of the relationship between earth and human earthling. Originally, food was the great connection. There were others — clothing, housing, wood for energy — but food made up the largest and most potent aspect of what we got from the earth.

That is no longer so. The human race has created an economy in which the many other products of the earth that are consumed by humans may outweigh food — in market value, if not in survival-importance. In such a modern economy, money in all its forms takes on much of the role that food originally had.

For this reason, we may, in our generation, need to apply Jewish teachings about food to other "consumables" that come from the earth, and also to the money that connects us with them.

MOST OF OUR strongest social values have their roots (or at least their analogues) in values expressed by Jewish tradition:

Oshek: The prohibition of oppressing workers, and the similar prohibition about exploiting customers. Its principles could be extended to prohibit eating the fruit of such oppression or exploitation.

Tza'ar ba'alei chayim: Respect for animals. It could be extended to prohibit eating meat, or to prohibit eating meat from animals that have been grown under super-productive "factory farm" conditions. It could also be extended to respect for the identity of plants — for example, by prohibiting the misuse of pesticides and of genetic recombination or the eating of foods that were grown by such misuses.

Bal tashchit: Living with, and not ruining, the earth. It could be extended to require the use of "natural" or "organic" foods — not foods grown with chemical pesticides.

Sh'mirat haguf: The protection of one's own body. It could be understood to prohibit eating foods that contain carcinogens and/or hormones, and quasi-food items like tobacco and overdoses of alcohol. This principle would also mandate attention to the problems of

177

anorexia or overeating that cause us deep physical and psychological pain and make food into a weapon that we use against ourselves.

Tzedakah: The sharing of food with the poor. It could be extended to prohibit the eating of any meal, or any communal festive meal, unless a proportion of its cost goes to buying food for the hungry. An extended version of this approach suggests that, in a world where protein is already distributed inequitably, it is unjust to channel large amounts of cheap grain into feeding animals to grow expensive meat protein — and that it is therefore unjust to eat meat at all.

Rodef tzedek and **Rodef shalom:** The obligation to pursue justice and peace. It might be understood to require the avoidance of food produced by companies that egregiously violate these values — for example, by manufacturing first-strike nuclear weapons.

B'rakhah and **Kedusha:** The traditional sense that those who eat must consciously affirm a sense of holiness and blessing. This might be understood to require that at the table we use old or new forms for heightening the attention we give to the Unity from which all food comes — whether we call it God or not. This would help us maintain an awareness of the sad fact that we must kill plants and/or animals to live.

It is important to note here that we have given only the barest sketch of these ethical principles that are embedded in Jewish tradition — no more, in fact, than a list. To draw on them in any serious way would mean to look more deeply at how the tradition shapes their content — not only at the specific rulings but at how they are arrived at. Our goal is not necessarily to follow the same paths of thought or decision, but to wrestle with a Judaism that draws on the wisdom of all the Jewish generations — not ours alone. Once we have done this, then indeed our generation must decide for itself.

The very decision to apply these ethical principles to the choice of what to eat would represent this process of consulting the tradition without being imprisoned by it. If we undertook such a study, we would first find that every one of these principles stands as an ethical norm in Jewish tradition — not only in the *aggadic* sense of symbol, metaphor, philosophy, but also in the law code, *halakha.* Then we would find that there are hints in the tradition that one is obligated not only to avoid doing these misdeeds, but also to avoid benefitting from them if they have been done by others.

We would also find, however, that there is no clear legal requirement to bring together the Jewish sense of the importance of food with these principles by forbidding the eating of the fruits of these misdeeds. We would also find that there is little in the tradition that would stand in the way of adding new ethical restrictions to what we allow ourselves to eat.

UP TO THIS point, we have focused on food alone as the nexus between human beings and the earth — but it is not the only one. From the Biblical era on, it has been understood that there were links other than food between earth and human, but none were addressed with as much care as the regulation of food.

Rain, for example, was seen as a crucial connection with the earth. Without it, no food could grow, and in the Land of Israel, this was sometimes a problem. One of the main concerns of Jewish liturgy is intense prayer for rain; the Talmud specifies an elaborate pattern of fasts and prayers in times of drought.

Clothing was another of these links with the earth, and the Torah notes a kind of kashrut of clothes — not mixing linen with wool. The rabbinic tradition did not greatly elaborate the rule.

Energy was another interface. Wood and olive oil were the main sources of light and heat. Olive oil took on a sacred aura — it was used for anointing sacred pillars in the earliest memories of the people and later for offerings at the Temple, for lighting the Temple Menorah (and thus took a central place in the origins of Hanukah), and for anointing kings (thus the name, "the Anointed One, Mashiach, Messiah" was given to the human being who would someday redeem history). The Talmud examines carefully the rules of making oil for sacred use. As for firewood, the Bible describes its gathering as the first occasion for a legal case to define the extent of the prohibitions on exploitation of the earth that apply on Shabbat.

Breathing was another earth-human link. God's most intimate name (*Exodus* 6: 2) may have been based on a breathing sound, and breath/wind became the metaphor for life, soul and spirit. Already in the rabbinic period, air pollution was occasionally a problem (when living downwind of a tannery, for example), but this was rare, and few rules were developed for the correct use of air.

In our own time, food is certainly not the only problematic link between human beings and our environment. Our water and air are often polluted, and our main sources of energy — fossils that can be replaced and renewed only over millions of years, and radiation — pose profound dangers to the life-web of the earth. Although food is still for many human beings the most urgent and perhaps the scarcest link to the earth, producing it takes up much smaller a proportion of our work and capital than it did before the modern age.

Today there are many products that we draw or make from the world around us that are crucial to our lives and health. Does it make sense to apply to them some rules of "*kashrut,*" and if so, how would we develop such rules? How would we enforce them?

Does it make sense for us now to draw on these basic principles to set new standards for what we actually consume — standards for an "ethical *kashrut*"? If we did, do we run the danger of obsessiveness, or even the danger that applying strict standards might result in drastically reducing the kinds of foods and other products we could use at all?

Perhaps we can learn a lesson from the way different types of Jews practice traditional *kashrut* today.

Different Jews do maintain different answers to the question, "Is this food kosher?" For ex-

Jews who find traditional *kashrut* an important link with Torah and Jewish peoplehood could continue to observe it while observing ethical *kashrut* as well; Jews who do not resonate to the traditional code could continue to leave it to one side while following the new path with its new way of connecting with Torah and Jewish peoplehood.

ample, some will only accept certain types of certification on packaged goods, while others are satisfied with reading labels to verify ingredients as kosher. Some people will drink only kosher wine, while others believe this category is no longer relevant. Some keep "biblical *kashrut*," only abstaining from Biblically forbidden foods. Some are willing to eat non-kosher foods in restaurants and in other people's homes, others are willing only to eat intrinsically kosher foods such as fish and vegetables on non-kosher utensils when they are away from home, while still others do not eat any cooked foods away from home.

A new *kashrut* that is rooted in ethical strands of Torah will also demand that people make choices about how to observe. For example: Some might treat the principle of *oshek* (not oppressing workers) as paramount, and choose to use only products that are grown or made without any oppression of food workers (from one's own backyard or neighborhood garden, or from a *kibbutz* where all workers are also owners and participants). Others may make the principle of *bal tashchit* (protection of the environment) paramount, and will put *oshek* in a secondary place — perhaps applying it only when specifically asked to do so by workers who are protesting their plight.

But there will also be some important differences between the way choices will work in an ethical *kashrut* and the way choices work in traditional *kashrut*. In the new approach, there will be so many ethical values to weigh that it may be rare to face a black-and-white choice in a particular product. This one is grown by union workers, that one with special care for the earth and water, another. . . . Choices will depend more on a balancing and synthesizing of the underlying values than on an absolute sense of Good and Bad; more on a sense of Both/And than of Either/Or.

What impact might adherence to this new approach to "ethical *kashrut*" have upon adherence to the traditional code of kosher food? Jews who find traditional *kashrut* an important link with Torah and Jewish peoplehood could continue to observe it while observing ethical *kashrut* as well; Jews who do not resonate to the traditional code could continue to leave it to one side while following the new path with its new way of connecting with Torah and Jewish peoplehood. Some who are newly observant of ethical *kashrut* may find that it leads them to find unexpected value in the traditional form. Others who have observed *kashrut* in traditional ways may find that the new one fulfills their Jewish sense more richly, and give up the ancient form.

In any case, this new approach to *kashrut* would be trying to deal with the issue of "distinctions" in a new way: not by separating only, but by consciously connecting. Connecting what is uniquely Jewish with what is shared and universal. Connecting Jewish categories with universal concerns. Consciously asserting Jewish reasons to avoid a product that others are also avoiding for similar but not identical reasons. Choosing not Either/Or but Both/And.

IN THE ANCIENT world, *kashrut* governed the earth-to-human side of the link between human life and the rest of the created world. On the human-to-earth side, the link was governed by rules of land use, including provisions for the poor and for periodic equalizations of land-holding, and by the prayers for rain.

In modern society, the human-to-earth link is not so much through the use of land as it is through the use of money. Rules about reserving the gleanings and the produce of the corners of a field for the poor, redistributing land once a generation, letting the land rest from its work every seventh year — all these need to be translated into the use of money and of "technological capital" if we are to preserve the same functional relationship of holiness between human beings and their environment.

In a sense, in our world the *kashrut* of food and other consumer products is holiness at retail; the *kashrut* of money would be holiness at wholesale.

There are some religious and cultural traditions that view money itself, or the effort to amass it, as intrinsically evil. There are others that see the possession of money — or large amounts of it — as intrinsic evidence of holiness and blessedness.

Most of Jewish thought sees money as a powerful tool for evil or good, depending on how it is used. There is deep Jewish experience with the *mitzvah* of *tzedakah* — sharing the just and righteous use of money not only to alleviate poverty but to help end it and create shared wealth — and with the use of money to protect Jewish rights, assist Jewish refugees, and help create the Jewish community in Israel. All this experience suggests that as the Jewish community stirs itself to protect its

---

In modern society, the human-to-earth link is not so much through the use of land as it is through the use of money. Rules about reserving the gleanings and the produce of the corners of a field for the poor, redistributing land once a generation, letting the land rest from its work every seventh year — all these need to be translated into the use of money and of "technological capital" if we are to preserve the same functional relationship of holiness between human beings and their environment.

own survival and that of the planet, the *seicheldik* (wise) use of money is an important tool. Knowing where not to spend money, as well as where it should be spent, is an element in both morality and politics.

Let us look at the different areas of possibility:

Work: How do we choose what companies to work for and what work to do? Should engineers, secretaries, scientists, public relations experts, nurses, be asking whether their work, for example, contributes to the danger of environmental degradation? Do Jewish tradition and the Jewish community offer any help in making such judgments? What help is most needed?

In the Summer, 1984 issue of *Reform Judaism*, Rabbi Laurence K. Milder raised such questions regarding scientists and nuclear weapons in an article, "If the Scientists Said No." Wrote Milder: "Until now, the Reform movement has been outspoken in its opposition to the arms race. Yet the question remains to be addressed whether the same religious convictions ought to prohibit one from working on the construction of those weapons whose deployment we oppose. Being disproportionately represented in the sciences and high-tech industries, we can be sure that the question would have far-reaching impact. A decision to refrain from such work would be a serious blow to the nuclear weapons industry. Any decision at all would be better than silence, which suggests that Judaism stops at the door of one's workplace."

How could the Jewish community, or parts of it, decide whether specific jobs were "kosher"? Suppose a community decided a specific job was not kosher; should and could the community provide financial help, temporary grants, low-interest loans, etc., to Jews who decide to leave such jobs for reasons of Torah and conscience? Should organizing toward such a fund be a goal of the Jewish community?

Investments: How do we judge where to invest money — in which money market funds, IRAs, etc.? What about institutional funds in which we may have a voice or could make for ourselves a voice — college endowments, pension funds, citybonds, etc.? In the last 10 years, there has arisen in the United States a network of people and groups concerned with "socially responsible investment" — that is, working out how to apply ethical standards to investment decisions. That network has brought into being socially responsible "screened" investment funds, which avoid investing money in what each considers the most socially irresponsible firms, and affirmative socially responsible investment funds, which seek to invest in new or small but financially viable businesses that in their eyes have major plus factors for social responsibility.

In the Jewish community, investment funds that might become "socially responsible" include community-worker and rabbinical association pension funds, synagogue endowments, building campaign accounts, pulpit flower funds, seminary endowments, etc. How would the community decide which investments are "kosher"?

Purchases: Should we, as individuals, when we choose from which companies to buy consumer goods, factor into our choice considerations of what else a specific company is producing? Are operations in South Africa, China, Chile — or in making nuclear weapons, dangerous petrochemicals — relevant? Should we ask our synagogues, pension funds, city and state governments, PTAs, to choose vendors on such a basis?

Rabbi Zalman Schachter-Shalomi has suggested that since, in our era, we consume many items other than food, the notion of *kashrut* should be expanded beyond food to many other products that we use. He asks: Is electric power generated by a nuclear plant "kosher"? More to the point, could we call into being a broader Commission for Eco-*Kashrut* that could reach out far beyond the Jewish community to define what products are so damaging to the earth that they ought not to be bought or consumed?

Taxes: Is it legitimate to challenge, protest, or prevent the use of our tax money to carry on activities that profoundly contradict Torah? If so, how do we define "profoundly contradict"? What weight do we give to the fact that our taxes and government expenditures are defined by elected representatives?

Tzedakah: How do we decide how much money we should give to "charity" and to which enterprises to give it? In the last 20 years, there have grown up not only new channels for *tzedakah*, such as Mazon (intended to feed the hungry) and the Jewish Fund for Justice (intended to help groups of the poor or powerless organize to win their own footing in the world), but also a relatively new (and old) form for *tzedakah*, the "*tzedakah* collective."

These groups meet together, face to face, to discuss possible recipients of *tzedakah*. The participants agree in advance on what proportion of their incomes they will give, and on a more or less collective process for deciding how to give it. The ambience is very different from what happens when individuals write checks to a national *tzedakah* organization, whether it is the United Jewish Appeal or the Jewish Fund for Justice; and usually the involvement of the participants is much deeper in learning what Jewish tradition teaches on *tzedakah*, as in learning about projects that might be *tzedakah* recipients.

Participants in these *tzedakah* collectives report that their involvement feels inspiring and their field results seem good; yet the number of such collectives seems still to be much lower than the number of *havurot* for study and prayer.

Two steps would encourage the growth of such direct-involvement *tzedakah* groups. One is face-to-face organizing by rabbis, Jewish teachers, and similar local Jewish community workers, to get groups of families to meet together to do *tzedakah*. The other is providing such groups with information not only on *tzedakah* decisions that groups like them are making, but also on Jewish aspects of the everyday use of money in their non-*tzedakah* lives: the "*kashrut* of money" for investment, purchasing, tax and workplace choices. If a packet of newsletters with such information were made available every month or two, first to rabbis to pass on to "*tzedakah* activists," and then to *tzedakah* collectives as they appeared, the chances would be much greater that Jewish values would be consciously applied to the use of money in many aspects of life.

HOW MIGHT WE GET this process going? If we were to draw further on the analogy with traditional kashrut, what we need is a kind of "living Talmud" — a group of people who are Jewishly knowledgeable, ethically sensitive, and willing to become reasonable experts on questions regarding food, other consumer products, and money — so that their advice would be taken seriously by large parts of the Jewish community.

Such a Commission on Ethical *Kashrut* might periodically issue reports and suggestions on specific matters, listing specific products and perhaps even brands that it regarded as "highly

---

How could the Jewish community, or parts of it, decide whether specific jobs were "kosher"? Suppose a community decided a specific job was not kosher; should and could the community provide financial help, temporary grants, low-interest loans, etc., to Jews who decide to leave such jobs for reasons of Torah and conscience?

---

recommended," and others it viewed as "to be avoided if at all possible."

How could such a Commission come into being? A process that is addressing these questions is already underway.

The first steps were taken by the Institute for Jewish Renewal in 1990. Together with Rabbis Marshall Meyer and Rolando Matalon of Congregation B'nai Jeshurun in New York, it called together a committee of Jews from every strand of the religious community and from secular organizations concerned with environmentally responsible purchasing and investing.

This committee decided that there is a broader consensus in the Jewish community around the urgency of addressing environmental dangers to the planet than there is around labor relations, racial or sexual equality, military involvement, or other similar ethical concerns. The committee was therefore prepared to focus on mobilizing Jews to direct their purchases and investments to dealing with environmental dangers, not with other issues.

Out of this decision emerged a proposal to use the name, "Eco-Kosher Project."

To some participants, this joining of a Greek prefix with a very new connotation to a Hebrew root with a very ancient one signalled precisely the fusion of the ancient with the post-modern that they felt necessary if the world environmental crisis is to be dealt with.

Others in the group were troubled: Might the use of the word "kosher" lead to problems? On the one hand, those in the Orthodox community, which had taken on the responsibilty for regulating traditional *kashrut,* expressed concern that the term "eco-kosher" might cause confusion. Might the Project, for environmental reasons, decide that what the tradition viewed as kosher was now "eco-treyf," or what the tradition viewed as treyf was now "eco-kosher"? On the other hand, some Reform Jews were concerned that members of the Reform movement, who had put great psychic energy into deciding that most of the categories of kosher food no longer had religious significance in the modern age, might reject the whole notion because its name echoed the traditional *kashrut.*

After long discussion, the committee decided to use "Eco-Kosher" because no alternative as aptly expressed the commitment to Jewish roots and values and the sense of a continuous daily practice and discipline. The committee also took two precautions:

1) to say explicitly that "eco-kosher" stood outside of and independent from traditional *kashrut,* in a different rather than competing sphere;

2) to carry out this assertion by leaving on one side, at least for the present, the main categories of "kosher" and "treyf" products — that is, meat and dairy foods — and instead focus on issues and products not addressed by traditional *kashrut.*

The Eco-Kosher Project's initial brochure began by saying: "What is Eco-Kosher? Are tomatoes that have been grown by drenching the earth in pesticides 'kosher' to eat at the synagogue's next wedding reception? Is newsprint that has been made by chopping down an ancient and irreplaceable forest 'kosher' to use for a Jewish newspaper? Are windows and doors so carelessly built that the warm air flows out through them and the furnace keeps burning all night — are such doors and windows 'kosher' for a Jewish Community Center building? Is a bank that invests the depositors' money in an oil company that befouls the ocean a 'kosher' place for a UJA to deposit its money?

"If by 'kosher' we mean a broader sense of 'good practice' that draws on the deep wellsprings of Jewish wisdom and tradition, then we believe that none of these ways of behaving is *eco-kosher.*"

The Project decided to focus on four categories of *individual* and *institutional* purchase and investment:

1) Foods outside the usual kosher/treyf categories — in particular, fresh and processed fruits and vegetables. In terms of the ways in which they are grown, packaged and marketed, which of these products are most sensitive to protection of the earth?

b) Household and congregational consumables other than food — in particular, paper products and cleaning products.

c) Finances — choices of checking and savings institutions, investments, etc.

d) No-cost or low-cost conservation and recycling of materials and energy.

The Project decided to begin by focusing on institutions that have buildings and sizable purchasing/investing patterns — for example, synagogues, schools, Hillel houses, camps, Jewish Community Centers, nursing homes and hospitals, Jewish journals and publishing houses. It also decided to approach two major strands of Jewish leadership: the "cultural-educational" staff (rabbis, school principals and teachers, JCC and camp program directors, Hillel directors, chaplains and editors) and the administrators and purchasing agents who are usually responsible for choosing banks, etc.

The Project decided that in judging what is eco-kosher, it would develop standards based both on the ethical, earth-preserving elements of Jewish tradition, and on contemporary secular work on protection of the environment.

The Project intends to explore whether the Jewish categories can be extended and intertwined to address a number of newer questions. For example, what about respect for the identity of plants as well as animals? Should *tza'ar ba'alei chayim* affect use of pesticides? Genetic recombination? Should *bal tashchit* be applied to nuclear reactors that leave permanent poisons in the earth?

What about a rhythmic pause (based on *shmitah* and *yovel*, the rhythm of allowing the earth to rest) in new engineering while we reexamine its effects? Or requiring an environmental impact statement before undertaking large corporate investments in new products? What about setting aside a special time each year for living lightly on the earth — like Sukkot with its simplest of shelters, Pesach with its simplest of breads?

The Project decided to draw as well upon the work of general groups like the Council on Economic Priorities, Green Seal, the Center for Corporate Responsibility, etc., and to encourage the Jewish community to apply these groups' work to the Jewish situation.

As it moves from developing these basic approaches to applying them in specific instances, and as it encourages the emergence of an "eco-kosher" mentality and practice in and beyond the Jewish community, the Eco-Kosher Project will draw not only on the specific content of Jewish tradition, but also on the processes by which the practical decisions emerged. In that sense, the Project sees the idea of an eco-kosher life-path as an extension of what it has meant for almost four millennia to be Jewish — into our era when the human race holds in its hands the choice of survival or destruction for the planet.

Can Jewish wisdom be of use to all the species, in choosing life at such a crisis?

The Eco-Kosher Project can be reached at 7318 Germantown Ave., Philadelphia, PA 19119, 215-247-9700.

Bibliography

Sources Used in this Essay

Ackelsberg, Martha, "Money and Class: Dealing with Difference in the Jewish Renewal Movement," 1989 paper for The Shefa Fund, Philadelphia.

Adelman, Clifford, "Women at Thirtysomething: Paradoxes of Attainment," June 1991 report for the U.S. Department of Education.

Alperovitz, Gar, "Toward a New Vision of Living Democracy, Beyond Socialism and Capitalism," *Israel Horizons*, Spring, 1992 (Vol. 40, No. 2).

Alperson, Myra, Alice Tepper Marlin, Jonathan Schorsch and Roslyn Will, *The Better World Investment Guide*, from the Council on Economic Priorities, 1991, Prentice Hall Press, New York.

Ausubel, Nathan, *A Treasury of Jewish Folklore.* 1948, Crown Publishers, New York.

Baron, Joseph L., *A Treasury of Jewish Quotations*, 1985, Jason Aronson, Inc., Northvale, NJ and London.

Blumenthal, David R., *God at the Center, Meditations on Jewish Spirituality*, 1988, Harper & Row, San Francisco.

Bush, Lawrence, *Babushkin's Catalogue of Jewish Inventions*, ill. by Dick Codor, 1988, Babushkin's Digest, Accord, New York.

Bronfman, Joanie, *Inherited Wealth: A Social-Psychological Perspective*, 1987 dissertation, Brandeis University.

Brooks, Karen, Judith Chalmer and Rebecca

Sherlock, "Celebrating the Cycles of the Sun and Moon Together," *Genesis 2*, Autumn, 1988 (Vol. 19, No. 3).

Bouyea, Laura, *Robin Hood Was Right: A Guide to Giving Your Money for Social Change*, 1977, The Vanguard Public Foundation, San Francisco.

Cohen, Arthur A., and Paul Mendes-Flohr, *Contemporary Jewish Religious Thought*, 1987, The Free Press, New York.

Cohen-Kiener, Andrea, "The *Sh'ma* and Ecology," *Genesis 2*, Spring, 1989 (Vol. 20, No. 1).

Davis, Dena, "On Not Eating Table Grapes," *Genesis 2*, Summer, 1988 (Vol. 19, No. 2).

Dekro, Jeffrey, "Energy Policy and Jewish Interests," *Jewish Currents*, June, 1982 (Vol. 36, No. 6).

Domhoff, G. William, and Richard L. Zweigenhaft, *Jews in the Protestant Establishment*, 1982, Praeger Publishers, New York.

Earth•Works Group, *The Recycler's Handbook.*, 1990, Earth•Works Group, Berkeley, CA.

Fackenheim, Emil L., *What Is Judaism? An Interpretation for the Present Age.* 1987, Summit Books, New York.

Feingold, Henry L., *A Time for Searching*, Vol. 4 of *The Jewish People in America.* 1992, Johns Hopkins University Press, Baltimore and London.

Fromm, Erich, *Psychoanalysis and Religion.* 1950, Yale University Press, New Haven, CT.

Garb, Maggie, "Saving the Inner Cities," *In These Times*, Aug. 5-18, 1992.

Ginzberg, Louis, *The Legends of the Jews.* 1989, Jewish Publication Society (15th ed.), Philadelphia.

Glatzer, Nahum N., *The Way of Response: Martin*

Buber, Selections from His Writings, 1966, Schocken Books, New York.

Green, Arthur, *Seek My Face, Speak My Name*. 1992, Jason Aronson, Northvale, NJ and London.

Heinze, Andrew R., *Adapting to Abundance, Jewish Immigrants, Mass Consumption and the Search for American Identity*, 1990, Columbia University Press, New York.

Henwood, Doug, "Business Ethics: Missing the Forest for the Trees," *Left Business Observer*, reprinted in *Utne Reader*, Jan./Feb., 1989.

Hollender, Jeffrey A., *How to Make the World a Better Place*, 1990, Quill/William Morrow, New York.

Holtz, Barry W., and Eduardo Rauch, eds., *The Melton Journal*, "Our Earth and Our Tradition." Spring, 1991 and Spring, 1992, Jewish Theological Seminary.

Jaffe, Eliezer David, "The Crisis in Jewish Philanthropy," *Tikkun*, Vol. 2, No. 4.

Kelly, Marjorie, "Revolution in the Marketplace," *Utne Reader*, Jan./Feb., 1989.

Kimelman, Reuven, *Tzedakah and Us*, 1991, CLAL, New York.

Kosmin, Barry A., and Paul Ritterband, eds., *Contemporary Jewish Philanthropy in America*, 1991, Rowman and Littlefield, Savage, MD.

Kramer, Judith R., and Leventman, Seymour, *Children of the Gilded Ghetto*, 1961, Yale University Press, New Haven, CT.

Krefetz, Gerald, *Jews and Money*, 1982, Ticknor and Fields, New York.

Kurzweil, Arthur, "Brother Can You Spare a Dime? The Treatment of Beggars According to Jewish Tradition," *Moment*, Nov., 1981 (Vol. 56, No. 10).

Lehrer, Chaia, "Those Old Working Class Values," *Bridges*, Spring, 1991 (Vol. 2, No. 1).

Lowry, Susan Meeker, *Economics As if the World Really Mattered*, 1988, New Society Publishers, Santa Cruz, CA.

Lydenberg, Steven D., Sean O'Brien Strub and Alice Tepper Marlin, *Rating America's Corporate Conscience*, from the Council on Economic Priorities. 1986, Addison-Wesley, Reading, MA.

Marlin, Alice Tepper, et al, *Shopping for a Better World*, 1991 edition, from the Council on Economic Priorities, New York.

Miedzian, Myriam, *Boys Will Be Boys: Breaking the Link Between Masculinity and Violence*, 1991, Doubleday, New York.

Milbank, Dana, "Being a Consumer Isn't Easy if You Boycott Everything," *Wall Street Journal*, April 24, 1991.

Mintz, Morton, "Tobacco Roads," *The Progressive*, May, 1991 (Vol. 55, No. 5).

Mogil, Christopher, and Anne Slepian, eds., *We Gave Away a Fortune*, 1992, New Society Publishers, Philadelphia.

Moskowitz, Milton, and Carol Townsend, "The 85 Best Companies for Working Mothers," *Working Mother*, Oct., 1991.

Nadir, Moishe, "My First Deposit," tr. from Yiddish by Lila B. Hassid, *Jewish Currents*, July-Aug., 1963 (Vol. 17, No. 8).

Nasar, Sylvia, "The Rich Get Richer, But Never the Same Way Twice," *New York Times*, Aug. 16, 1992.

Perlman, Myron, et al, *Chutzpah, A Jewish Liberation Anthology*, 1977, New Glide, Chicago.

Plaskow, Judith, *Standing Again at Sinai*, 1990, HarperCollins, San Francisco.

Reed, Adolph L., *The Jesse Jackson Phenomenon*, 1986, Yale University Press, New Haven.

Riemer, Jack, ed., *Jewish Reflections on Death*, 1974, Schocken Books, New York.

Plaut, W. Gunther, ed., *The Torah, A Modern Commentary*, 1981, UAHC Press, New York.

Schaefer, Arthur Gross, "Ten Commandments for the Synagogue," *Reform Judaism*, Fall, 1991 (Vol. 19, No. 4).

Schindler, Alexander M., "Reform Judaism 2001," *Reform Judaism*, Spring, 1991 (Vol. 19, No. 3); Presidential Address, Nov. 3, 1991.

Shorris, Earl, *Jews Without Mercy, A Lament*, 1982, Anchor Press/Doubleday, New York.

Siegel, Danny, *Gym Shoes and Irises: Personalized Tzedakah*, Books One and Two — 1982, 1988, Town House Press, Pittsboro, NC; *Where Heaven and Earth Touch. An Anthology of Midrash and Halachah* — 1989, Jason Aronson, Inc., Northvale, NJ and London.

Silberman, Charles, *A Certain People*, 1985. Summit Books, New York.

Silverman, William B., *The Sages Speak, Rabbinic Wisdom and Jewish Values*, 1989, Jason Aronson, Northvale, NJ and London.

Social Investment Forum, *A Guide to Forum Members*, 1992, Minneapolis, MN.

Snitow, Virginia, Letter to The Shefa Fund, 1991.

Sontag, Susan, *AIDS and Its Metaphors*, 1988, Farrar, Straus and Giroux, New York.

Tamari, Meir, *"With All Your Possessions" — Jewish Ethics and Economic Life*, 1987, The Free Press, New York.

Tasini, Jonathan, "Hearts of Gold," interview, *Mother Jones*, May, 1988.

Uchitelle, Louis, "Trapped in the Impoverished Middle Class," *New York Times*, Nov. 17, 1991.

Vorspan, Albert and David Saperstein, *Tough Choices*, 1992, UAHC Press, New York.

Waskow, Arthur, "Mystery, Wholeness and the Breath of Life," *Genesis 2*, April/May, 1986.

Wiesel, Elie, *Sages and Dreamers*, 1991, Summit Books, New York.

Yeskel, Felice, "Coming Out About Money," *Bridges*, Spring/Summer, 1992 (Vol. 3, No. 1).

Zweigenhaft, Richard L., *Who Gets to the Top? Executive Discrimination in the Eighties*. 1984, American Jewish Committee, New York.

Other Recommended Resources (see also page 68)

Books and Booklets

American Association of Fund-Raising Counsel, *Giving USA*, annual guide about philanthropic trends. 25 W. 43 St., New York, NY 10036.

Bingham, Sally, *Passion and Prejudice*, 1989, Random House, New York. An autobiography about growing up as a woman in a wealthy family.

Domini, Amy, *Ethical Investing: How to Make Profitable Investments Without Sacrificing Your Principles*, 1984, Addison-Wesley, Reading, MA.

Lappé, Frances Moore, *Rediscovering America's Values*, 1989, Ballantine Books, New York. A debate about economic and social values.

Lieberman, Annette, and Lindner, Vicki, *Unbalanced Accounts: How Women Can Overcome Their*

Fear of Money, 1988, Penguin, New York.

Millman, Marcia, *Warm Hearts & Cold Cash: The Intimate Dynamics of Families and Money*, 1991, Free Press, New York.

Needleman, Jacob: *Money and the Meaning of Life*, 1991, Doubleday, New York.

Odendahl, Teresa, *Charity Begins at Home: Generosity and Self-Interest Among the Philanthropic Elite*, 1990, Basic Books, New York.

Rabinowitz, Alan, *Social Change Philanthropy in America*, 1990, Quorum Books, New York.

Schneider, Susan Weidman, and Alan Drache, *Head and Heart: A Woman's Guide to Financial Independence*, 1991, Trilogy Books, Pasadena, CA.

Schneider, Susan Weidman, *Jewish and Female: Choices and Changes in Our Lives*, 1985, Simon & Schuster/Touchstone, New York.

Wachtel, Paul, *The Poverty of Affluence: A Psychological Portrait of the American Way of Life*, 1989, New Society Publishers, Philadelphia.

Zeitz, Baila, and Lorraine Dusky, *The Best Companies for Women*, 1988, Simon & Schuster, New York.

Articles and Journals

Community Economics, published quarterly by the Institute for Community Economics, 57 School Street, Springfield, MA 01105.

Family Business Review, issue on "Family Foundations," Winter, 1990 (Vol. 3, No. 4). Jossey Bass, Inc., 350 Sansome St., San Francisco, CA 94104

Family Therapy Networker, issue on "Money: Living With It, Living Without It," March/April, 1992 (Vol. 16, No. 2). 7705 13th St. NW, Washington, DC 20012.

Global Village News, newsletter of the Social Venture Network, a membership organization of entrepreneurs, investors, corporate leaders and social activists, 1388 Sutter St., Suite 1010, San Francisco, CA, 415-771-4308.

Kimelman, Reuven, "Leadership and Community in Judaism," *Tikkun*, Vol. 2, No. 5.

Lesbian Ethics, issue on class, Spring, 1991 (Vol. 4, No. 2), POB 4723, Albuquerque, NM 87196.

Parabola, the Magazine of Myth and Tradition, issue on "Money," Spring, 1991 (Vol. 16, No. 1), 656 Broadway, New York, NY 10012.

Redmond, Tim, "The Dirt on 'Clean' Investing," *San Francisco Bay Guardian*, March 14, 1990 (Vol. 24, No. 23).

Teltsch, Kathleen, "Shaking Up Old Ways of Benevolence," *New York Times*, Sept. 15, 1992.

Tenenbaum, Shelly, "Buying Chickens, Paying Bills: Jewish Women's Loan Societies," *Lilith*, Summer, 1991 (Vol. 16, No. 3), 250 W. 57th St., New York, NY 10107.

Wealth of Possibilities, newsletter of the Women Donors Network, Chela Blitt, ed., 3543 18th St., #9, San Francisco, CA 94110.

For a regularly updated bibliography of resources on social responsibility, we recommend "Taking Charge of Our Money, Our Values, and Our Lives," from Chrysalis Money Consultants and The Impact Project, 21 Linwood Street, Arlington, MA 02174, 617-648-0776.

About The Shefa Fund

THE SHEFA FUND (TSF) is a tax-exempt public foundation established in 1988 to provide seed and operating funding for innovative and transformational activities that are at the leading, controversial edge of Jewish communal concerns. TSF promotes ethical approaches to money and wealth by American Jews and Jewish institutions, and advocates financial social responsibility in their values, organizational structures and practices.

TSF also brings to funders the opportunity to connect deeply to their Jewish identities, to learn about the forces of progressive Jewish renewal in North America, and to form community with other funders. By conducting retreats, workshops and special meetings for groups of funders and activists to discuss personal and social dimensions of the "Torah of Money," TSF provides a framework for funders to explore issues of power, identity and self-esteem in psychological safety.

TSF grantmaking includes board-initiated and donor-advised grants. Organizations receiving funds from The Shefa Fund have included the Life Center for Jewish Renewal, the National Jewish AIDS Project, Americans for Peace Now, The Center for Democratic Renewal, The Shalom Center, *Lilith* magazine and Shomrei Adamah. Donor-advised grants have gone to the New Israel Fund, Mazon, the Jewish Fund for Justice, and P'nai Or, among other groups.

TSF's own board includes wealthy and non-wealthy people as full participants. TSF actively promotes the application of socially responsible criteria in the management of all its assets.

Most recently, TSF initiated the *Tzedek* (Justice) Economic Development Campaign, to promote visible American Jewish investment and participation in low-income community economic development throughout the United States. Towards this end, TSF has organized an Exploratory Project Board comprised of respected experts in community economic development, business and finance, social investment, philanthropy and Jewish communal affairs. This Board is developing a feasibility study of various strategies (e.g, community-based and controlled lending institutions, housing development tax credits, enterprise zones, program-related investments) that could be adopted to stimulate Jewish investment, by individuals and institutions, in low-income community development.

TSF is also deeply involved in its *Tzedakah* Development Project, aimed at promoting a "Torah of Money" in the broadest possible sector of the American Jewish community, and at helping to develop *tzedakah* collectives in Jewish communities across the country. *Jews, Money and Social Responsibility* is one major tool in that effort.

For information or to make contributions, contact The Shefa Fund, 7318 Germantown Avenue, Philadelphia, PA 19119, (215) 247-9704.

Index

SCRIPTURAL REFERENCES

ALL OTHER REFERENCES

196

Now that you've read
*Jews, Money and
Social Responsibility,*
why not buy copies for
your friends and relatives,
as holiday, graduation or birthday gifts?
**Help us develop and teach a
Torah of Money!**

And help yourself —
Join the leading edge of the Jewish
movement for social responsibility!
Organize your own money and values
for social change!
Make a profit and make a difference!

How?

**Contact The Shefa Fund for
information about our
exciting programs!**
Clip the coupon on this page
and return it to:
The Shefa Fund
7318 Germantown Avenue
Philadelphia, PA 19119-1792
Or give us a call today at:
(800) 92-SHEFA or (215) 247-9704